Personality and
Social Psychology

Personality and Social Psychology

Towards a Synthesis

Barbara Krahé

SAGE Publications

London · Newbury Park · New Delhi

SAGE Publications Ltd
6 Bonhill Street
London EC2A 4PU

SAGE Publications Inc
2455 Teller Road
Newbury Park, California 91320

SAGE Publications India Pvt Ltd
32, M-Block Market
Greater Kailash - I
New Delhi 110 048

British Library Cataloguing in Publication data

Krahé, Barbara
  Personality and Social Psychology:
  Towards a Synthesis
  I. Title
  302

ISBN 0 8039 8724 2
ISBN 0 8039 8725 0 pbk

Library of Congress catalog card number 92–53776

Typeset by Photoprint, Torquay, Devon
Printed in Great Britain by Biddles Ltd, Guildford, Surrey

For my children
Charlotte and Justin

Contents

Acknowledgements

As is probably true for most enterprises of this kind, the way to finishing this book was paved with both rewarding and disappointing personal experiences. At the end of the day, memories of the rewarding aspects prevail, and I gratefully acknowledge the support I received from institutions, colleagues and friends. In particular, I am grateful for two personal grants which greatly helped me in writing this book. My thanks are due to the Alexander von Humboldt Foundation for the Feodor Lynen Fellowship which facilitated the planning and beginning of the volume, and to the Deutsche Forschungsgemeinschaft for the Heisenberg Fellowship in the final stage of the book. I would like to thank Barbara Lloyd and Peter Smith at the University of Sussex and Hubert Feger at the Freie Universität Berlin for the hospitality with which they welcomed me in their departments during these periods. I owe special thanks to Bernd Six whose feedback on the manuscript as it was taking shape was of great help to me in clarifying the structure and contents of the book. I am also grateful to Sue Jones at Sage who accompanied the changing fate and appearance of the book with patience and understanding. Finally, I would like to take this opportunity to thank my husband Peter for his unfailing support and continuous encouragement, in this project as in all previous ones.

1

Persons and Situations: Cornerstones of Modern Personality Psychology

Almost 250 years ago, the English statesman and author, Lord Chesterfield, wrote in one of his famous *Letters to His Son*:

> Few men are of one plain, decided colour; most are mixed, shaded, and blended; and vary as much from different situations, as changeable silks do from different lights. (30 April 1752)

This view of human nature and its malleability poignantly anticipates the challenge that has faced the academic discipline of personality psychology from its inception to the present day. Personality psychologists and laypersons alike are aware of the fact that nobody feels, thinks, or acts in the same way across the multitude of situations encountered in the course of everyday life. People respond with flexibility to the different features of the social and physical world in which they live, and it would appear a hopeless task to try and predict exactly what each of a number of individuals will do in a particular situation. On the other hand, an individual's behaviour in general is not entirely unpredictable, nor is it ruled exclusively by the forces present in a given situation. Our experience with other people – as well as with ourselves – tells us that there is a certain regularity, consistency and uniqueness in the behaviours, thoughts and feelings of a person which define his or her 'personality'. Coming to terms with this intricate relationship between stability and change in individual behaviour is the central task of personality psychology.

Personality psychologists are committed to the creed that individuals can be characterized by enduring qualities that distinguish them from others and provide vital clues for understanding their behaviour in a wide range of situations. When we know a person well, we come to develop expectations about how the person will act in particular types of situations. These expectations are indispensable in guiding our interactions with the person, and they are typically expressed in the form of dispositional labels. Someone is said to be a 'friendly' or a 'conscientious' person, which means that he or she is expected to show friendly or conscientious behaviour

with some degree of consistency and predictability. Yet, predictability of behaviour on the basis of personal dispositions clearly has
its limits, set by the varying features of the situations in which
personality is expressed. A habitually friendly person may respond
with a rude remark to an unprovoked verbal insult, just as a
habitually conscientious individual may forget to keep an appointment after an emotionally upsetting experience with a friend. In
certain situations, as in many ceremonial events, cues or demands
for a particular kind of behaviour may even be so strong that
personal dispositions become negligible and behavioural conformity
is shown by all the persons involved.

Thus, the task of studying personality takes place within the
confines of a social world that poses its own constraints on the
manifestation of unique and enduring personal characteristics. It is
not surprising, therefore, that the issue of the relative importance of
personal dispositions and situational forces in explaining behaviour
has brought personality psychology into conflict with those psychological disciplines which regard behaviour primarily as a response to
the characteristic features of the setting in which it takes place. With
the growing prominence of learning theories stressing the dependency of behaviour on reinforcement and imitation processes, personality psychologists came under increasing pressure to produce
large-scale evidence of the stability and consistency of personal
dispositions and their reflections in behaviour.

As a result, the field of personality psychology was thrown into a
profound crisis of confidence some twenty years ago, fuelled by
powerful attacks on the trait concept and its role in capturing
consistency in individual behaviour across time and situations (for
historical reviews see Epstein and O'Brien, 1985; Tomkins, 1981).
The crisis found its reflection in questions like 'Where is the person
in personality research?' (Carlson, 1971), in the regular stock-
takings appearing in the *Annual Review of Psychology* (for example, Phares and Lamiell, 1977; Sechrest, 1976) and other critical
analyses of leading figures of the field (for example, Fiske, 1978a,b).
From all these different sources, a gloomy picture emerged as to the
current state and future prospects of personality psychology. In the
search for a new and more convincing identity that followed this
period of crisis, defining relations and claiming boundaries with
neighbouring disciplines, most notably social psychology, has
played an important role.

Among researchers in both fields, consensus is now growing that
personality and social psychology have indeed moved closer
together over the past years (Ajzen, 1987; Singer and Kolligian,
1987). Marked disagreement, however, exists on the issue of

whether this convergence is desirable and profitable for either or both of the parties involved. On a general level, three main views on this issue can be distinguished.

First, the *pessimistic* view according to which the commonalities between social and personality psychology exist mainly in the form of shared deficiencies and unresolved problems (for example, Carlson, 1971, 1984; Elms, 1975). As far as personality psychology was concerned, Carlson (1971: 217) concluded: 'That the person is not really studied in current personality research is clearly shown in the survey of the literature.' This statement was reiterated and extended to the field of social psychology in almost the same form over a decade later (Carlson, 1984). His verdict rested primarily on methodological considerations, accusing personality researchers of not meeting even the most basic criteria of adequate personality research (such as using biographical data or covering extended time spans) and social psychological inquiry (such as observing social interaction or assessing important social attitudes).

Even though one could disagree with one or the other of the methodological criteria which Carlson regarded as essential (see Kenrick, 1986), it is hard to dismiss the general point that both personality and social psychology have shown a substantial lack of correspondence between their subject matter and their predominant strategies of analysis.

Secondly, the *particularistic* view rejects the intrusion of social psychological thought into personality research in terms of military metaphors of invasion and usurpation (for example, Kenrick, 1986; Kenrick and Dantchik, 1983). Rather than searching for common aspects of both disciplines from a 'disinterested' point of view, it is clear that this perspective argues from a personality 'ingroup perspective' (see also Feshbach, 1984). Kenrick and Dantchik (1983) attribute the unpopularity of the trait concept to the social psychological bias in favour of situationist models of explanation. This bias, in turn, is seen as a product of the experimental methodology prevalent in social psychology and the influence of sociological thought. (Ironically, it is the very preference for individualism and individualistic explanations that is identified by Hogan and Emler (1978) as one of the ideological preferences of modern American *social* psychology.) Furthermore, Kenrick and Dantchik identify an obvious 'cognitive bias' in current social psychology which they regard as responsible for an overemphasis on the 'social construction' of personality (see Chapter 3). A similar lack of balance in favour of cognitive models is also seen in the interactionist model of personality which locates the interaction between person and environment at the level of *cognitive processes*.

Finally, social psychologists are accused of a preference for problem-oriented mini-theories and 'laundry lists' or ragbags of variables which has furthered the theoretical impoverishment of personality research. Thus, the particularistic view offers a largely negative appraisal of social psychological contributions which they regard, at best, as a mixed blessing for personality research.

Thirdly, several authors adopt an *optimistic* view which welcomes the convergence between the two fields as facilitating joint efforts to solve similar problems encountered by each of the two disciplines (for example, Blass, 1984; Kihlstrom, 1987; Sherman and Fazio, 1983). In the search for a common identity on conceptual grounds, the fate of the respective dispositional key concepts of personality and social psychology, namely 'attitude' and 'trait', is particularly informative. The critical assessments of Mischel (1968) of the trait concept and Wicker (1969) of the attitude concept referred to the same central problem: the lack of empirical evidence for the postulated consistency between a latent disposition (attitude or trait) and observable behaviour. Accordingly, both fields explored new ways of increasing the strength of the relation between disposition and behaviour. The ideas and methods resulting from these initially intradisciplinary efforts often also proved suitable for increasing the disposition–behaviour relation in the respective other field. Thus it was shown, for example, that self-monitoring and objective self-awareness are not only effective moderators of the attitude–behaviour relationship but also allow more specific predictions of trait–behaviour consistency. In the same way, the principle of aggregating behavioural measures across time or across multiple behavioural criteria turned out to be equally successful in strengthening the consistency between traits and behaviour and between attitudes and behaviour (Blass, 1984).

According to Sherman and Fazio (1983), the parallels between traits and attitudes are highlighted by recent efforts to expand the scope of dispositional models of behaviour prediction by including situational concepts. In the area of attitude–behaviour research, these efforts are reflected in 'contingent consistency' models of behaviour (Acock and Scott, 1980; Andrews and Kandel, 1979). In the area of personality, the modern interactionist perspective offers a new model of the interdependence of personal and situational factors to facilitate the prediction of behaviour. How the modern interactionist approach to behaviour prediction can be applied to the attitude–behaviour relationship has been shown by Kahle (1984). Similarly, Blass (1984) noted an increasing interdisciplinary consensus on the appropriateness of an interactionist perspective to explain and predict behaviour. This evaluation led him to describe modern interactionism as the 'natural bridge between social psychology and personality psychology'.

In terms of the three perspectives distinguished above, the present volume is clearly committed to the optimistic view that progress in the field of personality can profit and in fact has profited a great deal from developments in social psychology. What will become evident in every single chapter is the fact that personality psychology cannot afford to ignore the influence of situations on behaviour if it wants to arrive at a proper understanding of why individuals act the way they do and differ in a predictable fashion from others. It will also become obvious that personality psychologists have widely recognized the need for an overarching perspective on personality that includes both the characteristics of individual persons and those of the contexts (be they specific situations or more global environments) in which these individuals live.

Scope of the book

The present volume offers a critical introduction to recent research in the field of personality and social behaviour. The organization of the volume is based on what may be called a *concept-oriented* approach. New developments in personality research are discussed along the lines of general theoretical and methodological issues, and specific theories as well as domains of personality functioning are considered in the context of their relevance to these general issues. The decision to trace conceptual and methodological developments *across different domains of personality functioning* is made with the following objectives in mind:

1 To identify paradigmatic shifts, or changes of preferred theoretical constructs and methodological strategies, such as the acceptance of an interactionist view of personality or the renewed interest in the taxonomic analysis of traits.

2 To offer an evaluation of new methodological strategies aimed to improve empirical support for central concepts of personality theory, such as aggregation or the search for moderator variables of consistency, which is facilitated by looking at their advantanges and limitations across a range of personality constructs.

3 To identify deficits and unresolved problems, such as the lack of a 'psychology of situations' urgently required by the interactionist view of personality, which can be assessed in a more systematic and representative way if they are pursued through different research domains.

4   To identify new and promising developments which are not generally included in personality textbooks unless they have already acquired some form of 'canonization'. Here, special emphasis is placed on the growing interest in idiographic research strategies and the attempts at reconciling the objectives of nomothetic inquiry and idiographic assessment.

Thus, the volume will focus on the identification of recurrent conceptual and methodological issues, such as consistency and change or the role of cognitive factors in personality, which run as common threads through many of the otherwise so distinct domains of personality research. In particular, the aim is to convey an impression of the diverse developments which have emerged in response to the serious criticisms of the field in the late 1960s and early 1970s. The work discussed in the following chapters reflects a new sense of initiative and optimism, the first signs of which can be witnessed in the early collections of modern interactionist contributions to personality (Endler and Magnusson, 1976a; Magnusson and Endler, 1977a). As I hope to show, the last decade of personality research has been a prolific and innovative one. A distinctive feature of this period has been the increasing convergence between social psychology and personality psychology, particularly due to the progress of the work on social cognition in social psychology and the efforts to implement the research programme advanced by proponents of an interactionist view of personality. The thrust of these new developments has been not so much in the direction of exploring new domains of personality functioning as with finding new theoretical models and empirical strategies applicable to a wide range of themes and content areas.

Preview of the chapters

Current progress in personality research cannot be properly appreciated without at least a cursory examination of the problems and controversies that have dominated the field in its more recent history. This historical perspective is guided by the aim to illuminate the positions from which current research perspectives have emerged. Of central significance in this context is the issue of the cross-situational consistency of behaviour, giving rise to the persistent 'consistency controversy' from which personality psychology is only just beginning to recover.

The subsequent chapters are devoted to a discussion of theoretical and methodological developments that have been prompted by the criticisms and challenges of key concepts of personality theory. To begin with, recent suggestions for revitalizing the trait concept will be reviewed. Then, the interactionist perspective on personality will be discussed as the most significant theoretical response to the crisis of confidence in the early 1970s, followed by a review of the different methodological developments aimed to provide better strategies for measuring stability and change in an individual's personality.

Finally, the perspective is broadened beyond the boundaries of personality research to include approaches from related areas of psychology, most notably social psychology, which offer an answer to those problems not sufficiently recognized or elaborated by mainstream personality psychology. Particular emphasis will be placed in this context on the impact of situational forces on behaviour. It will be shown that the search for new theoretical models of personality must, and fortunately can, draw heavily on recent developments in social psychology.

Within this general framework, the individual chapters concentrate on the following issues. Chapter 2 will review one of the most fundamental, and at the same time most controversial, notions of personality research, the issue of consistency in personality. Virtually every conceptualization of personality includes the proposition that there is consistency in individual behaviour both temporally and cross-situationally. In what has become known as the 'consistency controversy', this key notion of personality has been challenged primarily on the grounds of inconclusive empirical evidence. Instead, the alternative view has argued that situational influences are the most powerful determinants of individual behaviour. The chapter will provide a critical discussion of the competing positions in this controversy, represented by trait psychologists and situationists respectively. While victory cannot be claimed by either party, the debate has stimulated the development of improved theoretical and methodological strategies in the search for consistency as well as the emergence of modern interactionism as a new framework for the study of personality.

In Chapter 3, trait psychologists' responses to the situationist challenge will be presented, guided by the aim to underline the theoretical significance of traits as central constructs for the analysis of individual differences. One line of development has led to the development of a basic trait taxonomy, capturing the central dimensions of the structure of personality. A second line seeks to show that individual differences on trait measures of personality can be explained, at least in part, by genetic differences of the persons involved. From yet another perspective, the nature of trait inferences is conceptualized as a process of social construction determined simultaneously by the qualities of the person observed and the descriptive language available to the observer.

The next two chapters are devoted to the 'modern interactionist' approach to personality which argues that behaviour is a joint function of both the person and the situation. Behind this straightforward formula lies the promise of a new and fruitful conceptualization of personality functioning which dismisses traditional trait approaches in favour of capturing the dynamic interplay between personal dispositions and situational characteristics in determining behaviour. Chapter 4 clarifies the basic tenets and methodological strategies of the interactionist approach, placing particular emphasis on the more recent theoretical and empirical developments of the interactionist model, including the role of situational variables and the emerging interactionist view of personality development.

Since the rediscovery of interactionism in the mid-1970s, a large amount of evidence has been accumulated to demonstrate the adequacy of this approach in accounting for individual behaviour in different personality domains. In Chapter 5, three research domains are examined in more detail which can be regarded as representative fields of application for the interactionist approach: anxiety, emotions, and prosocial behaviour. At the same time, unresolved problems will be discussed, most notably the failure to offer an adequate theoretical treatment of the 'psychological situation' and to develop methods which would be capable of capturing the proposed reciprocal interaction of persons and situations.

While modern interactionism reflects the search for a new conceptual framework, other responses to the consistency controversy have been more concerned with improving the methodological basis of studying personality. Recent developments can be classified in terms of their commitment to a nomothetic versus idiographic approach to personality measurement. After reviewing the longstanding debate about the adequacy of the two approaches, Chapter 6 presents various strategies designed to improve both the validity and reliability of consistency measurement. These approaches, which include the identification of moderator variables, the aggregation of measures over time and situations, and the use of peer reports, are located in the nomothetic mainstream of personality research.

However, recent years have witnessed an increasing interest in idiographic or person-centred methodologies designed to capture the uniqueness of the individual person. The central characteristic of these approaches, which are presented in Chapter 7, is that they treat the individual person as their unit of analysis rather than deriving inferences about individuals from sample-based data.

Significantly, the work discussed in this chapter is grounded in the attempt at bridging the gap between a strictly nomothetic and a strictly idiographic approach to the study of personality. In Chapter 8, the role of the situation as a concept for personality research is explored. Among the achievements of the interactionist approach to personality is its explicit recognition of the importance of the 'psychological situation' as a critical determinant of behaviour. The psychological meaning of situations for the individual is regarded as a crucial factor in predicting behaviour and accounting for behavioural regularities across situations. Following a brief introduction into attempts at defining and classifying situations in objective terms, the focus of this chapter is on two general lines of theorizing and research that have emerged from the interactionist perspective: the description and functional analysis of situations *as they are perceived* by the individual and the exploration of the process whereby individuals actively *choose and influence* the situations in which they find themselves.

The concluding Chapter 9 will pick up once more the issues discussed in the preceding chapters. The attempt is made to combine the work discussed in the preceding chapters into a more general picture of the state of personality research as it enters the last decade of the century which saw the rise of psychology as a scientific discipline. The progress achieved by the new theoretical and methodological developments will be assessed in a comparative appraisal of the promises and limitations contained in the different approaches. At this point it will be up to readers to decide for themselves if the field of personality has been successful in overcoming a state which was likened by Sechrest fifteen years ago to 'the apocryphal jet pilot who assured his passengers that while the plane was lost, it was at least making a good time' (1976: 22). The present volume seeks to foster the more optimistic view that as civil aviation is becoming increasingly safer and faster, personality research has made significant progress in consolidating its role as one of the core disciplines of psychology.

2

The Issue of Consistency in Personality:
Sixty Years of Controversy

How do personality psychologists define the subject matter of their discipline? Given the diversity of theories and methods that have characterized the field of personality psychology throughout its history, it is clear that there cannot be a single answer to this question. Nevertheless, it seems possible to extract three basic components of the meaning of *personality* that are endorsed by most researchers in this area regardless of their specific theoretical orientations:

1 Personality is the reflection of *individual uniqueness.*
2 Personality is *enduring* and *stable.*
3 Personality and its reflection in behaviour are *determined* by forces or dispositions assumed to reside within the individual.

These three cornerstones of a psychological understanding of personality are linked together by a still more general concept implied in each of them – the concept of *consistency*:

1 In order to capture the uniqueness of an individual's personality, that is, those personal qualities that distinguish him or her from others, one has to seek for consistent differences between individuals both across different situations and over time.
2 To demonstrate the stability and endurance of personality, evidence of intraindividual consistency is required, again both temporally and cross-situationally.
3 To explain a person's behaviour as the manifestation of some internal disposition, it is essential that the disposition can be shown to shape behaviour consistently and reliably in different situations.

Thus, the notion of consistency is tied inseparably to the very concept of personality, and its empirical validation is of crucial significance for the identity of personality psychology. As Loevinger and Knoll (1983: 196) put it: 'If there is no consistency in behavior, then the field of personality should disappear.' This special relationship between the concepts of consistency and personality holds the clue to understanding the vigour and persistence with which the so-called consistency controversy was led over almost sixty years before eventually calming down in the course of the 1980s. While personality theorists claimed that behaviour is largely determined by relatively stable, intrapsychic qualities of the person, this view was challenged by proponents of a situationist perspective. They, in turn, regarded the particular features of a situation as the principle determinants of individual behaviour in that situation. To resolve this issue, exchanges between the participants in the debate focused on one basic question: Is the evidence for consistent relationships between personal characteristics and behaviour conclusive enough to explain individual behaviour in terms of personality traits and other dispositional constructs and, by implication, to assign predictive power to these intrapersonal variables?

The present chapter reviews the main arguments in the person–situation debate and their impact on the current status of personality research. The debate reached a culmination point in Mischel's (1968) attack on the concept of consistency. His claim that there was no convincing evidence of consistency triggered a profound crisis of confidence in the field of personality (see, for example, Fiske, 1978b; Phares and Lamiell, 1977; Sechrest, 1976), from which it was slow to recover. As will be evident throughout this book, much of the current agenda for personality psychology can be traced directly to the consistency controversy. This is true not only for the modern interactionist perspective that emerged as a conceptual alternative to a purely trait-based model of personality (see Chapters 4 and 5). Holding on to a dispositional view of personality, other responses have been directed at revising the theoretical meaning of the trait concept (see Chapter 3) as well as the methodological strategies for assessing consistency (see Chapter 6). Still others have been led to call for a greater emphasis on the study of individual personalities (see Chapter 7) and on the search for a better understanding of the psychological as opposed to physical properties of situations as determinants of behaviour (see Chapter 8).

Meanings of consistency

Before entering into a more detailed discussion of the competing positions advanced in the course of the consistency debate, it is useful to take a look at the meaning of the term 'consistency'. There are different ways in which behaviour can be said to be consistent or inconsistent. Unfortunately, these different meanings have not always been made sufficiently clear and have acted as a source of ambiguity in evaluating empirical evidence for or against consistency (see also Caprara, 1987; Ozer, 1986). One basic distinction refers to the temporal versus cross-situational aspects of consistency. This section presents a summary of the meanings of the consistency concept involved in the controversy.

Temporal stability

One way of defining consistency of behaviour is in terms of its stability over time. To the extent that personality measures and corresponding behaviours show temporal stability, such evidence contradicts the situationist claim that behaviour is primarily a function of specific situational influences. There is conclusive evidence to suggest that individuals show considerable levels of stability in the course of their development. This is true for different types of personality constructs as well as different forms of personality assessment (see Conley (1984a) for a review). In the trait domain, studies using self-ratings (for example, Costa et al., 1980; Finn, 1986) and observer-ratings (for example, Costa and McCrae, 1988a; Huesman et al., 1984; Ozer and Gjerde, 1989) report correlations in the range of $r = 0.70$ and above across intervals of up to thirty years. Similar findings were obtained for other personality constructs, such as cognitive and attributional styles (for example, Block et al., 1981; Burns and Seligman, 1989). Piccione et al. (1989) assessed the stability of hypnotizability using objective behavioural indicators of a person's susceptibility to hypnosis and found retest correlations of $r = 0.71$ over a twenty-five-year period.

Studies assessing the stability of personality frequently rely on retests in which the same instruments are administered at different points in time. If the search for stability is to be extended beyond the level of personality attributes into the behavioural realm, the limitations of the retest strategy become obvious. In this case, retests are appropriate only if the way in which a personality characteristic is displayed in behaviour can be assumed to remain the same in the course of development. In the Piccione et al. study quoted above, for instance, one of the behavioural indicators of hypnotizability was the 'arm rigidity item' testing subjects' responsiveness to the hypnotic suggestion that their arm 'becomes as stiff as an iron bar which you cannot bend'. Criteria like this are likely to be relatively insensitive to developmental changes and can therefore be used to assess stability through retests over extended intervals.

However, there are many personality variables which are reflected in behaviour in phenotypically different forms in different developmental periods. Consider, for example, the trait of aggressiveness (Olweus, 1979). In children, this trait may be expressed behaviourally in the form of hitting another child or destroying a peer's toy. In order to assess the stability of an individual's level of aggressiveness, it would make little sense to look for these same behaviours twenty years later. Instead, a new behavioural repertoire needs to be defined that is an adequate representation of adult aggression. Thus, the search must be for genotypic continuities, that is, for those superficially different behaviours that nevertheless reflect a common underlying disposition. To achieve this task, 'we need to view development in terms of the organizations and reorganizations of behavior that take place in response to a series of salient developmental issues presented in the social environment' (Caspi, 1989: 86). Not all changes in behavioural patterns over time reflect instability, that is, lack of consistency. To the extent that such changes follow a systematic pattern over time, a more adequate interpretation would be to look at them as reflections of a continuous process of personality development. This view of personality as a dynamic exchange between personality and environmental demands has become more and more accepted in recent research and will be presented in detail in the final section of Chapter 4.

Altogether, the stability of personality characteristics over time has not been seriously disputed in the course of the consistency debate. Instead, the controversy has centred on a different meaning of consistency which refers to the regularity of behavioural responses *across different situations*. This became apparent once again in a series of exchanges between Mischel and Peake (1982a, 1983b) and Bem (1983b), Conley (1984b), Epstein (1983a), Funder (1983b) and Jackson and Paunonen (1985) over the relationship between temporal and cross-situational consistency. Mischel and Peake (1982a) found that behaviours in the domains of friendliness and conscientiousness showed high temporal stability in repeated occurrences of the same or similar situations but little consistency across different situations. From these findings, they derived a radical proposal: to conceptualize the perennial issue of consistency in personality solely in terms of temporal stability and to abandon once and for all the search for behavioural consistency across situations.

Cross-situational consistency

Cross-situational consistency has been defined in different ways, varying both in the degree of assumed behavioural invariance and the comparison level by which it is established (see for example, Argyle and Little, 1972; Magnusson and Endler, 1977b). Resolving the consistency issue has been hampered by the fact that the participants in the debate have not always been sufficiently clear (or

Table 2.1   Different conceptualizations of cross-situational consistency

Type of consistency	Level of comparison	Postulated by
absolute consistency	intra-individual	[attributed to] trait model
relative consistency	inter-individual	trait model
coherence	intra-individual	interactionism
specificity, i.e. no consistency	inter-individual	situationism

claimed to be misrepresented by their critics) about their respective understanding of cross-situational consistency (see Carlson, 1975; Funder, 1983a). Table 2.1 presents the different meanings that have played a role in the consistency controversy.

Absolute consistency: According to the concept of absolute consistency, a person is expected to display constant patterns of behaviour unaffected by situational factors. A person characterized as highly dominant on the basis of a trait measure of dominance should behave in an equally dominant fashion whenever the disposition is actualized. Conceptually, therefore, absolute consistency refers to the intra-individual stability of personality measures and behaviour across different situations. Empirically, however, absolute consistency is typically operationalized in terms of the stability of *group means* across situations, a procedure which does not furnish conclusions about stability at the individual level (Caspi and Bem, 1990: 550). It is the notion of absolute consistency against which the thrust of situationists' attack on the consistency concept has been directed. They argue that there is no or very little cross-situational consistency, since behaviour is largely determined by situational influences. Among these, reinforcement contingencies are seen as playing the most important role in the development and change of behavioural patterns (see, for example, Mischel, 1968). As Kenrick and Funder (1988: 24) note, however, the view that personality is reflected in absolute constancies in behaviour across different situations is not more than a 'straw man' that even proponents of the trait concept find unacceptable. Nevertheless, it is fair to say that trait psychologists generally regard the impact of situations on behaviour as much less important than that of personal dispositions. This is also true for the second meaning with which the concept of cross-situational consistency is used in the trait model.

Relative consistency: While relative consistency does not presuppose constancy of behavioural patterns within the individual, it requires the rank order of the behavioural patterns of different individuals to be stable across situations (Argyle and Little, 1972; Magnusson and Endler, 1977b). If Person A displays a higher level of dominant behaviour than Person B in one situation, then A is also expected to be more dominant than B in another situation, although their absolute levels of dominant behaviours in both situations may well be different. This means that relative consistency acknowledges behavioural variation as a function of the situation. However, the impact of situational influences is assumed not to affect the rank order between individuals so any observed differences in behaviour can be attributed to personality variables. To obtain evidence for relative consistency an individual difference approach is required permitting an individual's behaviour to be assessed against that of relevant others across different situations. Although most widely accepted as a basis for empirical research, there are obvious problems involved in relying on inter-individual comparisons to establish consistency. It may be the case, for example, that two persons out of a group of four show dramatic changes in their behaviour from one situation to the next, while the behaviour of the other two remains more or less constant. As a result, different rank orders of the four individuals are likely to emerge in the two situations, producing low correlations between the two rank orders and thereby suggesting little evidence of relative consistency. What conclusions would this evidence suggest? One would clearly be mistaken in concluding that the four members of this hypothetical sample were inconsistent in their behaviours, since two of them were in fact quite consistent. Rather, it can be concluded that not all of them were equally responsive to the different features of the two situations. This latter interpretation, however, is at odds with the criterion of stable rank orders as an index of consistency. What follows from this reasoning is that the concept of relative consistency is not an adequate strategy for capturing the proposed cross-situational stability of behaviour as a function of individual qualities (see Lerner and Tubman (1989) for a similar point). What is needed, instead, is a conceptualization of consistency that incorporates both the importance of personal dispositions and the differential sensitivity of individual behaviour to situational influences.

Coherence: Such a definition of consistency is entailed in the concept of coherence introduced as part of the interactionist model of personality. In this approach, behaviour is regarded as being determined by the interaction of personal characteristics and situational features (Magnusson and Endler, 1977b). According to the interactionist understanding of consistency, individual behaviour is assumed to be coherent across situations in the sense of being an inherently lawful expression of the individual's personal qualities and cognitive activities. What is central to this third meaning of consistency is that it allows for both stability and change of behaviour so long as they follow a systematic and hence individually predictable pattern. In order to identify cross-situational coherence, the following type of information is required (see Magnusson and Endler, 1977b: 10): (a) information about the individual's disposition to react in the respective kind of situation; (b) information about the individual's interpretation of the situation; and, (c) a psychological model about the link between response dispositions and situational meaning as determinants of individual behaviour. If, for example, a person is studied who (a) tends to respond with dominant behaviours to situations where his or her authority is challenged and (b) interprets the respective situations as belonging to that category, then one would expect cross-situational coherence under (c) the theoretical assumption that behaviour is similar across situations if the situations involved are perceived as similar by the individual. Defining cross-situational consistency in terms of coherence appears to be the most promising avenue for solving the consistency problem. Recently, Larsen (1989) advocated the study of a 'hybrid' kind of consistency that involves both fluid and fixed patterns of personality characteristics and in which it is the *pattern of change that is consistent* (Larsen, 1989: 180). However, as the discussion of the modern interactionist approach to personality in Chapters 4 and 5 will reveal, the large-scale search for coherent patterns of personality still awaits being launched.

This brief review of the different meanings assigned to the concept of consistency has shown that even at the definitional level, there has been plenty of room for ambiguity as well as substantive disagreement. Now it is time to look more closely at the theoretical approaches as well as empirical paradigms involved in the debate.

The beginnings of the controversy

In 1928, Hartshorne and May published the first part of a large-scale investigation into the consistency of personality in children. Their study, in conjunction with Allport's (1937) criticism of its rationale and findings, is generally regarded as marking the beginning of the consistency controversy in personality psychology. These two early contributions clearly spelled out the basic conceptual and empirical issues that were to dominate the debate between trait psychologists and situationists over the next five decades.

Challenging the trait model: the case of dishonesty
As part of their extensive *Studies in the Nature of Character*,
Hartshorne and May (1928) examined the cross-situational consistency of children's dishonest behaviour. More than 10,000 school
children participated in the study which addressed three types of
deceptive behaviour: cheating, stealing, and lying. Each of the three
types was represented by several behavioural indicators, for
example, stealing money in a party situation, a play situation, or a
classroom situation. In an elaborate design, the children were
provided with opportunities to perform different deceptive activities, supposedly without the risk of being found out, and their
behaviour was unobtrusively recorded. To assess the consistency
with which the children either showed or refrained from deceitful
behaviour, correlations were computed between the different measures across the whole sample. The obtained correlations ranged
from a minimum of $r = -0.003$ to a maximum of $r = 0.312$
(Hartshorne and May, 1928: 383).

From this pattern of low correlations, the authors concluded that
there was little support for a stable, intrinsic disposition towards
dishonesty that would lead to the consistent performance of deceptive behaviour in different situations. Whether or not a child acts in a
deceitful manner depends, as they interpreted their findings, primarily on the specific features of the situation. As a consequence,
psychologists seeking to understand and predict behaviour in
different situations should direct their efforts towards identifying
those situational qualities responsible for encouraging or suppress-
ing dishonest behaviours.

The Hartshorne and May study is generally quoted as prime
empirical evidence against the assumption of cross-situational
consistency. At the same time, however, there have been criticisms
of their statistical analyses and interpretations (see, for example,
Burton, 1963; Epstein and O'Brien, 1985; Maller, 1934). Among
the early critics was Allport (1937) who highlighted some fundamental flaws in approaching the consistency issue in this way.

Dishonesty revisited: Allport (1937)
In his discussion of the Hartshorne and May study, Allport
uncovered several implicit and thus untested premises in their
design that cast doubt on the authors' interpretation of their
findings. Since the same points can be made with regard to many
subsequent studies addressing the consistency issue, it is worth
taking a closer look at his line of reasoning.

As noted above, Hartshorne and May's central message was that there is little evidence for consistency in children's deceptive behaviour across situations. Allport's critical analysis concentrates on the fact that this conclusion was derived from low correlations between the frequencies of various deceptive behaviours *averaged across respondents*. Such a procedure, Allport notes, is fraught with two basic problems.

The first problem concerns the issue of selecting behavioural indicators for the underlying trait of dishonesty. In order to assess consistency on the basis of data aggregated across a large sample of respondents, one has to be certain that the behaviours selected as trait indicators are, indeed, representative of one and the same trait dimension for the sample as a whole. Unless the link between traits and their behavioural indicators is established explicitly, the possibility cannot be ruled out that, for some respondents, some of the behaviours may have been representative of a trait other than dishonesty. To illustrate this point, consider the following example: Hartshorne and May regarded lying and stealing as conceptually equivalent behavioural criteria for dishonesty. Yet it is not unlikely that for part of the children in their sample the two behaviours had different psychological meanings, and should have been regarded as belonging to two different trait categories. A child could have lied to protect her- or himself against an anticipated punishment, but had no reason for stealing money from a classmate because she or he received ample pocket money. As long as such differential responses to situations follow a systematic, temporally stable pattern, it would be wrong to label a child inconsistent who tells a lie in one situation but fails to steal money in another. This important, but generally neglected issue was repeated more recently by Bem (1983c: 568) who stressed once again that the 'traditional inference of inconsistency is not an inference about individuals but a statement about the disagreement between a group of individuals and an investigator over which behaviors and which situations may properly be classified into common equivalence classes.'

Allport's second line of criticism referred to a closely related point. He noted that Hartshorne and May's unit of analysis was the sample of children as a whole. This database, he argued, only facilitates inter-individual comparisons and is mute with regard to consistency at the intra-individual level. More specifically, he made the point that their low correlations revealed no more than the fact that the behavioural patterns of the children did not vary in the same way across the selected situations. Consequently, Allport claimed that an adequate examination of the postulated intra-individual consistency of behaviour calls for an idiographic meth-

odology. In such an approach the subjective definition of equivalence classes of behaviours and situations would be of central
importance (see Allport, 1937: 280). Unfortunately, Allport's plea
for a greater emphasis on the individual in the search for consistency
failed to make a deep impact on the majority of researchers
addressing the consistency issues in the subsequent decades. Their
focus remained on the search for relative consistency, firmly rooted
in the individual difference paradigm. Over the last ten years or so,
however, a renewed concern with a person-centred perspective on
consistency has gradually emerged that is clearly indebted to
Allport's critical analysis. In this vein, Mischel (1979: 742) reminded
trait psychologists of the fact 'that individuals organize and pattern
their behavioral consistencies and discriminations in terms of their
subjectively perceived equivalencies and their personal meanings,
not those of the trait psychologist who categorizes them.'

Following the early contributions by Allport, Hartshorne and
May, trait theorists and situationists became increasingly polarized
over the issue of behavioural consistency versus specificity. At the
theoretical level, the controversy centred on the explanatory value of
dispositional concepts: to what extent can a person's behavioural
performance be traced back to the operation of some latent
disposition within the individual? At the *methodological level*, the
fact that the parties involved based their arguments on different
methods must be seen as a major reason for the failure to obtain a
conclusive body of evidence that would have facilitated the settle-
ment of the debate. The next two sections summarize the main
features of the trait approach and the situationist perspective as they
have been presented in the course of the consistency debate.

The traditional trait position

Defining and explaining personality in terms of traits has a long and
reputable tradition in personality psychology. After Allport, whose
proper identification as a trait psychologist was recently re-
examined by Zuroff (1986), many prominent theorists – such as
Cattell (1950), Eysenck (1952) and Guilford (1959) in their factor
analytic models – have relied on personality traits as their basic units
of analysis. The present section will not attempt to discuss these
models since thorough discussions are widely available in personality textbooks (for example, Abramson, 1980; Mischel, 1986;
Peterson, 1988). Instead, this section begins by identifying some
core assumptions shared by the different varieties of the trait
approach and then discusses two alternative conceptualizations of

traits as either summary labels for observed behaviours or personal dispositions in the sense of latent response tendencies.

There are at least three general features associated with the use of traits as theoretical constructs in personality research (see Levy (1983) and Brody (1988) for critical discussions of the trait model):

1 Traits are invoked as differential constructs to explain why people differ from each other in their responses to identical or similar situations.
2 A person's behaviour is assumed to show relative temporal and cross-situational consistency due to the operation of some latent internal disposition.
3 Research based on the trait concept typically employs personality testing in the form of trait ratings and relies on correlational methods in the analysis of data.

These common assumptions should not, however, obscure the fact that the trait concept has been defined in different ways by different theoretical models. One broad distinction refers to the use of traits as summary labels for stable and consistent *behaviour patterns* on the one hand and the conceptualization of traits as *latent dispositions* on the other. Hirschberg (1978) refers to the two perspectives as the 'summary view' and the 'dispositional view' of the trait concept.

The summary view of traits
According to this view, trait concepts serve the purpose of summarizing similar behaviours under a common label so as to facilitate the interpretation of behavioural patterns. Thus, traits are used primarily for descriptive purposes aimed at reducing the variety of specific behavioural acts into more manageable units (Mischel, 1973). They are not intended to provide *explanations* for observed regularities of behaviour nor to be used as a basis for *predicting* future behaviour. By definition, this means that trait categories can only be used retrospectively since they require that trait-relevant behaviours have actually been observed. Consequently, a trait ascription is made if a sufficient number of behavioural instances have been recorded that can be grouped together and interpreted as expressions of one common personality category.

Thus, the summary view relies on manifest behavioural evidence as a basis for ascribing a trait to a person. Because of this feature, there is no need for the summary view to concern itself with the situational properties facilitating or inhibiting the performance of certain relevant behavioural acts. To put it simply, if someone shows a variety of behaviours pertaining to the trait category of friendliness, then the trait is ascribed to the person. The stronger the behavioural evidence, the more compelling the trait ascription. In contrast, if a person fails to show evidence of friendly behaviour in a given period of observation, a trait ascription in terms of friendliness will not be made.

This straightforward way of assessing personality traits, however, rests on a problematic premise: it assumes that the person is free to choose between performing or not performing actions that are expressive of the trait in question. It is only under this condition that observed behaviours provide a conclusive basis for or against the ascription of that trait. The problem becomes particularly salient in interpreting non-occurrences of trait-relevant behaviours, often quoted as evidence against the trait concept. Thus, for example, it may be a mistake *not* to ascribe traits such as 'generous' or 'brave' to a person on the grounds of insufficient evidence of corresponding behaviours. Individuals may not have the opportunity to act bravely simply because they rarely find themselves in situations where bravery is called for or are unable to behave generously because they lack the necessary resources.

A related criticism refers to the problem that the summary view is unable to deal with those personality characteristics whose translation into behaviour is suppressed by normative constraints (Hirschberg, 1978). This is true for many negatively valued traits like jealousy or avarice, which a person might not choose to express in behavioural terms for fear of social rejection or other unwanted repercussions. Allport's (1966) reminder that the non-occurrence of trait-consistent behaviour as well as the occurrence of trait-inconsistent behaviour do not necessarily preclude the ascription of a trait is clearly relevant to this point.

Thus, the summary view of traits fails to recognize both low frequency of occurrence of trait-relevant situations and trait-irrelevant constraints on behaviour as alternative causes for what may appear as lack of behavioural evidence for a particular trait. In recent years, a more refined version of the summary view was introduced by Buss and Craik (1980, 1984) in their 'act frequency approach' to personality which will be discussed more fully in connection with other recent advances in personality measurement in Chapter 6. In particular, they offered a stringent methodological rationale for establishing the strength of act trends indicative of a given trait. The main improvement is that behavioural indicators of a given trait are sampled empirically and assessed in terms of their average frequency as well as their typicality as indicators of the trait in question. A further advantage is that each trait domain is represented by multiple acts. This means that the ascription of a trait to a person does *not* require the person to show one particular act with high frequency so long as he or she shows a sufficient number of acts within a category.

The dispositional view of traits

Unlike the summary view which focused on the descriptive qualities of trait categories, the more widely accepted dispositional view treats traits as hypothetical constructs designed to explain and predict regularities in behaviour. It is this version of the trait approach which has been the primary target of criticisms from the situationist side. According to the dispositional view, traits cannot be inferred directly from behavioural observation. Rather, they are regarded as latent tendencies which dispose the person to behave in a particular way *if he or she meets with situations that actualize the respective disposition* (Allport, 1937: 48). Traits are claimed to have a causal role in eliciting specific patterns of individual behaviour as well as producing individual differences in the way people react to a given situation. The dispositional view avoids some of the problems of the summary view by emphasizing the potential instead of the actual manifestation of traits in behaviour. Traits as latent dispositions are assumed to find their expression in overt behaviour in a linear way: the greater the strength of the underlying trait, the more pervasive and/or intense the corresponding behavioural manifestations. In this view, the relationship between traits and behaviour is a probabilistic one. This means, as Epstein (1979) points out, that a trait refers to a generalized tendency of a person to behave in a certain way over a sufficient sample of situations. Clearly, it does not imply that the person will show trait-relevant behaviour in all situations or even in all instances of one and the same situation.

By treating the impact of traits on behaviour as contingent upon the trait-actualizing features of the situation, the dispositional view needs to consider the situational properties that elicit the behavioural expression of a particular trait. For example, what are the situations that facilitate the manifestation of conscientious or dominant behaviours expected from a person with a strong trait of conscientiousness or dominance? Unfortunately, trait psychologists have largely neglected the task of establishing a functional link between traits and the situations most likely to actualize them (Brody, 1988: 8). Support for the dispositional view of traits is typically defined in terms of evidence for the *relative consistency* of behaviour across situations. As noted above, the concept of relative consistency acknowledges that different situations may have different effects on the trait-specific behaviour of individuals. However, since relative consistency only requires the rank order of individuals to remain invariant against situational changes, a more fine-grained analysis of the way situations affect the manifestation of traits behaviour may have seemed dispensable. As will be seen in Chapter 4, the failure to specify the relationship between traits and situations was an important aspect in the disillusionment with the traditional trait concept which prompted the modern interactionist perspective on personality.

The controversy surrounding the dispositional view of traits has centred less on conceptual than on empirical issues. Trait theorists and their situationist critics fundamentally disagreed in their interpretations of the available evidence examining the relationship between trait measures and behaviour across situations. Mischel's (1968) book *Personality and Assessment* stands out as one of the most powerful attacks on the empirical foundations of the trait concept. Reviewing a wide range of personality domains, he concluded that there was very little support for the notion of consistency in personality except in certain areas of intellectual functioning. While some recent authors have been critical of Mischel's analysis (for example, Levy, 1983), advocates of the trait concept have generally found it hard to fight off this powerful attack on the very foundations of their field. As Epstein (1979: 1103) notes not without sarcasm: 'The arguments in defense of traits are, for the most part, speculations that if things had been done differently, stability in personality might have been demonstrated.'

Given this situation, one has to ask why personality theorists have been so persistent in their efforts to defend the notions of traits and consistency. One answer to this question lies in what has become known as the 'consistency paradox'. In this paradox, intuitive beliefs that our own as well as other persons' behaviour shows considerable consistency in different situations clash with the failure to support these beliefs through systematic empirical research. In everyday life, these intuitive beliefs often prove successful in understanding and predicting the behaviour of others. Therefore, they tend to be quite robust, with even personality psychologists continuing to believe that their intuitions are right and the research wrong (Bem, 1983a; Buss, 1989: 1379). How strong, then, is the case against the deeply entrenched belief in the notion of consistency?

Assessing the evidence bearing on the issues of stability and consistency as a function of personal dispositions is not an easy task. Problems are due in large part to the fact that findings supporting the trait concept are frequently based on different methodological strategies and different types of data than those quoted against it. Therefore, one has to look very carefully at the ways in which support for both the trait and the situationist positions is sought in empirical research. Building upon a distinction first made by Cattell (1957), Block (1977) adopts such a fine-grained perspective by discussing the evidence for and against consistency as a function of three different data sources.

The first type of data, termed *O*- or *R-data*, provides information obtained through *observer ratings* of an individual's personality. Included in this category are ratings by peers and other knowledgeable informants, such as clinicians and teachers, who are in a position to provide valid information about the person under investigation. As Block himself as well as subsequent authors (for example, Deluty, 1985; Koretzky et al., 1978; McCrae, 1982; Woodruffe, 1984, 1985) were able to show, studies relying on R-data provide convincing evidence for the stability and consistency of personality traits and their corresponding behaviours in a variety of personality domains.

The impact of this evidence for the consistency issue is challenged, however, by the increasingly popular view that traits should not be conceived of as categories denoting qualities of the person observed. Instead, it is argued, traits are more adequately conceptualized as categories utilized by the observer to organize and structure his or her cognitive activities and to 'construct' observed behaviour patterns as being consistent (for example, Hampson, 1988; Mischel and Peake, 1983a; Shweder, 1975). If one accepts this view, which will be examined in more detail in the next chapter, the validity of observer ratings as sources of information about the personality of others becomes dubious unless they can be shown to converge with information from other data sources.

A second widely used type of data, *S-data*, contain *self-reports* about an individual's behaviour, feelings as well as broad personality dispositions. S-data are often used to relate latent trait-measures to specific state-measures, and the correspondence between traits and states is interpreted as an index of consistency. In the domain of anxiety-provoking situations, for example, self-report measures of trait anxiety have been shown to be significantly related to measures of state anxiety obtained in actual anxiety-provoking situations (see, for example, Spielberger, 1972). Moreover, S-data have been used successfully in the validation of trait concepts by showing their links with other relevant variables. For example, Snyder and Ickes (1985) quote evidence suggesting that questionnaire measures of authoritarianism are strongly related to a variety of self-reported attitudes, such as rejecting minority groups and holding conservative political attitudes.

It should be noted that even among those personality theorists defending the trait concept, reliance on S-data is regarded as problematic. They acknowledge the problem that S-data may tell us little more about consistency than that individuals are consistent in their beliefs about themselves which is 'a far cry from demonstrating that the behaviour itself is consistent.' (Epstein, 1979: 1100). In defence of S-data, however, one can point to a number of studies which demonstrated significant correlations between self-ratings and observer ratings of different personality variables (for example, Block, 1977; Cheek, 1982; Edwards and Klockars, 1981).

A third category of data is composed of *T-data* based on objective behavioural information obtained in standardized *test* or laboratory situations. According to Block (1977: 45) evidence for consistency based on T-data is 'extremely erratic, sometimes positive but often not'. Therefore, it is not surprising that the relationship between T-data and the two other data categories is also far from systematic. Empirical strategies leading to T-data are clearly favoured over the first two data types by the proponents of the situationist perspective. This explains why the failure to obtain evidence for consistency on the basis of T-data has had such a profound impact on the controversy. Within the domain of T-data, two types of studies can be identified from which calls for the rejection of the consistency concept have been derived (Alston, 1975: 34).

The first type are studies showing low correlations, within one class of situations, between different trait indicators, for example, low intercorrelations between different forms of dominant behaviours in similar situations. As Alston argues, these studies are not directly relevant to the issue of consistency, since it would not be required that a person showed a variety of different forms of trait-related behaviour so long as he or she consistently showed one type of behaviour or another.

The second type are studies showing low correlations between similar forms of trait-relevant behaviours in different situations, for example, low correlations between certain dominant acts under different situational circumstances. These studies do speak to the issue of consistency, because in order to be consistent a person would be expected to show similar patterns of behaviour across different situations. Yet, since findings from those studies are always based on average levels of behavioural performance observed in a larger sample, they only permit the conclusion that people in general do not tend to act consistently in the domain under study. Despite the fact that no interpretation can be justly derived from these data about individual members of the sample, as Lamiell (1981) has pointed out, evidence against the consistency concept is often misleadingly worded in an 'individualistic' mode.

The claim by advocates of the situationist model that T-data show greater objectivity and should therefore be given more weight than findings derived from self- and observer-ratings has been questioned by several authors. Looking for correspondence between the three types of data in the domain of aggressiveness, Olweus (1980) draws attention to the fact that the psychometric properties of T-data, such as their retest reliability, as well as their relationship with other theoretically relevant variables remain unexamined in the majority of studies using them. He therefore rejects the claim made by Mischel (1977: 335) that the failure to predict T-data from S- or R-data should be treated as evidence against the consistency of personality traits and behaviour. Funder (1983a: 357) points out that no single strategy of personality assessment can be claimed to be superior on an a priori basis and concludes: 'The different sources of personality must therefore serve as criteria *for each other.*' However, as Kagan (1988) notes, the meaning of a personality attribute is shaped to a significant degree by the source of evidence from which it originates. Failure to recognize this link often leads to uncritical comparisons of personality constructs across different data sources which may lead to unwarranted inferences of inconsistency: 'Most of the time, personality theorists compare individuals on degree of possession of an abstract, hypothetical quality, such as hostility, anxiety, or sadness. If the categorizations are based on different sources of evidence, it is possible that there is no one core quality but several different ones.' (Kagan, 1988: 619).

Problems with both views
As the review of the different data sources has shown, evidence for or against the dispositional view of traits is ambiguous. An obvious response to this state of affairs is to embark on the development of improved methods leading to more conclusive evidence for consistency in personality. While this task has been addressed on a large scale over the last ten years (see Chapters 6 and 7), a number of conceptual problems with the traditional understanding of traits remain to be addressed at a theoretical level.

A general problem is the essentially a-theoretical nature of both the summary view and the dispositional view, as pointed out by Hirschberg (1978), Levy (1983) and Snyder and Ickes (1985), among others. These critics argue that so far traits have been largely treated as isolated constructs and little effort has been made to study the relationship between different traits. Traits are often treated as handy constructs to invoke whenever regularities in individual behaviour and interindividual differences are observed. Yet little is gained in terms of conceptual analysis until the traits themselves are subjected to further theorizing in the context of other relevant constructs. This argument is not aimed at rejecting altogether the potential usefulness of the trait concept in the attempt to understand personality and individual behaviour, as advocated in some radical suggestions (for example, Nisbett, 1980). Rather, sympathetic critics such as Alston (1975), Hirschberg (1978) and Levy (1983) argue that traits do have a place in personality research if they are integrated into an explanatory network in which their interaction with other variables like cognitive functioning or motivational factors has to be defined. Attempts at exploring the genetic bases of personality traits illustrate a way of advancing the theoretical analysis of the trait concept (see Chapter 3).

There is another, more specific conceptual problem affecting the use of traits as descriptive labels as well as the accumulation of evidence for or against the trait concept. This problem refers to the sampling of behavioural indicators which are then combined into a common trait category (summary view) or serve as a basis for inferring the strength of an underlying disposition (dispositional view). In trait research, as in everyday impression formation, a decision needs to be made about how many confirming behavioural instances are required in order to warrant the ascription of a trait to a person and how many disconfirming instances are permitted before a trait is rejected and/or its opposite invoked as a psychological description of the person. There are two aspects involved in this issue. First, the explicit recognition of normative behavioural base-rates: how common and widespread are the different behavioural criteria. Secondly, the diagnostic value of these criteria with respect to the generalized trait: how much impact has the presence, or absence, of particular behaviours on ascribing a trait to a person. Meehl (1986) suggests that attributions of a trait to an individual are guided jointly by three types of considerations: the *frequency* of trait-relevant behaviours, the *intensity* or extremity of a single behaviour, and the *pervasity* with which trait-relevant behaviours emerge over a wide range of situations.

Elaborating on these issues, Rorer and Widiger (1983) note that traits differ in terms of their base-rates as well as the 'ascription rules' associated with them. For example, only very few positive instances, such as attacking a policeman during a rally, are sufficient to ascribe the trait 'violent' to a person, whereas negative evidence, such as the failure to observe violent behaviours, would not be enough to characterize the person as non-violent or even peaceable. In contrast, for other traits, such as 'friendly' or 'honest', few negative behavioural instances, such as, not returning a polite greeting or not taking a found wallet to the police, are sufficient for denying the respective attribute to the person. These examples illustrate that the outcome of trait attributions is not determined solely by behaviour which actually occurs but to a large extent by the very nature of the ascription rules used to link behavioural evidence to trait interpretations. Rothbart and Park (1986) provided empirical support for this line of reasoning. They demonstrated that trait terms vary in the number of instances required for their confirmation or disconfirmation, and that this variation is systematically linked to the favourability of the trait terms. Using a sample of 150 trait adjectives, favourable traits, such as honest, intelligent or kind, were shown to require a larger number of instances to be confirmed and a smaller number of instances to be disconfirmed than unfavourable traits, such as cruel, malicious or sly, which are 'easy to acquire but hard to loose' (Rothbart and Park, 1986: 137).

Whether traits are used as summary labels for observed behaviour or assigned the status of explanatory constructs, they refer to ordinary language as their basic frame of reference (see also Chapter 3). Therefore, it is vital to recognize that the conventions of everyday language contain specific ascription rules which are conceptually independent of, and yet exert a powerful influence on, the psychological meaning of trait descriptions.

The situationist challenge

In the previous sections, repeated reference has been made to the situationist critique of trait-based research in personality. Now it is time for a more detailed examination of the situationist position in its own right. Over and above its significance as a challenge to the trait model, situationism has played a constructive role in personality psychology by contributing concepts and methods to the emerging modern interactionist view which embraces central features of both the trait approach and the situationist model into a common conceptual framework. Rather than denoting a unified theoretical orientation, 'situationism' is a summary term (see Bowers, 1973; Edwards and Endler, 1983). It comprises such diverse viewpoints as radical behaviourism, which explains behaviour exclusively in terms of reinforcing factors present in the environment (for example, Skinner, 1963), and social learning theories which acknowledge the importance of intrapersonal, and in particular cognitive, variables to varying degrees (for example, Bandura, 1969; Mischel, 1973). Nevertheless, it is possible to extract some common theoretical and methodological assumptions shared by the different varieties of situationism. Situationists would generally agree that:

1 Behaviour is highly situation-specific, not cross-situationally consistent.
2 Individual differences within a situation are attributed primarily to measurement error rather than broad internal dispositions.
3 Observed response patterns can be causally linked to the stimuli present in the situation.
4 The experiment is the most appropriate method for discovering such stimulus–response links.

These four assertions stand in marked contrast to the basic tenets of the trait approach. To assess the strengths and weaknesses of the situationist perspective as a conceptual alternative to the trait approach, we need to take a closer look at each postulate.

First, as far as the person–situation debate is concerned, the core proposition of situationism states that there is little consistency in behaviour. Since situational factors are seen as the most powerful determinants of behaviour, different situations should produce different behaviours. Temporal stability is expected only to the extent that the central features of the situation reinforcing particular behaviours recur or remain constant. As Bandura (1986: 12) puts it: 'Whether social behavior is invariant or changes over time depends, partly, on the degree of continuity of social conditions over the time span.' Moreover, it is suggested that discriminativeness in behaviour should not be regarded in negative terms as a lack of consistency but as a highly adaptive process allowing the person to respond flexibly to situational changes. In contrast, cross-situationally consistent, or indiscriminate, patterns of behaviour are seen as indicative of the individual's inability to cope with environmental demands (Mischel (1984a); and see Phares and Lamiell (1977) for a similar argument). In support of this view, Wright and Mischel (1987) quote evidence that emotionally disturbed boys showed higher levels of consistency in their aggressive and withdrawal behaviour in situations demanding high levels of cognitive and self-regulatory competencies than in less demanding situations.

Secondly, if behaviour is determined by situational variables, then it follows that individual differences within any one situation should be minimal and be treated as error variance. This postulate takes a somewhat modified form in social learning theories which acknowledge the role of person variables, such as cognitive competencies and attention processes, as mediating variables between situation and behaviour (Bandura, 1986; Mischel, 1990). Situational stimuli are regarded as affecting behaviour through the mediation of internal variables which regulate both the interpretation of objective stimuli and the ensuing behavioural response. Thus, social learning theories allow some room for individual differences due to internal mediators between stimulus and response, even though, as Mischel (1973) points out, they are likely to manifest themselves only if the situational stimuli are weak and ambiguous. What remains, however, is the rejection of the view, entailed in the concept of relative consistency, that individual differences within a situation are the result of differences in broad personality traits actualized in that situation.

Thirdly, according to the situationist position, the processes regulating individual behaviour can only be properly understood if causal relationships are specified between overt behaviour and its antecedent conditions in the form of stimulus–response (S–R) links. For an S–R link to be established in the domain of aggressiveness, for instance, evidence is required that changes in the situation, such as the availability of aggressive cues and models, produce systematic changes in the amount of aggressive behaviour displayed by the subjects (see, for example, Bandura et al., 1963). The impact of aggressive stimuli on eliciting aggressive responses was demonstrated in a well-known study by Berkowitz and LePage (1967). They showed that subjects gave significantly more electric shocks to a person who had previously frustrated them when the shocks were administered in the presence of a gun (aggressive stimulus condition) than in the presence of a badminton racket (neutral stimulus condition).

However, as Bowers (1973) points out in his critical analysis of situationism, observing a link between stimuli as independent variables and responses as dependent variables is by no means a causal explanation of why certain stimuli bring about certain responses. In his view, it is one of the metaphysical fallacies of the situationist position to mistake the observation that antecedents cause consequences for an explanation of the principles accounting for the observed relationship. Quoting an analogy from the natural sciences, Bowers illustrates that scientific explanation requires theoretical perspectives to be imposed on observed regularities: to say that 'letting go' of an apple 'causes' it to fall to the ground is not an adequate causal explanation unless the principle of gravitation is brought in. In the same way, explanation in psychology must go beyond the mere identification of observed regularities and advance theoretical models in which the conditions producing the regularities are explained. From this point of view, there is no reason why situational variables facilitating the observation of S–R links should be assigned a superior quality as building blocks for a theory of individual behaviour and personality than any other type of construct, including traits, goals or other personal variables.

The fourth general assumption is that in order to establish stimulus–response links as required by the situationist model, a methodology is needed which examines the effect of an independent variable on a dependent one. This is best achieved by experimental manipulations, and thus the experiment is generally accepted as the method of choice for situationism. In this way, for instance, Mischel's social behaviour theory 'seeks order and regularity in the form of general rules that relate environmental changes to behavior changes' (1968: 150). It is worth noting in this context that the newly emerging 'situational strategy' in personality research identified by Snyder and Ickes (1985) reverses this traditional perspective by focusing on the way in which the behaviour of individuals affects and brings about change in their environments (see Chapter 8).

Situationists' reliance on the experiment in challenging the trait model and obtaining evidence for the determination of behaviour by situational features is based, in Bowers's (1973) view, on another 'metaphysical assumption'. This is reflected in the tendency to misidentify a particular theoretical perspective, the S–R model, with a particular methodological strategy, the experiment. The problem involved in this misidentification is that an essentially 'neutral' method, which in principle can be employed in the service of a diversity of theoretical orientations interested in the relationship between independent and dependent variables, is charged with specific theoretical stipulations. As a consequence, Bowers rejects the situationist claim that the failure to find behavioural consistency in experimental settings constitutes conclusive evidence against the trait model. After all, it is obvious that the very nature of experimental designs contains a systematic bias in favour of the situationist model (see, for example, Bowers, 1973; Kenrick and Dantchik, 1983). Two aspects of the experiment are of particular importance here.

First, it is an explicit aim of experimental procedures to minimize differences between subjects due to personal qualities. Randomization both in sampling participants and in allocating them to the different experimental treatments is generally employed as a strategy to ensure that interindividual differences are cancelled out. This precaution is a necessary requirement for observed behavioural differences to be attributed conclusively to the effectiveness of the experimental manipulation, that is, the variation of situational conditions.

Secondly, the aim of experimentation is to discover the co-variation of a dependent variable with an independent variable. Thus, the focus is on the effect of different treatments on subjects' behaviour, which implies a general orientation towards uncovering change rather than stability. Successful manipulations are those that produce noticeable differences between experimental conditions, that is, change across situations. Conversely, failure to observe significant behavioural differences across situations is usually attributed to inadequacies of the experimental treatment rather than the operation of some generalized personal disposition.

The commitment of situationism as a theoretical perspective to the experiment as its corresponding methodological approach has led its proponents to declare their approach superior to the trait approach with its mainly correlational studies. However, Bowers's methodological reasoning as well as the discussion in this chapter of evidence from R-, S-, and T-data illustrate that there is no convincing basis for such a claim.

In tracing the history of the consistency debate, it has become increasingly clear that it is not only a matter of the opposition between two theoretical views on how to conceptualize the forces that shape a person's behaviour. It is also a history of disagreement over the methodology most adequate to settle the issue of consistency. This dual nature of the controversy had the unfortunate effect that much effort was wasted in attempts at refuting one approach with the methods of the other (see also Funder and Ozer, 1983; Magnusson, 1990a). In recent years, however, new initiatives have been launched to overcome the deadlock and explore alternative conceptual and methodological avenues for addressing the issue of consistency. Some of these approaches will be outlined in the next section before being presented in detail in subsequent chapters.

Proposed solutions

Looking at the progress of personality psychology over the last ten years or so, it becomes obvious that researchers have been concerned in large part with addressing the fundamental problems raised in the course of the consistency debate. The contributions to three special issues of the *Journal of Personality* (West, 1983, 1986a; West and Graziano, 1989a) as well as two recent surveys of the field (Buss and Cantor, 1989; Pervin, 1990a) portray an impressive picture of these developments.

By way of a broad classification, three lines of development can be distinguished, each of which will be introduced briefly in this section:

1 One line of development is directed at defending the utility of traits as basic units for personality research from different theoretical angles.

2 In a second group of contributions, ways of delineating the scope of the consistency concept are explored by looking for subgroups of persons, situations and trait–behaviour relationships associated with high levels of consistency.

3 A third line of progress is aimed at forging a link between the trait model and the situationist view by studying individual behaviour as a function of the reciprocal interaction between the person and the situation.

No personality psychology without the trait concept

'If there is to be a speciality called personality, its unique and therefore defining characteristic is traits.' With these words, Buss (1989: 1378) sums up his critical review of the claim that traits are unimportant and could be abandoned without great loss for the future development of personality research. His statement derives support from a growing body of research defending the utility of traits as analytical constructs in the study of personality. Among these efforts, three main orientations can be discerned.

Searching for basic trait dimensions that allow a parsimonious yet comprehensive description of personality and individual differences: It has long been recognized that everyday language provides the repertoire to which both laypersons and professional psychologists refer in their descriptions of personality. In their classic study, Allport and Odbert (1936) tried to reduce the enormous number of trait adjectives in everyday English into a manageable set of personality categories. Their study not only informed Cattell's (1950) factor analytical theory of personality; it also provided the starting point for a recently expanding interest in the taxonomic analysis of personality categories that led to the emergence of the famous 'Big Five' factors in personality (see Digman (1990) for a review). Committed to the method of factor analysis (Briggs and Cheek, 1986), these research efforts converge on the finding that personality can be represented at the trait level by five factors or dimensions. Whether trait attributes are phrased in everyday language or derived from personality questionnaires in the form of self-reports and ratings, it appears feasible to condense them into descriptions of personality along five broad dimensions. Despite some disagreement as to the interpretation of individual factors, they are frequently labelled 'extraversion/introversion' (I), 'friendliness/hostility' (II), 'conscientiousness' (III), 'neuroticism/

emotional stability' (IV), and 'intellect' (V) (see Digman, 1990: 424). The consistent emergence of a five-factor structure has been welcomed by personality psychologists as a big step forward in the search for a taxonomy of broad and comprehensive dimensions for capturing individual differences and for illuminating the structure of personality (John, 1990).

Exploring the genetic determinants of personality traits: A second line of development in defence of the trait concept seeks to explore the biological bases of trait-specific behaviour and individual differences. The field of behaviour genetics is one discipline at the interface of personality psychology and biology that has been involved in these efforts. Behavioural genetic methods, such as twin and adoption studies, facilitate the assessment of the extent to which traits are due to genetic, hereditary factors as opposed to shared environmental influences (Plomin et al., 1990). Summarizing a large body of recent research, Loehlin et al. (1988) argue that there is conclusive evidence for identical twins to show substantially higher similarities than fraternal twins with regard to their standing on various personality dimensions. Since environmental factors can be assumed to affect both groups to the same extent (Plomin, 1986), the higher similarities among identical twins are attributable to the operation of genetic factors. Behaviour geneticists are concerned with explaining traits in relation to the genetic make-up of individuals and thus refer to more immediate or 'proximate' biological influences on personality. In contrast, a second line within the biological perspective is directed at uncovering 'ultimate' causes of personality by demonstrating the evolutionary development of certain traits. The basic argument of this so-called sociobiological approach is that natural selection, that is, pressures from the environment of a species, favours the emergence of traits that are adaptive in dealing with those environmental demands (Kenrick et al., 1985). For example, high levels of dominance are instrumental in achieving status and social power. Thus, the genetic bases for that trait are proposed to be favoured by natural selection, with the genetic make-up of a highly dominant person standing a greater chance of being transmitted to the next generation. Altogether, placing the issue of trait-specific behaviour into a biological context is guided by the aim to underscore the importance of traits as basic units of analysis for personality research.

Conceptualizing traits as socially defined categories by which impressions of personality are 'constructed': This constructivist perspective, which has its roots in the field of social cognition, presents a distinctly different understanding of traits and consistency. Rather than referring to dispositional qualities of the individual, traits are conceptualized as cognitive categories used by the perceiver to interpret an individual's behaviour across different situations. For example, the statement that 'Paul is a conscientious person' indicates that the speaker witnessed a number of different activities by Paul that he or she interprets as belonging to the category of conscientious behaviours. Everyday language and the socially agreed meaning of dispositional labels, such as 'extrovert', 'hostile' or 'neurotic', provide the frame of reference for such trait ascriptions. According to this view, therefore, consistency is *construed* by the perceiver rather than *manifested* by the individual. The innovative aspect of this approach compared to the traditional understanding of traits lies in the proposition that judgements of an individual's personality are dependent as much on the interpretative activity of the perceiver as on the observed behaviour itself. This means that the task of the personality theorist shifts from explaining why consistency does or does not show up in individual behaviour to exploring the principles whereby perceptions of consistency or inconsistency are formed (Bem, 1983a; Hampson, 1988; Mischel, 1979).

The when and where of consistency
A second line of recent research in defence of consistency holds on to the concept of traits as latent constructs disposing the individual towards acting in a particular way. Its emphasis is on substituting the general hypothesis that traits determine behaviour by the more specific hypothesis that consistency may be expected for some individuals and/or under certain conditions. Consensus has grown between trait psychologists and situationists that there is stability as well as change in individual behaviour and that both provide important clues to our understanding of personality (see Mischel, 1983; Pervin, 1984c: 28f.). As McClelland (1981: 101) puts it: 'What we are interested in is not consistency *per se* but in lawfulness, in understanding and predicting behavior.' The crucial question to ask, therefore, is when and why individuals either show flexible behavioural responses to different situations or display consistency in terms of systematic relationships between latent personal variables and overt behaviour. At least four different strategies have been pursued in recent years to address this issue.

The search for subgroups of people characterized by high levels of cross-situational consistency: Two essential steps are involved in this strategy: first, groups of individuals have to be identified who reliably show high levels of behavioural consistency in different trait domains, and secondly, an explanation has to be advanced accounting for the observed differences in consistency levels. In order to explain individual differences in consistency, different *moderator variables* have been proposed as affecting the link between personal dispositions and behavioural consistency. Bem and Allen (1974), for example, suggested that a person's global self-rating of consistency ('How much do you vary in your behaviour from one situation to another?') can be used to distinguish between consistent and inconsistent individuals in particular trait domains. Among other variables that have been examined as moderator variables of consistency are 'self-monitoring' (Snyder, 1987) and 'public vs. private self-consciousness' (Scheier, 1980), with low self-monitors and persons with high private self-consciousness showing higher levels of consistency. At a more general level, Baumeister and Tice (1988) introduced the concept of metatraits. A 'metatrait' is defined as the trait of having or not having a particular trait, thus indicating whether or not a given trait category is applicable to the description of an individual's personality. Metatraits are proposed to act as moderators of trait-behaviour consistency in that only 'traited' individuals are expected to show substantial levels of consistency.

The search for subgroups of situations which facilitate the influence of personal dispositions on behaviour: Here, the most urgent task is to develop taxonomies of situations so that situations can be classified in terms of their constraints on individual behaviour, and, by implication, on the emergence of individual differences (see also Chapter 8). We have already mentioned Mischel's (1973) distinction between strong and weak situations, whereby strong situations are highly structured, contain unambiguous clues as to the appropriate responses and thus elicit highly similar response patterns from the individuals present. Dweck and Legett (1988) stress that consensus in people's choices between different goals available in a given situation is likely to increase to the extent that the situation offers strong cues in favour of a certain goal (for example, gaining social approval). Similarly, Price and Bouffard (1974) have classified situations in terms of the number and type of different activities socially acceptable in the respective situations (for example, at church, in a lecture, etc.). The greater the variety of acceptable behaviours within situations, the greater the likelihood that there will be intra-individual as well as inter-individual variability in behaviour.

The search for representative behavioural referents for a trait: This strategy is based on the claim, advocated most eloquently by Epstein (1979, 1980), that the evidence marshalled against the validity of traits as latent dispositions is to a large extent compromised by inadequate operationalizations of the link between traits and behaviour. In particular, failure of traits to predict single instances of behaviour is rejected as pertinent evidence, as it is argued that traits as broad dispositions can only be expected to predict *classes* of behaviour. In terms of Epstein's (1979: 1105) general hypothesis: 'Stability can be demonstrated over a wide range of variables as long as the behavior in question is averaged over a sufficient number of occurrences.' Two related tasks derive from this line of reasoning for a more adequate examination of the trait concept (see Chapter 6). First, individual behaviour has to be measured over a sufficient number of instances to reduce the effect of measurement error involved in single instances of behaviour. Secondly, the behavioural criteria have to be established as representative referents for the trait in question. As Moskowitz (1982) as well as Epstein and O'Brien (1985) point out, the relationship of different behavioural criteria to a trait critically depends on how well these criteria are representative of the trait.

The search for consistency at the level of the individual: This strategy, too, is concerned with a more adequate translation of theoretical concepts into research paradigms. Its basic argument is that the concept of consistency, referring to individual qualities and behavioural patterns, requires a methodology which permits unambiguous conclusions about the individual person. This is an explicit rejection of the predominant individual difference paradigm where consistency in the behaviour of individuals is expressed in terms of the stability of their rank order over time and situations. Compared with the first three strategies, research based on a person-centred approach is only just beginning to take shape. Its advantages continue to be vigorously debated by both critics and proponents of the traditional nomothetic approach to the problem of consistency (see, for example, Harris, 1980; Lamiell, 1981; Paunonen and Jackson, 1985; see also Chapter 7).

Person–situation interactions

The most ambitious response to the challenge of the consistency concept is to be found in the modern interactionist perspective on personality. The aim of this perspective is to develop a new comprehensive framework for personality research in which individual behaviour is seen as resulting from the reciprocal interaction between personal qualities and the features of the situation. Recognition of the importance of person–situation interactions in accounting for individual behaviour is not new as shown, for instance, by Lewin's (1936) well-known formula of $B = f(P,S)$. In the course of the consistency debate, however, the portrayal of trait versus situationist models in terms of competing, essentially incompatible, explanations of behaviour has diverted attention away from the study of person–situation interactions (Ekehammar, 1974). It was not until the field of personality experienced a severe crisis of confidence in the aftermath of Mischel's attack on the trait concept that concern with developing an interactionist research programme for personality theory was revived. Since the mid-1970s a 'modern' interactionist view of personality has emerged and quickly expanded into a widely accepted platform for empirical research in a variety of personality domains (Magnusson and Endler, 1977a; Pervin and Lewis, 1978). The major advantage of the modern interactionist approach is that it dismisses the traditional conflict between situationism and trait psychology. The opposition between traits and situations is declared a 'pseudo issue' (Endler, 1973) which needs to be transcended in favour of a theoretical model that treats individual dispositions and situational features as equally necessary and mutually dependent conditions of individual behaviour. Chapters 4 and 5 will look in detail at the theoretical and methodological foundations of the modern interactionist model of personality and offer a critical appraisal of the empirical research it has generated over the last decade. Kenrick and Dantchik (1983: 292) described the modern interactionist view as 'a happy compromise that allows both parties in a dispute to conclude that they were right after all.' The discussion in Chapters 4 and 5 will be guided by the question whether this is all there is to interactionism or whether it does have a potential for uniting the two parties in a joint endeavour to develop a new paradigm for the study of personality.

Summary

Why is it that the concept of consistency occupies such a central and yet contentious role in personality theory and research? What is there about the meaning of consistency that has made it the object of such a long-standing controversy? The present chapter has attempted to offer an answer to these questions and highlight suggestions for approaching the issue of consistency in a more fruitful way.

The chapter began by looking at the different meanings in which the term consistency is employed in personality research in order to clarify what exactly is at issue in the controversy. We saw that the extreme view of 'absolute consistency' was never seriously endorsed by any great number of personality theorists. Yet, it also became clear that the generally accepted meaning of consistency in terms of 'relative consistency' entails conceptual problems that need to be more fully recognized. As an alternative, still to be put to empirical test, the interactionist concept of 'coherence' was discussed as a reformulation of the consistency concept.

A brief recapitulation of the historical beginnings followed next, identifying some of the arguments taken up and elaborated in the subsequent stages of the debate. Against this background the traditional formulations of the trait approach and the situationist approach, which represent the competing positions in the consistency debate, were examined. It was argued that two distinct understandings of the trait concept have been involved, both of which stress the stability and consistency of behaviour across situations and over time. The 'summary view' limits the value of traits to describing observed behavioural regularities and facilitating predictions only in terms of projecting observed patterns into the future. The 'dispositional view', on the other hand, regards traits as broad response dispositions which have a causal impact on overt behaviour. Both views, however, are faced with the task of interpreting behavioural evidence as indicative (or not) of a particular trait. This process involves ascription rules, not inherent in the behaviour itself, which so far have not been taken sufficiently into account by trait researchers. Moreover, the need was stressed to explore more fully the relationship of traits with other psychological variables to make them part of a comprehensive network of personality theory.

The discussion of the situationist model focused only on those aspects immediately relevant to the person–situation debate. Since the situationist challenge of the trait concept is not so much directed at the theoretical assertions of the trait approach as at its empirical foundations, evidence from different data sources was examined as to its impact on rejecting the influence of traits on individual behaviour. This analysis revealed that the picture portrayed by the different sources is ambiguous as far as consistency is concerned. Additional problems of interpretation are created by the strong reliance of the situationist argument on experimental methods which, by their very nature, are geared towards the discovery of change rather than stability.

The final section, therefore, looked at recent proposals for redefining and resolving the issue of stability and consistency in personality. From the literature available to date, three general strategies seem to emerge. The first involves approaches directed at providing a more adequate conceptualization of traits. They focus on the task of identifying basic trait dimensions as building blocks of a trait-theory of personality, on demonstrating that traits have a biological basis and on explicating the role of traits as cognitive categories applied by the observer to the behaviour of another person. According to this latter approach, consistency is construed through social interaction rather than manifested by the individual person. A second line of progress in the consistency debate is aimed at discovering more specifically when and why behaviour is consistent or inconsistent. This strategy includes the identification of those types of persons and situations for whom consistency is most likely to be observed along with a greater concern with formalizing the relationship between traits as global personality constructs and specific behavioural instances. Finally, the modern interactionist perspective on personality was identified as the most far-reaching development prompted by the consistency debate. Here, a new paradigm is envisaged where the clue to understanding individual behaviour is seen as lying in the continuous, reciprocal interaction between personal characteristics and situations. Most notably, the concept of situation now needs to become an integral part of theorizing in personality psychology.

3

In Defence of Traits: New (and Revived) Perspectives

Despite its troubled history, the trait concept presents itself in remarkably good shape at the beginning of the 1990s. For one, there have been cogent refutations of many of the criticisms levelled against the use of traits in personality psychology (see, for example, Buss, 1989; Kenrick and Funder, 1988). At the same time, new avenues for the elaboration of a trait-based view of personality have been explored in recent years, leading to an extensive and many-sided body of research. These efforts are based on the conviction that traits should be retained as dispositional categories particularly suited for conceptualizing individual differences in behaviour as well as stable personality profiles over time. Different aspects of the utility of traits as core units of analysis for personality psychology have been stressed as part of these efforts. One line of research is devoted to the identification of a limited set of basic trait dimensions facilitating a comprehensive description and interpretation of individual differences. Another branch of research seeks to corroborate the validity of the trait concept by exploring genetic bases of trait-specific differences between persons. Finally, a fundamentally different viewpoint is adopted by a group of contributions which look at traits as 'social constructions' in the sense of interactive constructs that are shaped both by the behaviour of the person in question and the interpretative activities of the observer. These three lines of development will be reviewed in the present chapter.

In addition to these developments, other authors have suggested reconceptualizations of the trait concept that stress specific aspects of the dispositional basis of behaviour. Athay and Darley (1981), for instance, proposed an interaction-centred theory of personaliy in which 'interaction competencies' are postulated as central dispositions accounting for individual differences in behaviour. Kreitler and Kreitler (1990) advocate a cognitive approach in which traits are conceptualized in terms of an individual's preferred tendencies for assigning meaning to his or her experiential world. Read et al. (1990) have emphasized the significance of goal-directed aspects as defining features of traits. Their evidence suggests that trait inferences are made with greater confidence from those behavioural manifestations that are closely linked to the goals associated with a given trait.

Basic trait dimensions: the Big Five

Judging from the large number of recent publications alone, research on the 'Big Five' factors of personality is certainly one of the most prolific, if not *the* most prolific, area in current personality psychology (see the comprehensive reviews by Digman (1990) and John (1990) as well as a special issue of the *Journal of Personality* (1991)). This intense interest is grounded in the conviction that the identification of a limited number of personality-descriptive factors or dimensions is a most desirable goal towards developing a unifying framework for the analysis of a diverse range of concepts and issues in the field of personality. As a point of departure, this line of research has adopted the proposition that natural, everyday language contains the elements from which a scientific taxonomy of personality-descriptive attributes can be derived. Therefore, dictionaries containing the full lexical repertoire of a language community are drawn upon as major sources of information for establishing the central aspects of personality description (however, see Hofstee (1990) for an analysis of the problems involved in this strategy). Personality questionnaires, which are by far the most commonly used instruments in the study of personality through both self-reports and observer ratings, reflect the close association between everyday language and the language of personality measurement. While the items of a questionnaire or lists of attributes provide information about personality at a descriptive level, investigators are ultimately concerned with identifying the central underlying factors or dimensions along which individual differences can be conceptualized. The method of *factor analysis* has been the preferred statistical instrument for achieving this aim. As Briggs and Cheek (1986: 107–108) describe it, 'factor analysis is a way of grouping correlated variables, a way of reducing a set of redundant variables, and a way of identifying what it is that a set of variables shares in common.' Thus, factor analysis is a means of providing the investigator with information about the optimal number of factors for capturing the pattern of individual differences reflected in responses to the questionnaire items, whereby the aim is to explain as much of the difference (that is, variance in questionnaire responses) with as few factors as possible. Buss and Finn (1987) refer to this procedure for systematizing traits as 'empirical classification' since it relies on demonstrated relationships between traits.

In contrast, 'conceptual classifications' are derived from specific theoretical models, whereby the link between particular traits is postulated on conceptual grounds (for example, Jung's (1923) system of personality types and Buss and Finn's own distinction between instrumental, affective, and cognitive traits and the independent dimension of social versus non-social traits).

The search for taxonomic systems to describe and categorize individuals in terms of their personality characteristics has a long tradition in personality psychology which is traced in a recent paper by John et al. (1988). The best-known early example of this so-called *lexical approach* to the study of personality is provided by Allport and Odbert's (1936) classic study in which they compiled a list of almost 18,000 attributes drawn from the 1925 edition of *Webster's New International Dictionary.*[1] These attributes were subsequently grouped by the authors into four categories (traits, states, evaluative terms, and a miscellaneous category), with trait terms making up about 25 per cent of the attributes.

The next step in the ancestry of the current interest in trait taxonomies is Cattell's (1943) revision and substantial reduction of Allport and Odbert's initial list. After eliminating redundant and unfamiliar terms, about 4500 terms remained which, in turn, were condensed on the basis of semantic similarity into 171 synonym groups (160 traits and 11 abilities), mostly represented by bipolar scales. Subsequent clustering procedures further reduced this list to a set of 35 variables used by Cattell as input for his factor-analytical theory of personality which specifies 16 primary personality factors (see Cattell, 1950).

A study by Fiske (1949), which tried unsuccessfully to replicate the complex factor structure of Cattell's analyses, marks the beginning of a continuing series of studies suggesting a total of five factors as the optimal number of personality-descriptive categories. Other milestones in the emergence of a five-factor structure of personality were the studies of Tupes and Christal (1961) and Norman (1963), before the consistency controversy revived by Mischel's (1968) attack on the trait concept led to a decline of interest in the factor-analytical study of personality. In the course of the 1980s however, the issue was resumed and quickly expanded into a major line of progress in mainstream personality psychology.

Today, there is an impressive body of evidence converging on the finding that the domain of dispositional variables, as measured by self-reports and observer ratings, can be adequately described by five broad constructs, dubbed the 'Big Five' (Goldberg, 1981). As Peabody (1987) and Goldberg (1990) demonstrated in their two series of studies, the five-factor structure is not dependent on a specific lexicon of trait-descriptive terms, such as derived from Cattell's work, but emerges with reasonable clarity across independently sampled lists of attributes. Beyond this numerical point, however, there is, and always has been, some divergence of opinion on how the five factors should be interpreted in substantive, psychological terms. It should be noted in this context that factor analysis, as a statistical procedure, provides the investigator with clear and established guidelines on the *number* of factors to be extracted on the basis of a given correlational structure of the items. In contrast, he or she has considerable leeway in interpreting the psychological *meaning* of factors. The labelling of factor solutions is a largely intuitive process whereby the investigator typically inspects the items with high loadings on a given factor and then chooses a label that in his or her view contains the gist of the total range of items making up the factor. Thus, it is not surprising that different studies have arrived at different qualitative interpretations of their obtained five-factor solutions. Table 3.1 presents a summary of the factor labels suggested by a representative range of studies over the last forty years.

An inspection of Table 3.1 reveals that agreement in factor labellings varies across the five factors. The first factor (I) shows a high similarity of factor labels across studies and is commonly interpreted as referring to *extroversion versus introversion*. The second factor (II) also captures individual differences relevant to social interaction and is generally assigned the labels of *friendliness* or *agreeableness*. A less clear-cut picture emerges for the third factor (III). This factor broadly refers to the individual's characteristic way of dealing with the tasks of his or her life and is most frequently interpreted as a *conscientiousness* factor.[2] The fourth factor (IV) is again consensually perceived as relating to individual differences in *emotional stability versus neuroticism*. Finally, the fifth factor (V) pertains to different aspects of intellectual functioning and a general *openness to experience*. This latter aspect, as John (1990: 77) points out, distinguishes the fifth factor as a personality construct rather than a construct pertaining to ability.

Thus, despite obvious discrepancies in the labelling of individual factors, it does seem possible to define a consensual interpretation of the Big Five. It should be noted, though, that the factor labels suggested by earlier studies have certainly served as guidelines for subsequent investigators in interpreting their factor solutions, creating a more homogeneous picture than would have resulted in the case of totally independent or 'blind' factor labellings in the later studies. Another source of inflated convergence lies in the fact that all studies, even though they employ a wide range of different

Table 3.1   Interpretations of the 'Big Five' factor structure

	I	II	III	IV	V
Fiske (1949)	social adaptability	conformity	will to achieve[a]	emotional control	inquiring intellect
Eysenck (1970)	extroversion	psychoticism		neuroticism	
Tupes and Christal (1961)	surgency	agreeableness	dependability	emotionality	culture
Norman (1963)	surgency	agreeableness	conscientiousness	emotional	culture
Borgatta (1964)	assertiveness	likeability	task interest	emotionality	intelligence
Cattell (1957)	exvia	cortertia	superego strength	anxiety	intelligence
Guilford (1975)	social activity	paranoid disposition	thinking introversion	emotional stability	
Digman (1988)	extroversion	friendly compliance	will to achieve	neuroticism	intellect
Hogan (1986)	sociability and ambition	likeability	prudence	adjustment	intellectance
Costa and McCrae (1985)	extroversion	agreeableness	conscientiousness	neuroticism	openness
Peabody and Goldberg (1989)	power	love	work	affect	intellect
Buss and Plomin (1984)	activity	sociability	impulsivity	emotionality	
Tellegen (1985)	positive emotionality		constraint	negative emotionality	
Lorr (1986)	interpersonal involvement	level of socialization	self-control	emotional stability	independent

[a] Not in the original analysis but noted in a re-analysis by Digman and Takemoto-Chock (1981).

Source: reproduced, with permission, from the *Annual Review of Psychology*, 41 (Digman, 1990). © 1990 by Annual Reviews Inc.

personality questionnaires and rating systems, are ultimately rooted in the everyday lexicon of personality-descriptive terms. Therefore, it seems reasonable to attribute some proportion of overlap in the factor interpretations to the semantic similarity of this common input (see Waller and Ben-Porath (1987) for a similar point). What is clear from these last considerations is that the identification of five basic or 'big' personality factors does not, in itself, contribute to a better understanding of the psychological principles underlying individual differences. It does, however, provide a unifying system for looking at diverse issue and concepts relating to personality and individual differences whose utility needs to be demonstrated with respect to information from other sources (McCrae, 1990).

   To begin with, there is evidence from a variety of studies that factor solutions obtained on the basis of a broad range of different personality questionnaires can be mapped quite well onto the Big

Five structure (for example, Noller et al. (1987); and see also John (1990: Table 3.4) for a summary). Costa and McCrae (1985) developed a personality inventory specifically designed to represent the Big Five. This instrument, the NEO-PI, has been used by numerous studies to assess the extent to which other personality measures corresponded to, that is, were correlated with the five-factor model. It is available in two versions, allowing the collection of both self-reports and observer ratings. An important feature of the NEO-PI is that it is not based on trait attributes sampled from natural language but includes personality scales widely used by personality researchers. This representation of the five-factor model has been found to show substantial congruence with some of the most prominent personality scales. This is true for Gough and Heilbrun's (1980) *Adjective Check List* (ACL) (Piedmont et al. (1991); however, see Livneh and Livneh (1989) for a failed attempt at recovering the Big Five from ACL responses) and Jackson's (1984) *Personality Research Form* based on Murray's (1938) list of need concepts (Costa and McCrae, 1988b). In each case, response patterns to the instrument in question could be meaningfully grouped within the framework of the five-factor model. Trapnell and Wiggins (1990) further underline the integrative function of the five-factor structure by designing a personality inventory for the combined assessment of the Big Five and Wiggins's (1979) circumplex structure of personality attributes (see also McCrae and Costa, 1989).

In a recent study, Botwin and Buss (1989) confirmed the five-factor structure for act composites, that is, sets of *behavioural* referents for each factor, in both self- and spouse ratings. Despite some discrepancies in the interpretation of the factors, the authors interpret their findings as providing compelling support for the five-factor model, given that they are based on a distinctly different source of information (behaviour as opposed to traits). Moreover, they found that the act composites defining each factor showed meaningful correlations with trait ratings obtained from six independent sources (self, partner, father, mother, friend and interviewers) on a series of standard personality questionnaires. That is, individuals who characteristically behave in an extroverted fashion (those with high self- or spouse-reported act composites of extroverted behaviour) also receive high ratings on trait measures of extroversion obtained from different raters. As the work by Digman and his co-workers (Digman, 1989; Digman and Inouye, 1986) shows, the five-factor structure is not limited to the description of adult personality but also emerges consistently in trait ratings of children by their teachers.

Further support for the generality of the five-factor structure comes from studies using languages other than English. John (1990) summarizes findings from studies using German and Dutch personality questionnaires which also come up with a consistent and replicable five-factor structure (see also Borkenau and Ostendorf, 1990). In one of these studies, Borkenau (1988) also used act reports in the form of behaviour-descriptive terms, instead of personality attributes. A sample of eight judges (German native speakers) were requested to rate each of 120 activities in terms of their prototypicality for 40 traits representing or 'marking' the Big Five. A factor analysis, performed on the basis of the intercorrelations of the prototypicality ratings across the 40 traits, yielded clear support for the five-factor structure. Evidence for the cross-cultural generality of the Big Five beyond Western cultures has been found in a study by Church and Katigbak (1989), conducted with a sample of Filipino subjects in Manila. Additional studies replicating the five-factor model with samples of Japanese and Filipino students are quoted by Digman (1990: 433).

As far as the external validity of the five-factor model is concerned, some studies have examined the relationship between the Big Five and measures of psychological well-being. In one such study, McCrae and Costa (1991) found that *extroversion* is associated with positive well-being and general positive affect, whereas *neuroticism* is clearly linked with negative affect and less well-being. At the same time, they found evidence of a positive link between both *agreeableness* and *conscientiousness* and general well-being, which they interpret in terms of the instrumental significance of these two factors in promoting well-being. In his analysis of 'personal projects', Little (1989) found that the stress and difficulty associated with persons' handling of their life projects are significantly related to the 'extroversion' factor as measured by the NEO-PI. Conversely, the enjoyment and control dimensions of personal projects showed significant relationships with the 'conscientiousness' factor (see Chapter 7 for a discussion of the personal project approach).

From what has been said so far, there seems to be an unreservedly positive appraisal of the research corroborating the Big Five factor structure of personality. As Digman concludes: 'At a minimum, research on the five-factor model has given us a useful set of very broad dimensions that characterize individual differences. These dimensions can be measured with high reliability and impressive validity. Taken together, they provide a good answer to the question of personality *structure*' (1990: 436). There are, nevertheless, occasional dissenting voices who are reluctant to accept the five-factor model as *the* key to a better understanding of the structure of personality (for example, Briggs, 1989; Waller and Ben-Porath, 1987).

Briggs expresses concern, among other things, about the lack of correspondence in the factor interpretations derived from different studies. This problem, as noted above, arises from the fact that the technique of factor analysis does not provide precise specifications of the *meaning* of factors. One might add that this imprecise specification is a problem not only because it leads to discrepancies in factor interpretations. It is problematic also because it may lead to apparent *correspondences* arising from the investigators' desire to harmonize their data with the existing five-factor pattern in spite of alternative, possibly more adequate, interpretations of a particular factor solution. In short, since the labelling of factor solutions is essentially an intuitive process, assessing the level of convergence or discrepancy across different studies remains somewhat ambiguous. Again, one has to resort to quantitative indices to establish the overlap or convergence between an obtained factor solution and the five factors as established in previous research. If the factors in a new data set show a substantial correlation with independent measures of the Big Five, they are typically interpreted in terms of the existing factor labels. However, since there are no clear-cut criteria for deciding when agreement with the existing five factor labels is good enough to abandon the search for alternative interpretations, the replicability of exactly the Big Five as named above remains a difficult question. The problem is aggravated by the absence of a theoretical model or rationale from which the Big Five, as they are known today, have been derived. As the five factors are the result of an 'empirical classification' rather than a 'conceptual' one (see Buss and Finn, above), their underlying item- or attribute-structure is defined solely in quantitative (correlational) terms, and any substantive relationship between them can only be identified post hoc in an inductive way.

The fact that the five-factor model has emerged from the analysis of trait attributes represented in natural language gives rise to another fundamental concern. This issue refers to the question of whether the Big Five are, indeed, psychological constructs pertaining to the description of individual persons or whether they merely reflect semantic relationships in the language from which they are derived. To illustrate the problem, consider the following case. A sample of raters is presented with a measure known to lead to the five-factor structure, for example, a comprehensive list of trait-descriptive adjectives (for example, McCrae and Costa, 1985). Rather than using this list to describe themselves or another person they know well, these raters are instructed to judge the attributes either in terms of their similarity in meaning or as descriptors of another person whom they do not know at all. What if ratings under the latter two instructions also yield the well-known five-factor structure? In that case, it is difficult to argue that the relationships among items (or factors) tell us anything about psychological characteristics of specific persons. Instead, they reflect inherent properties of language, shared by all competent members of a language community, which will emerge with high regularity and reliability no matter to whom they are applied. While there are several studies demonstrating a close resemblance of factor solutions derived from trait ratings by strangers and well-acquainted observers which support this last line of reasoning (for example, D'Andrade, 1965; Passini and Norman, 1966; Watson, 1989), the matter is clearly more complicated. In a comprehensive review of the issues involved, Borkenau (in press, a) points out that the level of acquaintanceship, and hence the availability of information on which trait ratings can be based, has an effect on the extent of self–other agreement as well as inter-observer agreement (see also Funder and Colvin, 1988). These findings cannot be accounted for by a merely language-based interpretation of the five-factor structure. Thus, it seems that while linguistic conventions play an important role in shaping people's ratings of personality, subsequently cast into the five-factor structure, such ratings also have a psychological substance in the sense that they reflect the raters' knowledge of the person to be rated, be it themselves or a well-acquainted other (see the final section of this chapter for a more general discussion of the role of language in trait measurement).

From yet another perspective, research on the Big Five has been challenged in terms of its potential contribution towards *explaining* individual differences in personality functioning. As Digman himself admits immediately following his optimistic summary quoted above, 'the *why* of personality is something else' (1990: 436). Identifying the causal factors responsible for the appearance of stable individual differences is beyond the scope of the taxonomic analysis of personality. This issue, however, is at the heart of another prominent line of development, to be reviewed in the next section, which is directed at clarifying the genetic basis of personality.

The biological basis of traits

In the attempt to expand the conceptual repertoire of personality psychology, reference to biological models of personality and individual differences has become increasingly popular in recent years. This development stems, in part, from dissatisfaction with the largely phenotypic orientation of personality research, which locates the study of personality at the level of manifest reactions (such as questionnaire responses, ratings, or observations of behaviour), and often falls short of providing conclusive explanations for empirically observed relationships.

In contrast, adopting a biological orientation is advocated as a means of answering crucial questions on the 'why' of personality and individual differences. This development is represented by two major lines of inquiry. The first is located in the field of behavioural genetics which offers a perspective on personality facilitating the assessment of the genetic roots of individual differences (Loehlin et al., 1988; Plomin and Rende, 1991). The second line of inquiry complements this approach by providing explanations for genetic differences in terms of natural selection and adaptation. In a sense, one can say that behavioural genetics refer to the *ontogenetic* or *proximate* aspects of biological influences on the life of individual persons, while evolutionary psychology is concerned with the *phylogenetic* or *ultimate* aspects of the emergence of genetic differences in the history of a species. Without ignoring the uniqueness of the individual, the evolutionary perspective is more concerned with the processes that explain why members of a species have developed *similar* patterns of behaviour in the course of their history (Tooby and Cosmides, 1990) or why characteristic differences have emerged between defined *groups* of people (for example, Kenrick's (1989) work on sex differences in parental investment; see also Rushton (1990)).

In the present section, we will focus on the behavioural genetic approach because it is more specifically directed at the trait concept and the causal analysis of trait-based differences between individuals. The potential contribution of evolutionary psychology as a 'metatheory' casting new light on a diversity of issues in the field of personality will be reviewed in Chapter 9.

The question of the relative importance of genetic and environmental origins of individual differences has been one of the most intriguing issues in psychology generally and in personality psychology in particular. After all, deciding whether personality is primarily determined by genetic factors or largely the result of socialization processes is not merely of scientific relevance but has direct implications in the sociopolitical domain. In the 1970s, this became evident in the highly politicized and emotionalized debate over the impact of genetic factors on intelligence. Stressing the role of genetic variables in accounting for phenotypic differences in intelligence, as measured by intelligence tests, was seen (not entirely without reason) as cementing racial and class differences in intelligence and undermining the development of compensatory education programmes. As the case of intelligence illustrates, the issue has frequently been phrased in terms of a 'nature versus nurture' controversy in the past, and genetic influence has been taken to imply stable and immutable levels of ability or personality. More recently, it seems that research exploring the contribution of genetic factors to the emergence of personality differences has become less ideologically suspicious and is developing into a broad research tradition in personality psychology (see, for example, Brody, 1988: ch. 3; Plomin et al., 1990). It is important to note at the outset that the behavioural genetic approach is concerned with the causes of *differences* in individual behaviour, not with the causes of individual behaviour per se.

The basic proposition underlying this approach can be described as follows. Individual differences in the manifestation of trait-specific behaviour at the phenotypic level (for example, in terms of verbal responses to personality measures or in terms of overt behaviour) can be linked in a systematic fashion to the underlying genetic make-up of the individuals involved. In order to address this proposition, two methodologies have been widely used by recent research, both individually and in combination: the comparative analysis of identical (monozygotic, MZ) and fraternal (dizygotic, DZ) twins and the study of adopted and natural children growing up in one family (see Plomin (1986) for a survey of behavioural genetic methods).

Results from a wide range of twin studies conducted with large samples and in different countries show impressive evidence for the genetic origins of individual differences on two central traits: extroversion and neuroticism (for reviews see Eysenck, 1990; Loehlin, 1989; Loehlin et al., 1988). As noted by Plomin et al. (1990), evidence concerning other traits is less conclusive, although it generally supports the impact of genotypic differences on the manifestation of phenotypic differences. For example, studies suggesting a genetic basis for individual differences in aggression have been reviewed by Huesman and Eron (1989).

As to the strength of genotypic influences, MZ correlations are typically in the range of $r = 0.50$ to $r = 0.60$ on measures of extroversion and slightly lower on measures of neuroticism. DZ correlations, in contrast, rarely exceed a score of $r = 0.25$ in both trait domains. What the extroversion and neuroticism findings show, then, is that correlations between MZ twins on measures of these traits are frequently more than twice as high than correlations between DZ twins. Heritability estimates are subsequently derived from these data by doubling the difference in correlations between the MZ and the DZ groups (see Rowe (1989) for a more detailed explanation).[3]

Compared with the twin research, studies using the adoption paradigm indicate less genetic influence in accounting for individual differences. In this paradigm, correlations of trait measures between biological parents and their adopted-away children are compared against trait correlations between adoptive parents and adopted children. In families involving both natural and adopted children, differences in trait correlations between parents and adopted children, parents and their natural children, and natural children and their adopted siblings can be analysed. These analyses consistently reveal far lower levels of heritability estimates in the range of about 20 per cent, which is about half the magnitude suggested by the twin studies (see Loehlin et al., 1988). How can this difference be explained?

Twin studies typically compare MZ and DZ twins in terms of their phenotypic similarities, such as responses to the items of a personality questionnaire, and then attribute observed differences *between the two groups* to underlying differences in the level of genotypic similarity among MZ and DZ twins. This procedure rests on the assumption that there are no systematic differences between MZ and DZ twins in terms of the similarity of environmental influences to which the two groups are exposed. For instance, if it were the case that MZ twins are typically dressed alike by their parents whereas DZ twins are not, then differences in behaviour between the two groups could no longer be attributed conclusively to differences in their genetic make-up but could also be the result of differential treatment elicited from their social environment. It must be reasonable to assume, of course, that such treatment inequalities affect the manifestation of the specific personality trait(s) in question (see Rowe, 1987). Given the widespread reliance on self-report measures of traits as a basis for inferring heritability, the issue is complicated further by the possibility that MZ twins may *perceive* themselves as more similar than DZ twins (Plomin, 1986: 234). Either way, a polarization effect may be assumed to operate in such a way that MZ similarity is increased relative to DZ similarity (assimilation effect) or that DZ similarity is decreased relative to MZ similarity (contrast effect).

This ambiguity is avoided by studies combining the twin and adoption approach in one design. Such a design involves the comparison of MZ and DZ twins reared together and apart, whereby the influence of environmental and genetic factors can be assessed more conclusively. Comparing MZ and DZ twins raised together corresponds to the classic twin study design in which the environment is assumed to be the same for both groups. In contrast, comparisons between MZ twins raised together or apart and between DZ twins raised together or apart represents the 'adoption' situation and provides information about the relative impact of non-shared environmental influences. Several studies using this combined paradigm confirm, across a wide range of traits, that DZ twin correlations are substantially lower than MZ correlations (for example, Pedersen et al., 1988; Tellegen et al., 1988; and see Plomin et al. (1990: Table 9.2) for a summary). This is true, in particular, for the difference between MZ and DZ twins *reared together*, which has been found to be higher than the corresponding difference between MZ and DZ twins *reared apart*. At the same time, differences between twins as a function of environmental factors (being reared together or apart) are far more pronounced for MZ than for DZ twins. In combination, these findings support the view that the heritability estimates derived from differences between MZ and DZ correlations in twin studies may be inflated, partly because of differences in the level of environmental similarity between the two groups. The fact that MZ correlations appear to be more affected by the difference in rearing environment (together versus apart) than DZ correlations, suggests that the crucial assumption of equal environments for MZ and DZ twins underlying the classical twin study design may not be valid. Thus, Plomin et al. (1990) argue that heritability estimates of around 20 per cent emerging from adoption studies are probably more accurate reflections of the true extent of genetic influence than the figure of around 40 per cent resulting from twin studies.

While earlier research has concentrated on the genetic bases of individual differences on single traits, patterns of trait *covariations* have been a more recent focus of attention among behavioural geneticists. Multivariate analyses have been used to pinpoint common genetic influences on two or more traits. To the extent that trait correlations can be linked to shared genetic influences, the behavioural genetic approach can provide an explanation of personality structure. In this respect, it can be seen as a direct complement to the taxonomic work described in the previous section where the emphasis was on identifying the major dimensions of personality structure. The aim is to explain the phenotypic correlations between traits (as reflected, for example, in responses to different scales of a personality inventory) as a function of genes exerting a parallel influence on the traits involved. The complex reasoning behind this approach which is beyond the scope of the present discussion, is explicated in detail by Plomin (1986) and Rowe (1989).

So far, evidence referring to the role of genetic differences in accounting for phenotypic differences between individuals has been considered. Little has been said about the significance of *environmental influences* except for the fact that the assumption of equal environments is a crucial prerequisite for comparing trait correlations for MZ and DZ twins. Analysing the impact of environmental differences on the manifestation of personality similarities or differences is another central aspect of the behavioural genetic approach to the study of personality. After all, given that something between 20 per cent and 40 per cent of phenotypic variance (that is, individual differences on trait or behaviour measures) appears to be attributable to genetic factors, a substantial proportion of variance (between 60 per cent and 80 per cent) remains to be accounted for. Allowing for a certain amount of error variance, environmental influences suggest themselves as most important candidates for explanation and are estimated to account for about 50 per cent of the individual difference variance. There are two main approaches for demonstrating the impact of environmental factors on individual differences. One is the study of MZ twins reared apart. Since their genetic make-up is identical, observed phenotypic differences can be traced to environmental factors. This would be true especially if phenotypic differences could be shown to increase as a function of age, that is, time spent in different environments.[4] Even though few studies have addressed the latter issue, it seems on the basis of the available evidence that neither MZ correlations nor differences between MZ and DZ correlations change with age (Rowe, 1989), speaking against environmental factors as major determinants of phenotypic differences in personality. The second, complementary source of information is provided by the study of adopted children and their siblings or adoptive parents. Since adoptees are genetically unrelated to the members of the family in which they grow up, observed similarities in their personalities suggest the operation of environmental influences.

In order to obtain a conclusive picture of the role of the environment in explaining personality differences, two types of environmental influences need to be distinguished (for example, Rowe, 1987). The first type of influence, called *between family* or *shared environment*, refers to those environmental conditions peculiar to one family which are assumed to affect the members of the family in the same way. In contrast, the second type, *within family* or *non-shared environment* influence, refers to environmental experiences idiosyncratic to the individual members of one family.

Concerning the relative importance of these two types of influence, there is conclusive evidence that the impact of shared environmental factors on personality is small (Plomin et al., 1990; Rowe, 1989; Tellegen et al., 1988). This conclusion is based on consistently low correlations of personality scores between biological siblings and between adopted children and their siblings. Loehlin et al. (1990) recently reported a study in which they investigated personality change in two samples of adopted and non-adopted children over a period of ten years. In addition to personality ratings of the children by their parents on both occasions, they collected personality data, at the beginning of the ten-year period, from both parents (for the non-adopted sample) and from adoptive parents and biological mothers (for the adopted sample). Their analyses revealed that personality change in the adopted children could not be predicted on the basis of the personalities of either the adoptive parents or the biological mothers, suggesting non-shared environmental experiences as a major source of personality development and change (see also Bouchard and McGue, 1990; Plomin and Nesselroade, 1990). No conclusive answer is offered by the Loehlin et al. (1990) study to the question of whether adopted siblings tend to become more similar over time, which would be another indicator of shared environmental influences. While increasing similarities were found for some traits, other traits failed to show a corresponding pattern. Thus, while it is undisputed that environmental influences account for much of the variance in phenotypically manifested personality, it seems equally clear that the crucial influences are those that operate individually on each member of a family rather than affecting all siblings in a similar way.

What should have become clear from the present discussion is that the behavioural genetic approach not only specifies the impact of genetic similarity on personality, namely the 'nature' side of personality development, it also serves to clarify the relevance of environmental origins of individual differences, as implied in the 'nurture' side of the problem. Here, behavioural genetic findings suggest that the impact of the shared family environment may have been overestimated at the expense of the specific socialization experiences made by the individual siblings. From both angles, the behavioural genetic approach has illustrated the utility of traits as units of analysis for capturing the relative contribution of genetic and environmental sources of individual differences in personality.

Like the taxonomic approach discussed in the previous section, the behavioural genetic approach is based on a conceptualization of traits as substantive psychological constructs referring to latent properties of the individuals to whom they are applied. Such a view implies that data based on trait measures provide information, genotypic as well as phenotypic, about individuals that is conceptually independent of the source from which it is derived. Ideally, self-reports should converge with observer ratings, and different operationalizations of a trait should lead to similar conclusions. Even the finding, quoted above, that the degree of acquaintanceship between raters and target persons affects both interrater agreement and self–peer agreement is compatible with the view that traits are essentially properties of the target which may be more or less discernible to others. The next section looks at a line of research which advocates a radically different understanding of the trait concept. In this work, traits are conceptualized as socially constructed categories for personality description and impression formation which reflect not only the qualities of the target person but also the cognitive activities of the observer, both embedded in the conventions of natural language.

Traits as social constructions

In its traditional form, personality psychology as a scientific discipline is based on the premise that 'personality' is a construct referring to the characteristic qualities of a person as well as his or her characteristic way of differing from others. It is only under this premise that it makes sense to look for the genetic roots of personality or to study how particular personality variables interact with particular situational properties in producing behaviour. Thus, scientific or 'explicit' personality psychology is concerned primarily with the 'actor' whose measurable characteristics and behaviours constitute the subject matter of the discipline (see Ross's (1987) personality textbook for a recent example). A concurrent, though clearly less central, line of thought has concentrated on people's implicit or lay conceptions of personality. From this perspective, the emphasis is on the way in which 'observers' form impressions about the personality of others against the backdrop of their intuitive assumptions of personality functioning and trait interrelations. Since the classic studies of Thorndike (1920), it is generally accepted that *trait perception* may not be an accurate reflection of empirical *trait relationships*. Thorndike demonstrated that a person described by certain positive (or negative) characteristics is likely to be attributed other congruent (positive or negative) characteristics, for which there is no empirical basis, through the operation of a kind of *halo effect*. The question of the relationship between such intuitive or implicit perceptions of personality and the characteristic features of individuals revealed through the methods of explicit psychology has sometimes been phrased in terms of a 'realism–idealism issue' (Schneider et al., 1979). From a realist position, consensual perceptions of trait interrelations are interpreted as reflecting the actual covariation of traits in people. In contrast, the idealist position argues that they have little to do with actually observed trait patterns and are informed by other sources, primarily language. To complicate matters even further, a third perspective on personality needs to be considered which focuses on the person as 'self-observer' of his or her own qualities and behaviours. The self-observer is in the unique position of having a maximum of information about his or her characteristic ways of thinking, feeling, and acting. He or she uses this information in an instrumental way to sustain a certain self-concept and to convey a certain impression about the self to others (Baumeister, 1982; and see Chapter 8 for a discussion of social identity construction).

While the perspectives of actor, observer and self have been the object of largely independent, sometimes competing research traditions in the past, the emerging *constructionist* view seeks to embrace the three aspects into a unified perspective on personality (Gergen and Davis, 1985; Hampson, 1988). This view is part of a general epistemological orientation questioning the traditional position that psychological inquiry directly maps or reflects an objectively definable reality. Rooted in the seminal work of Berger and Luckmann (1966), the core assumption of the social constructionist view is summarized as follows by one of its most prominent current representatives:

> The terms in which the world is understood are social artifacts, products of historically situated interchanges among people. From the constructionist position the process of understanding is not automatically driven by the forces of nature, but is the result of an active, cooperative enterprise of persons in relationship. (Gergen, 1985: 267)

One implication of the social constructionist position is to challenge the idea that psychological theories are sustained or abandoned on the basis of empirical data supporting or disconfirming their validity. Instead, preference for certain theoretical accounts is explained primarily as a result of social negotiation processes. Views and theories are upheld in spite of disconfirming evidence or given up in spite of supportive data, depending on the predilections of the 'community of interlocutors' who use them (Gergen, 1985: 268). As Shweder and Miller (1985: 41) elaborate, social construction theories 'argue that people categorize the world the way they do because they have participated in social practices, institutions, and other forms of symbolic action (for example, language) that presuppose or in some way make salient those categorizations.' The cultural and social relativity of knowledge about the world becomes apparent, for example, in the cross-cultural work reported by Shweder and Miller (1985). In their comparative analysis of conceptions of 'the person', they point out that the traditional duty-based moral code of Hindu communities is associated with a strong emphasis on social roles, whereas the prevailing rights-based code of ethics among Americans assigns central importance to the individual person (see also Shweder and Bourne, 1984).

In the personality domain, 'social constructionism' denotes a general orientation comprising different approaches. These approaches share the basic credo that personality does not have an objective reality independent of the person observing it and the cultural and historical context in which both actor and observer are located: 'From the constructionist view, personality is seen as the combination of three equally important components: the *actor*, the *observer*, and the *self-observer*' (Hampson, 1988: 196). The process of personality construction is regarded as a form of communication through which actor, observer, and self-observer ideally arrive at a shared personality impression about the actor: 'In this sense, personality should not be located *within* persons, but *between* or *among* persons' (Hampson, 1988: 205–206).

Looking at personality construction as a process of communication, it is clear that the social constructionist perspective needs to assign crucial importance to the *language* of personality description (Gergen, 1985: 271). Language is centrally involved in the process of forming impressions of personality consistency on the basis of an individual's behaviour. Statements such as 'Paul is conscientious' reflect the perceiver's witnessing a number of different activities by Paul which he or she assigns to the category of conscientious behaviour reflecting the underlying disposition of conscientiousness. In this sense, consistency is *construed* by the perceiver (including the person observing his or her own behaviours) rather than *manifested* by the individual. This means that the task of the personality psychologist shifts from explaining why consistency does (or does not) occur to explaining how inferences of consistency or inconsistency are derived from instances of behaviour (Bem, 1983a; Mischel, 1979).

Different approaches have been developed to address this issue. Cantor and Mischel's (1979a) work on 'cognitive prototypes', for example, examines the structure of the semantic categories used in the process of trait description. They argue that the language of personality description contains consensually defined person categories, such as extroverts and neurotics. Such categories are located at different levels of a hierarchy of generality or abstraction: broad, inclusive constructs (for example, 'emotionally unstable person') representing the superordinate level are followed by middle level categories (for example, 'criminal madman') and specific subordinate categories (for example, 'rapist'). Following the studies of Rosch (1975) on the categorization of objects in natural language, these person-descriptive categories are conceived as having fuzzy boundaries rather than being mutually exclusive. This means that each category contains both highly typical and less typical members, with the less typical members sharing a number of characteristics with the members of adjacent categories. The meaning of a category is best captured by a 'prototype' or 'ideal member' possessing a large number of features typically associated with the category. In terms of its functional significance, the prototype is thought to serve as a cognitive schema that is readily accessible in information processing, facilitating faster and more confident handling of prototype-consistent information (see, for example, Brewer et al., 1981; Cantor and Mischel, 1979b; Cohen, 1983).

The extent to which the behaviour of a person resembles the prototype forms the basis for deciding whether or not the respective category will be applied to him or her. Thus, in our example above, assigning Paul to the category of 'conscientious people' would be a matter of how many of his characteristic attributes are part of the 'conscientiousness prototype' relative to the attributes that are either irrelevant to or incompatible with the prototype. This process, in which both verifying and falsifying information are considered, presupposes that observers can base their judgement on detailed information about Paul as the target person, facilitating a 'full view' on his personality. It is not uncommon, however, for personality judgements to be made on the basis of limited information providing no more than a 'restricted view' on the target's personality. In this case, Cantor and Mischel (1979a) argue, estimates of the prototypicality of the target person with respect to a given category rest primarily on the identification of particular, highly central attributes, that is, on verifying evidence alone (however, see Chapter 2 on the problem of interpreting trait-inconsistent behaviours and non-occurrences of trait-specific behaviours). In both instances, personality descriptions relying on prototypes are informed jointly by the attributes and behaviours of the person to be described and the cognitive categories invoked by the observer on the basis of his or her knowledge of the consensual meaning of those attributes and behaviours. Thus, Cantor and Mischel's theorizing and research clearly reflects the social constructionist position that person perception is 'a function of an inter-action between the beliefs of observers and the characteristics of the observed' (Cantor and Mischel, 1979a, 45–46).

In her contributions to the social constructionist analysis of personality, Hampson (1989; Hampson et al., 1986) also builds upon Rosch's work on object categorization in natural language but extends it into a different direction. She notes that Cantor and Mischel's analysis has concentrated on nouns as linguistic input for person prototypes. In contrast, her focus is on the semantic structure of personality descriptions based on trait adjectives. This distinction is an important one because it is associated with different vantage points: 'Nouns categorise people, whereas traits categorise behaviours' (Hampson, 1988: 202; see also Semin and Fiedler (1988, 1991) for further research on the implications of different linguistic categories for personality description).

Thus, to analyse the semantic structure of trait categories, it is essential to look in detail at the behaviours that make up the category in question. In the attempt to understand the meaning of traits, two aspects need to be distinguished: the *descriptive* aspect, referring to the contents of the behaviours asssociated with the trait, and the *evaluative* aspect, referring to the social desirability of those behaviours. Stating that 'Paul is conscientious' means, at a descript-ive level, that he is likely to turn up in time for his classes, never forgets an appointment, or whatever other behaviours serve as indicators of conscientiousness. At the evaluative level, the state-ment implies that Paul has a quality that is generally regarded as positive and desirable. The two aspects of trait meaning can be assessed independently as well as in combination, as illustrated in a study by Hampson et al. (1987). Their aim was to establish normative values of the breadth of different trait categories, whereby category breadth (or bandwidth) is defined in terms of the range of descriptively different behaviour subsumed by a trait label. While broad categories have the advantage of comprising a diverse spectrum of behaviours, their disadvantage is that they are relat-ively low in *fidelity*, that is, informativeness on exactly which aspects of behaviour are central to the trait inference.

Starting from a list of 573 personality-descriptive adjectives (derived, in part, from the taxonomic work reviewed in the first part of this chapter), Hampson et al. asked a sample of British subjects to indicate the semantic breadth (that is, the diversity of behaviours associated with a term) of each attribute on a seven-point rating scale. In a separate step, the same subjects rated the social desirability of each trait term. The results of the study confirm the proposition that trait terms can be arranged along a continuum of category breadth. Moreover, they provide a quantitative score for each attribute indicating its relative position on the continuum. The broad end of the continuum was found to be occupied by traits such as 'good', 'nice' and 'normal', whereas the narrow end was represented by terms such as 'prompt', 'unpunctual', and 'silent'. At the same time, each term was assigned a social desirability value based on the subjects' mean ratings. Here, terms such as 'cruel', 'dishonest', 'spiteful' and 'uncaring' received the lowest desirability ratings, while terms such as 'honest', 'kind', 'reliable' and 'truthful' marked the positive end of the dimension. The correlation between category breadth and social desirability was moderate and revealed that desirable traits are generally broader than undesirable ones. This suggests that, in English at least, more fine-grained distinctions are available for describing negative behaviours of people. Moreover, when the findings were related to those of a parallel study with US subjects, the overall pattern of category-breadth and social desirability values was quite similar (correlations were $r = 0.75$ for the category-breadth values and 0.97 for the social desirability ratings). At the same time, some interesting differences between the two language communities emerged:

> For example, the British ratings were substantially broader than the American ratings for traits such as *natural, pleasant, merry, mannerly,* and *spirited*; the American ratings were substantially broader than the British for traits such as *dominant, cynical, ethical,* and *honest*. . . . The terms with the largest discrepancies [in social desirability] between American and British norms are *aggressive, cunning, self-seeking, simple,* and *earnest,* with the Americans evaluating these characteristics more positively than the British. (Hampson et al., 1987: 244–245)

Thus, the findings illustrate that even within the same language, cultural differences between the respective user communities exert a subtle influence on the meaning of personality-descriptive attributes. This is clear evidence against the 'realist' position that personality descriptions are immediate reflections of the qualities of the individual in question. In contrast, impressions about personality are shaped to a significant degree by the descriptive categories available to the observer by virtue of his or her membership in a particular language community.

While Hampson et al. (1987) demonstrated that category breadth and social desirability are important dimensions of trait categories, the impact of these dimensions on personality descriptions in everyday discourse is explored in their subsequent work. John et al. (1991) present a series of studies showing that the selection of traits to describe target persons can be predicted on the basis of a trade-off between breadth and fidelity. Especially when asked to generate spontaneous personality descriptions, subjects show a clear preference for trait terms with an optimal balance between breadth and fidelity such as 'dominant' (being as broad as possible while still sufficiently descriptive of behaviour) at the expense of both subordinate traits such as 'bossy' (lower breadth and higher fidelity) and superordinate terms such as 'unpleasant' (higher breadth but little fidelity).

Interestingly, Hampson (1989) reports evidence that the preference for broader traits was not dependent on the familiarity between target and observer, but that it was mediated by the observer's liking for the target. When asked to describe liked and disliked others in both positive and negative terms, observers tended to select broad desirable and narrow undesirable traits for targets they liked, while they described disliked targets by broad undesirable and narrow desirable qualities. Thus, subjects skilfully used category breadth as an indirect means of conveying evaluative impressions about the personalities of others. Together with recent studies extending the perspective from single to multiple traits (Hampson, 1990; Casselden and Hampson, in press), these findings support the importance of the semantic characteristics of trait categories for the 'construction of personality'. It is clear that impressions of personality are neither independent of behavioural information about a target person nor unaffected by the properties of the available language in which such impressions are cast. The fact that individuals are able to reconcile incongruent or conflicting trait information into a coherent personality impression but find it difficult to do so (Casselden and Hampson, in press) corroborates this dual basis of personality description. Moreover, aspects of the relationship between target and observer, for example, liking, play a role in the choice of strategies for conveying particular impressions about the personalities of others.

In their analysis of central dimensions underlying the categorization of trait terms, Hampson et al.'s studies are subject to two limitations. First, they treat traits as well as their behavioural referents as decontextualized attributes, disregarding the fact that trait attributions typically include implicit or explicit propositions about the conditions under which trait-specific behaviour is likely to be manifested. Secondly, the behavioural referents specified for different trait categories are provided by raters in the form of verbal labels rather than being derived from observations of actual behaviour. This means that both behaviours and traits are measured in the same response mode, that is, everyday language, whereby nothing can be said about the external validity of the trait-referent behaviours. These two issues are addressed by Wright and Mischel (1988) who present a 'conditional view' of dispositional categories. Their general argument is that when people use trait terms to characterize patterns of behaviour, they do so against the background of socially shared knowledge about the contexts relevant to the elicitation of trait-specific behaviour. Thus, to say that somebody is a 'shy person' is a statement about the person's likely behaviour in certain types of contexts (such as social situations involving the presence of strangers or powerful others). Such if–then relations, or condition–behaviour contingencies, are regarded as constituent features of trait terms, reflecting the user's awareness that individual behaviour varies in a systematic way across situations rather than being stable or consistent in an absolute sense. Thus, dispositional constructs are conceived of as consisting of three components: a set of conditions, a set of behaviours, and a set of if–then rules linking conditions and behaviours.

Wright and Mischel (1988) conducted a study to explore the use of qualifiers or 'hedges' in trait attributions made by children and adults for targets with whom they were highly familiar. The setting for the study was provided by a summer camp for socially mal-adjusted boys. On the basis of extensive behavioural observations of the children, *aggressiveness* and *social withdrawal* emerged as salient trait categories, and prototypical behaviours could be identi-fied for each of the two traits. These behavioural records allowed the selection of representative target persons for each trait (for instance, the child with the highest overall frequency of aggressive or withdrawn behaviours) in two age groups: 8-year-olds and 12-year-olds. To measure trait attributions, personality descriptions were elicited for each target from two groups of observers in the form of open-ended interviews. One group of observers consisted of the targets' respective age-mates, while the second group consisted of adult counsellors working at the camp. Thus, both groups of observers had detailed first-hand knowledge of the targets' behav-iour. The focus of the analysis was on examining the spontaneous behavioural descriptions and trait attributions offered by the two groups of observers. In particular, the data were coded for the frequency of *probability qualifiers* and *conditionals* to test the proposition that trait attributions are not made in context-free form but take account of the conditions under which trait-specific behaviour is likely to occur. Probability qualifiers, such as 'some-times' or 'always', reflect observers' general awareness that behav-iour is variable across situations. Conditionals, such as 'if in situation *x* then behaviour *y*', are more precise qualifiers in that they specify particular sets of circumstances under which high probabil-ities of trait-related behaviours are expected.

Wright and Mischel proposed that the development of conditional trait knowledge proceeds from more global probability qualifiers to more specific conditionals which should be reflected in systematic differences between peer and adult observers' descriptions of their target persons. This hypothesis received clear support from the data: children of both age groups used a higher proportion of uncertainty statements in describing their peers' behaviour than did the adult observers. Conversely, adults used a significantly higher proportion of certainty statements and conditional qualifiers. The overall frequency of explicit qualifiers, however, was low even among the adult observers. In interpreting this latter finding, Wright and Mischel suggest that observers can largely build upon shared social knowledge of the limiting conditions of certain trait-specific behaviour (for example, the audience can be assumed to know that characterizing somebody as shy refers to his or her behaviour in social situations and not in solitary ones). Explicit qualifiers are reserved for those cases that might otherwise be ambiguous (for example, somebody is shy only when interacting with an attractive member of the opposite sex).

Altogether, the findings of Wright and Mischel (1988; see also Shoda et al., 1989) are in accordance with the social constructionist view that dispositional statements are determined jointly by the behavioural performance of the target person and the interpretative activities of the observer. They show that trait information is organized in everyday language in a way that reflects the user's understanding of both consistency and discriminativeness of trait-relevant behaviour. Therefore, the authors challenge the idea that evidence of consistency in personality description can be enhanced by aggregating behavioural indicators into 'overall behavioural tendencies' (see also the summary view discussed in Chapter 2) without considering the conditional hedges associated with the different behaviours involved in the aggregation.

The study by Wright and Mischel is also directly relevant to another line of argument which adopts a radically different view of the role of language in impression formation. In his 'systematic distortion hypothesis', Shweder (1982) questions the view endorsed by both the traditional trait model and the social constructionist approach that statements about trait relationships are linked to actual empirical relationships between dispositional and behavioural measures. Instead, he argues that estimates of trait co-occurrences, as derived from self- or peer-ratings, reflect semantic relationships without any reference to the qualities of the target person. That is, high correlations between different traits are interpreted as reflecting 'what goes with what' according to linguistic conventions rather than 'what goes with whom' in the sense of substantive individual differences. One source of evidence on which the systematic distortion hypothesis was built was the finding that trait correlations derived from ratings of informed others closely resembled those of strangers who had no direct knowledge about the target. As was noted in the discussion of the 'Big Five' personality factors in the first section of this chapter, very similar five-factor structures emerged from personality ratings of strangers and well-acquainted peers. However, recent reviewers (for example, Borkenau, in press, a; Kenrick and Funder, 1988) have concluded that the systematic distortion hypothesis cannot be upheld in the light of the evidence available to date. First, the correspondence between judgements of semantic similarity and personality ratings was shown to vary as a function of the linguistic category employed, being relatively high for descriptions using adjectives and low for descriptions using verbs (for example, Semin and Greenslade, 1985). Secondly, agreement between raters was found to be higher when they rated familiar target persons as compared to strangers (for example, Funder and Colvin, 1988). Another study (Mervielde and Pot, 1989) showed that ratings of two perceivers rating the same target were more closely related than ratings of two targets by the same perceiver, suggesting that target effects are more important than perceiver effects in personality ratings. Both findings indicate that factors other than the consensually shared semantic meaning of the descriptive attributes must have been involved in the ratings. Third, studies comparing different forms of personality measurement, such as direct observation and peer ratings, found convergent patterns of individual differences across the different approaches (for example, Small et al., 1983). In the Wright and Mischel (1988) study, peers' and adult observers' descriptions of the targets' personalities in terms of the two trait dimensions of aggressiveness and withdrawal corresponded almost perfectly with classifications of the targets on the basis of independent behavioural observations.

The discussion surrounding the systematic distortion hypotheses has illustrated once more that neither the 'realist' position that impression formation is primarily a function of the qualities of the target person nor the 'idealist' position that it is located entirely in the head of the perceiver stand up to closer scrutiny. In short, personality is neither 'found' nor 'imagined'. Instead, there is a growing body of evidence supporting the social constructionist argument that inferences about personality are shaped jointly by the behaviours shown by a person and the interpretative constructs applied to them by competent members of a given language community.

Summary

The present chapter has reviewed three lines of response to the challenge of the trait concept in the course of the consistency controversy. Grounded in the conviction that traits are indispensable constructs for the study of personality and individual differences, these efforts are directed towards refining and consolidating the conceptual understanding of traits from different perspectives.

The first perspective examined in this chapter emphasized the potential of traits as an organizing framework for the systematic analysis of individual differences. To the extent that a limited set of trait dimensions can be shown to emerge consistently from a variety of personality measures, these dimensions can be used as a tool for capturing the structure of personality. Building upon a research tradition that started over five decades ago, the current concern with establishing a broad trait taxonomy has led to the identification of a five-factor structure of personality in which the majority of specific trait categories can be accommodated. Despite a certain amount of ambiguity on how best to label the Big Five, this work has proved useful in providing personality psychology with a well-founded descriptive platform from which to approach the task of *explaining* personality structure.

This task is at the core of the second perspective reviewed in this chapter which seeks to explore the genetic roots of individual differences in personality. Again, this perspective is not an entirely new one but takes up a line of research that had become entangled for a while in a more general ideological argument. By separating the relative impact of genetic and environmental influences on an individual's personality profile, it was hoped to strengthen the case in favour of traits as central units of analysis. Indeed, the behavioural genetic approach has yielded consistent evidence that traits have a hereditary basis, even though this basis is generally estimated to be less powerful in accounting for individual differences than the specific socialization experiences (that is, non-shared environmental influences) made by the individual. As a by-product of their analyses, behavioural geneticists have provided clear evidence that the influence of the common family environment in which siblings grow up is negligible compared with both genetic factors and idiosyncratic environmental experiences, a finding which is clearly at odds with widely held intuitive beliefs.

From the social constructionist perspective discussed in the last section of the chapter, the two previous approaches may be criticized for overemphasizing the *target* of personality measurement, that is, the individual under study, at the expense of both the *language* of personality description and the *observer* applying this language to the behaviour and qualities of the target. In contrast, social constructionists regard inferences about personality as products of a socially and culturally mediated process whereby an observer (as layperson or psychologist) applies a consensually shared meaning system (namely, language) to the categorization and interpretation of behavioural data. Since language is considered to be the primary vehicle for conveying personality impressions, it follows that studying the linguistic properties of trait terms becomes a central objective. In this vein, the principles of trait categorization have been conceptualized with reference to a prototype model in which trait-referent behaviours are characterized in terms of their centrality in defining the category in question. From a slightly different angle, the dimensions of category breadth and descriptive versus evaluative content were shown to be useful in identifying a breadth/fidelity trade-off underlying people's preference for trait descriptions at a relatively broad level of abstraction. Another line of work stressed the fact that trait terms do not only provide summary labels for observed behaviours but also contain implicit conditional information about the situations likely to elicit trait-specific behaviour. This information, while acquired as part of a person's linguistic competence, is by no means independent from the conditions governing the actual manifestation of trait-specific behaviour. Thus, from a social constructionist view, there is little support for the contention that perceptions of consistency and trait interrelations are purely semantic artefacts with no immediate reference to observable data.

Altogether, the work reviewed in the present chapter attests to the utility of the trait concept in understanding personality. At the same time, there is general agreement that traits must not be studied in isolation from the features of the situations and environments in which the person acts and lives. In this sense, even though the focus is clearly on the person side, the new variants of the trait approach introduced above can furnish a significant contribution to the modern interactionist perspective on personality which is discussed in the next two chapters.

Notes

1   John (1990: 83) reserves the term 'lexical approach' for studies concerned with the analysis of trait *adjectives*. Recent research, however, has pointed to the

significance of other linguistic categories, such as verbs and nouns, in the search for a taxonomic description of personality (for example, Angleitner et al., 1990; De Raad and Hoskins, 1990). Furthermore, a number of studies contributing to the Big Five literature have employed personality questionnaires where the personality-descriptive terms are typically presented to respondents in sentence form (for example, Costa and McCrae, 1985; McCrae and Costa, 1987). It is in this broader sense that the lexical approach to the study of personality is discussed in this section.

2   Digman (1989) suggests to label this factor 'will to achieve' because of its significant relationship with formal criteria of educational and occupational achievement.

3   If MZ correlations are more than twice the magnitude of DZ correlations, this calculation leads to heritability estimates for the trait in question that are higher than the correlations obtained for the MZ twins. To illustrate this point, consider the following data from Loehlin and Nichols (1976). In their sample, they obtained correlations for extraversion of $r = 0.62$ for MZ females and $r = 0.28$ for DZ females. Doubling the differences between the two correlations leads to a heritability estimate of 0.68, which is higher than the MZ correlation itself. This pattern needs to be explained, since the level of MZ correlations theoretically defines the upper level of similarity due to additive genetic influence. As MZ twins are identical in terms of their genetic make-up, further theorizing is required to explain heritability estimates exceeding the MZ twin correlations (see Plomin et al., 1990: 229ff.).

4   As Plomin (1986) points out, selective placement of adopted children (that is, placing children with adoptive children similar to their biological parents) is based primarily on criteria of social class and intelligence (and, one can add, race), and is unlikely to lead to confounding effects in the personality domain. Bouchard and McGue (1990) addressed the potentially biasing effect of selective placement empirically by analysing twin correlations on a measure of family environment. Even though correlations were generally positive and some were also significant, their overall magnitude was found to be small, suggesting that placement effects do not seriously distort comparisons between twins reared together and apart.

4
Modern Interactionism: An Alternative Framework for Personality Research

Explaining personality and social behaviour in terms of the joint influence of individual qualities and situational influences has a long, though discontinuous history in personality research. In the 1920s and 1930s, authors such as Kantor (1924, 1926), Koffka (1935), and most notably Lewin (1936) advanced models of individual behaviour in which the reciprocal interaction of the person and the situation was a key idea. Yet while some of these contributions exerted a continuous influence in certain areas of psychology, such as Lewin's work in the study of group processes, they have failed to sustain a similar impact in personality psychology (see Ekehammar, 1974; Heilizer, 1980). In the course of the consistency controversy, the conflict between trait psychologists and situationists diverted attention away from the task of elaborating the early interactionist propositions. So, even though the importance of person–situation interactions for explaining individual behaviour was first highlighted a long time ago, it was not until the mid-1970s that the study of these interactions was addressed systematically in personality research. In an attempt to progress beyond the positions advanced in the consistency debate, a 'modern' interactionist perspective on personality and social behaviour began to take shape. Within a few years, this perspective became so widely accepted that, as Pervin (1989a: 352) stated, 'most personality psychologists now are interactionists'.

Emerging research perspectives within the interactionist framework are documented in various specialized books and journal issues (for example, Endler and Magnusson, 1976a; Kahle, 1979; Magnusson and Endler, 1977a; Magnusson and Allen, 1983a; Pervin and Lewis, 1978; Spokane, 1987). However, relatively little coverage is given to modern interactionism in the personality textbook literature directed at a readership not necessarily familiar with the issues at the core of this approach (see, however, Pervin (1984c) for an exception). Therefore, the present volume devotes two chapters to the modern interactionist perspective to offer a detailed discussion of its distinctive features, achievements, and shortcomings.

The present chapter will review the main theoretical postulates and methods of the interactionist approach. In the first section, different meanings of the term 'interaction' are distinguished which lead to different strategies of data collection and analysis. The second section examines how situational variables are incorporated into the interactionist reconceptualization of personality. The third section is devoted to the analysis of personality development and change from an interactionist perspective. Particular attention will be given to studies which follow patterns of personality development over longer periods of time employing longitudinal research designs.

Focusing on specific areas of interactionist research, Chapter 5 presents a review of three main areas of empirical work. The domains of *anxiety*, *emotions*, and *prosocial behaviour* are selected as representative examples of how to implement a perspective on personality that is committed to studying the interdependence of personal and situational determinants of individual behaviour. Following a summary of the major research contributions in each of these areas, the final section of Chapter 5 sums up the discussion of the modern interactionist approach by presenting a critical appraisal of its achievements so far. Is modern interactionism still alive and well or does it show signs of attrition signalling its fading impact on personality psychology in the 1990s?

The fundamentals of modern interactionism

Rather than denoting a single, well-defined theory of personality, 'modern interactionism' stands for a variety of research perspectives. What these perspectives share is the basic hypothesis that behaviour is a joint function of personal characteristics and the features of a given situation. They differ, however, over the exact nature of the two essential ingredients as well as the ways in which their interaction should be conceptualized and measured (Buss, 1977). The consensual core of the modern interactionist approach is captured in four basic postulates (see Magnusson and Endler, 1977b: 4):

1 Actual behaviour is a function of a continuous process of multidirectional interaction or feedback between the individual and the situations he or she encounters.
2 The individual is an intentional, active agent in this interaction process.
3 On the person side of the interaction, cognitive and motivational factors are essential determinants of behaviour.

4   On the situation side, the psychological meaning of situations for the individual is the important determining factor.

From these general postulates, two essential tasks follow for the implementation of an interactionist research paradigm (Endler, 1983). The first is to study exactly how person and situation variables interact in eliciting behaviour. This involves not only to demonstrate that a substantial proportion of variance in behaviour is attributable to the interactive effect of personal and situational characteristics. It also means to identify the psychological principles by which such interactions can be explained and, ultimately, predicted. The second task is to describe and classify stimuli, situations and environments in a systematic way. In accordance with the fourth postulate quoted above, the emphasis here is on understanding the process whereby objective situational cues are transformed by the individual into subjectively meaningful representations of his or her social world. In addition, this task includes the search for a comprehensive taxonomy of situations to complement the analysis of individual differences on the person side.

Before exploring how far modern interactionism has progressed over the past fifteen years in addressing these tasks, let us first take a look at the particular way in which personality is defined in the context of the interactionist model.

Defining personality
After what has been said so far about the interactionist approach, it almost goes without saying that it entails a definition of personality which emphasizes the interdependency of personal and situational determinants of behaviour. Few interactionist authors have offered an explicit definition of personality, but one definition which seems to be shared implicitly by many researchers in the field is the following:

> *Personality* is a person's coherent manner of interacting with himself or herself and with his or her environment. (Endler, 1983: 179)

However straightforward this definition may appear, it is different in at least two significant respects from the traditional definition of personality sketched at the beginning of Chapter 2 and endorsed, for example, by the advocates of the trait approach.

Firstly, no reference is made in the above definition to the differential aspect of personality stressing those characteristics of an individual that characterize him or her relative to other people. Instead, the emphasis is on discovering lawfulness in individual behaviour, which implies a different, namely *intra-individual*, level of analysis. At this level, the major task is to identify coherent, that is, idiographically predictable, patterns of individual behaviour across situations and over time (see Chapter 2 and also Magnusson, 1976).

Secondly, by including the individual's interaction with himself or herself (that is, interaction of variables *within* the person) as a defining aspect of personality, it becomes necessary to introduce different types of person variables which interact within the individual to produce coherent patterns of behaviour. One basic distinction here is that between *reaction variables* and *mediating variables* (Magnusson, 1976).

Reaction variables refer to different types of responses which the individual may show as a result of the interaction between situational stimuli and their internal processing. Four main categories of reaction variables are distinguished: *overt observable behaviour*, for example, helping another person; *physiological responses*, for example, heart rate; *covert reactions*, for example, emotional responses; and *artificial behaviour*, for example, responding to experimental instructions. In looking for coherence at the level of reaction variables, therefore, it is important to consider the regularity of behaviour patterns both within and across different types of reaction variables.

Whether or not the individual shows a certain response in a given situation is determined to a large extent by the operation of a latent mediating process in which situational information is selected and interpreted in relation to the individual's cognitive and affective predispositions. Three types of mediating variables are assumed to be involved in this process. They are not directly accessible but have to be inferred from the person's responses (for example, Edwards and Endler, 1983): (a) the *content* of the mediating process, that is, the meaning which is attached to the selected situational information on the basis of either stored social knowledge or information inherent in the specific situation; (b) the cognitive *structure* into which that content is integrated; that is, the person's intellectual capacity and cognitive schemata which link a particular content with other already existing contents in a meaningful way; and (c) *motivational variables* which explain why the process of selecting and interpreting certain situational cues is instigated and sustained; for example, the person's momentary needs. A similar and partly overlapping set of variables is proposed in Mischel's cognitive social learning theory as 'person variables' influencing the acquisition and performance of social behaviour (Mischel, 1986).

An example from the domain of prosocial behaviour may serve to illustrate the proposed functioning of these variables as mediators between external situational cues and an individual's response to them. Imagine a person suddenly confronted with an elderly man who has fallen down in the street. The decision to engage in some form of helping behaviour as well as the actual performance of the helping act are seen as being *mediated* by (a) the meaning assigned to the situation as involving a person in need of help as opposed to involving a drunk no longer able to walk properly; (b) the individual's cognitive competence to link this meaning to other relevant contents, for example, cognitive scripts containing knowledge of appropriate responses to situations where helping is required; and (c) the person's motivation (including emotional states, prosocial attitudes, needs, etc.) which may lead him or her either to direct attention to the person on the ground and then embark on the process of interpreting the situation or ignoring the situation and walking past.

What this example shows is that the modern interactionist view, like the trait approach, assumes that latent variables within the person have a significant effect on overt behaviour and explain why people respond differently to the same situational cues. However, unlike the trait approach, these latent variables are not conceived of as stable dispositions but as interdependent facets of a flexible inner system for matching incoming situational information with an individually characteristic form of response.

Types of interaction and their measurement
In contrasting their approach with other models of personality, advocates of interactionism draw particular attention to the distinction between personality theories and measurement models (see, for example, Magnusson, 1976). A personality theory consists of a set of *psychological hypotheses* about the role of personal dispositions, needs, motives, etc. in relation to individual behaviour. On the other hand, a measurement model, according to Magnusson, is a model about the *link between certain psychological hypotheses and their corresponding empirical measures*. The measurement model determines which strategies of data collection and analysis are selected to substantiate the theory empirically. A single psychological theory can endorse and employ different measurement models, each leading to different types of operationalizations and, by implication, different types of evidence for or against the proposed psychological hypotheses. The importance of observing this distinction with regard to the modern interactionist approach becomes evident if one looks at the meanings attached to the key concept of 'interaction' (see Olweus, 1977). At the level of personality theory, the psychological meaning of 'interaction' refers to the joint impact of personal and situational qualities on social behav-

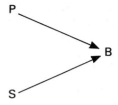

Figure 4.1   *Mechanistic interaction of person (P) and situation (S) variables on behaviour (B)*

iour. This psychological meaning has been represented by at least two different meanings of 'interaction' at the level of measurement models. Each of them has specific methodological implications and consequences (see Buss (1977) and Howard (1979) for controversial assessments of this issue).

The first type of interaction is called *mechanistic* or *statistical* interaction, assuming unidirectional influences of person and situation variables on behaviour. Inherent in this view is a clear distinction between independent and dependent variables and the assumption of a linear combination of person and situation variables in their effect on behaviour (see Figure 4.1).[1] The corresponding methodological framework to capture this type of interaction is the analysis of variance (ANOVA) model. It allows the investigator to quantify (though not to explain!) the proportion of the total behavioural variance which is accounted for by the interactive effect of person and situation variables and to compare it with the proportion of variance due to the person and situation main effects. This strategy of apportioning behavioural variance into the relative contributions of person and environment factors has remained in constant use despite numerous criticisms (for example, Golding, 1975; Olweus, 1977). Recently, it has received further attention by research in the context of behavioural–genetic methods seeking to apportion the influence of genetic versus environmental factors as determinants of individual differences (see Chapter 3).

To collect the data required by the variance components strategy, interactionist researchers have strongly relied on one particular type of instrument called situation–response inventory. S–R inventories are composed of two integral parts – a set of situation categories and a set of response scales. Subjects are required to describe their responses separately for each situation category. Thus, S–R inventories differ from traditional personality inventories in that they measure people's responses conditional upon the specific features of the situation category (see, for example, Dworkin and Kihlstrom,

Table 4.1   *The S–R Inventory of General Trait Anxiousness*

Situations	Responses
• You are in situations involving interaction with other people	• Seek experiences like this
	• Perspire
• You are in situations where you are about to encounter physical harm	• Have an 'uneasy feeling'
	• Feel exhilarated and thrilled
• You are in a new or strange situation	• Get fluttering feeling in stomach
	• Feel tense
• You are involved in your daily routines	• Enjoy these situations
	• Heart beats faster
	• Feel anxious

1978; Endler and Hunt, 1968). A typical example of the S–R format, which was first introduced by Endler et al. (1962), is the 'S–R Inventory of General Trait Anxiousness' (S–R GTA). This measure was developed by Endler and Okada (1975) to test the interactionist model of multidimensional trait anxiety. The S–R GTA consists of four general situations and nine modes of response displayed in Table 4.1.

For each situation, subjects are asked to indicate, on a five-point scale, the extent to which they typically show each of the nine responses. On the basis of this information, one can assess the influence of differences between individuals, situations, and response modes (that is, the main effects due to persons, situations and responses) and, more importantly, the following statistical interactions: the interaction between individuals and response modes; the interaction between individuals and situations; the interaction between situations and response modes; and the three-way interaction of individuals, response modes, and situations. Interactionists usually interpret evidence from S–R inventories to be supportive of their theoretical claims if the proportion of variance accounted for by the interactions exceeds the proportion of variance accounted for by the main effects.

A critical analysis of research based on S–R inventories has been presented by Furnham and Jaspers (1983; see also Golding, 1977). A central criticism refers to the issue of how persons, situations and response modes are sampled as 'input' for a particular S–R inventory. Furnham and Jaspers argue that the strength of the various variance components can easily be influenced a priori by selecting either very homogeneous or very heterogeneous samples of persons, situations and responses which are bound to result in correspondingly low or high variance components. Accordingly, they conclude that 'the implicit or explicit theories of the experimenters, as regards P × S interaction, may have been confirmed by a non-

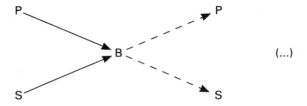

Figure 4.2   *Dynamic interaction of person, situation, and behaviour*

random unrepresentative sampling of Ss and questionnaire items'
(Furnham and Jaspers, 1983: 640).

The variance component strategy and the S–R inventory are both
linked to the analysis of statistical, unidirectional interactions. In
contrast, the second meaning in which the psychological concept of
interaction is represented at the measurement level refers to the
process of *dynamic* or *reciprocal* interaction. This meaning of the
term 'interaction', which some authors refer to as 'transaction' (for
example, Pervin, 1968), designates the continuous and reciprocal
interaction between behaviour and both person and situation
variables (see Figure 4.2).

Emphasizing the reciprocal influence of persons, situations and
behaviour in this way, the distinction between independent and
dependent variables cannot and need not be upheld. Instead, it is
acknowledged that through their behaviour people affect and
modify not only the situations in which they act but also their own
internal cognitive and emotional states – each of which were
involved in prompting the behaviour in the first place.

One example of research committed to the dynamic meaning of
interaction is provided by the work of Peterson (1979) on interpersonal relationships. One should note that in the context of
personal relationships, the 'situation' is constituted by the presence
and behaviour of one or more other persons. Peterson asked
married couples to agree, at the end of each day of the investigation
period, on their most important interaction in the course of the day.
Each partner then provided an independent account of that interaction guided by three questions: What were the conditions under
which the interaction took place? How did it start? What happened
next? These free-response interaction records were subjected to a
complex coding process in which they were judged in terms of their
main acts as well as the message (meaning) and the dominant affect
associated with each act. On this basis, a detailed inspection of
'interaction cycles', each consisting of an action by one partner and
a reaction by the other, was possible. The following passage

illustrates one of the many ways in which such information facilitates the understanding of the dynamic interaction between person and situation:

> Two common cycles have to do with behavior in task situations. In one set, the partners cooperate. In the other they do not. The main difference between the two cycles is in the way the initiating statement is made. When cooperation occurs, the request usually involves an assumption of mutual responsibility and shared effort. 'Let's get this job of ours done.' Refusals to cooperate were usually brought on by 'dumping'. One partner assumed the other should do all or most of the work: 'Let's you get going.' The 'dumpee' disagreed, with feeling. (Peterson, 1979: 49)

Another perspective from which to study the reciprocal influence of person, situation and behaviour is illustrated in research on the 'Social Relations Model' (Malloy and Kenny, 1986). The model rests on the assumption that individuals not only respond in their characteristic ways to situational conditions but also function as social stimuli for the behaviour of others. Accordingly, social interaction is regarded as a paradigmatic case of dynamic person–environment interactions. Depending on the analytical perspective, the actor may either be looked at as the 'person' influenced by the partner's behaviour representing the 'situation' or vice versa, with the specific relationship between actor and partner being conceived of as the 'interaction' term. Thus, the social relations model deals with dyadic interactions as its basic units of analysis whereby the behaviour of one member is influenced by and, at the same time, influences the behaviour of the other member. This results in interrelated, non-independent patterns of behavioural data for each of the two partners. By combining observations obtained for different dyads, the model can be extended to multiple member interactions.

The non-independence of behavioural observations would present a serious methodological problem for traditional analysis of variance procedures aiming to separate the effects due to the person and the situation (represented here by the interaction partner). In contrast, it is treated by the social relations model as a significant source of information with regard to the reciprocal nature of person–situation interactions. To exploit this source, the model offers a formal mathematical rationale for the analysis of non-independent data patterns resulting from multiple interactions. The formal model, which is rooted in the logic of the general analysis of variance design (for details see Malloy and Kenny, 1986, 208ff.), allows the investigator to identify the relative strength of the following variance components:

1 The *actor* component, representing the person's behavioural

tendencies averaged across multiple interaction partners (for example, the frequency with which the person shows dominant behaviours towards different partners).

2 The *partner* component, reflecting the extent to which an individual elicits similar responses from a variety of social interactions (for example, the frequency with which the person elicits submissive behaviours from different partners).

2 The *relationship* component, expressing the uniqueness of the interaction between two partners on any one occasion which is purged of the influence of both actor and partner effects (for example, the frequency with which the two partners smile at each other if their overall tendencies of smiling to and eliciting smiles from other partners on different occasions is partialled out).

In a study testing the social relations model, Miller et al. (1983) investigated the determinants of subjects' self-disclosure on a variety of topics classified as involving either high or low intimacy. In this context, the *actor* effect was defined in terms of each subject's willingness to disclose across a large number of partners. The *partner* effect was defined as the readiness of all the participants to disclose to that particular partner. The *relationship* effect referred to the amount of self-disclosure displayed by any one subject towards any particular partner. When the proportions of variance accounted for by each of the three components were computed, an interesting pattern of results emerged. Only a minimal proportion of the variance, namely 1 per cent, was due to the generalized partner effect for both high and low intimacy topics, suggesting that at least in their sample there were no individuals who consistently encouraged high self-disclosure from others. The amounts of variance accounted for by the actor and relationship components were substantially higher although affected significantly by the intimacy of the topic. For the highly intimate topics, 14 per cent of the variance were attributable to the person's general tendency towards self-disclosure, while 86 per cent were due to the relationship component (confounded, however, with error variance). For the low intimacy topics, the actor component became more important with 39 per cent of the variance, while the relationship component was reduced to 60 per cent. This suggests that a person's general openness towards self-disclosure is an important predictor of actual self-disclosure when the topic is less intimate or ego-involving. In contrast, the willingness to discuss intimate topics is determined almost exclusively by the specific nature of the relationship between two partners.

Although the dynamic concept of interaction is regarded as more central to the theoretical framework of the interactionist model, the vast majority of empirical research available today has relied on the analysis of unidirectional statistical interactions of person and situation variables on behaviour. The main reason for this discrepancy between programmatic claims and empirical practice is generally seen in the lack of appropriate measurement models and methods capable of capturing the continuous interplay between internal qualities, situational properties and overt behaviour.

As an important step towards addressing this inadequacy, Bem (1983c) pleads for the construction of a 'triple typology' of persons, situations, and behaviours. Such a typology would have to specify what types of situations and behaviours are psychologically equivalent for what kinds of persons. It could then provide a basis for understanding the particular patterns of similarity and differences in individual behaviour across time and situations which is at the core of the concept of coherence in personality.

The role of situation variables

Up to this point, little more has been said about the place of situation variables in the interactionist model than that situations are seen to affect behaviour through their interaction with specific person variables. It is certainly true to say that much less effort has been devoted to the task of exploring the situation side of the interaction compared with the person side. Therefore, far from offering a unified 'psychology of situations', this review of the interactionist treatment of situation variables will be limited to outlining some building blocks of a systematic analysis of situations as required by the study of dynamic person–situation interactions (see also Furnham and Argyle, 1981; Magnusson, 1981a). A more extensive discussion of the role of situation variables in current personality research beyond the modern interactionist approach will be presented in Chapter 8.

As a point of departure for the present analysis, consider again the fourth general postulate of modern interactionism (see above) which states that 'on the situation side [of the interaction], the psychological meaning of situations for the individual is the important determining factor.' According to this proposition, therefore, the focus of the interactionist analysis of situation variables should be on the *subjective* interpretation of situational stimuli rather than on their *objective* properties which can be described in physical terms. The same set of objectively defined features of a situation, like being introduced to an attractive member of the opposite sex at a party, will be transformed into completely different subjective situations by a habitually shy person and a socially skilful extrovert. As a consequence, there is every reason to expect that the two persons will also show considerable differences in their behaviour (Gormly, 1983).

Thus, one strategy for the study of the 'psychological situation' that has been advocated by interactionists is a *stimulus-analytical approach* aimed at describing and classifying situations in terms of their perceived meaning. According to the rationale of this approach, situations are regarded as similar to the extent that they are interpreted by the individual in a similar way, such as two anxiety-provoking situations being perceived as equally threatening, unpleasant, or aversive. This strategy is complemented by a *response-analytical approach* whereby situations are classified in terms of the responses they elicit from the individual. According to this approach, two anxiety-provoking situations would be similar to the extent that they produce similar responses, such as accelerated heart rate, trembling hands, or attempts to escape from the situation. Depending on the level of complexity of the investigated responses, Magnusson and Stattin (1982) further differentiate the response-analytical approach into a *reaction approach* focusing on spontaneous affective or physical responses and an *action approach* addressing more complex, global actions.

The relationship between an individual's perception of and responses to various situations has been examined in several studies of the Stockholm group (Ekehammar et al., 1975; Magnusson and Ekehammar, 1975, 1978). Generally, these studies found a substantial degree of correspondence between perceived situational similarity and response patterns for those situations. They suggest that individuals tend to show similar behavioural patterns across situations to the extent they assign similar interpretations to the situations involved. In a study by Krahé (1986), an idiographic methodology was employed to assess the correspondence between perceived situational similarity and behavioural similarity. Participants first listed a number of anxiety-provoking situations from their past experience and then described these situations both in terms of their perceived similarity and in terms of the characteristic responses shown in them. Compared with findings from earlier studies, where nomothetically defined sets of situations were presented to the participants, this evidence shows that the intra-individual correspondence between situation perception and behaviour increases significantly when situations are sampled from each participant's personal experience. The findings thus support the interactionist claim that the subjective meaning assigned to a particular situation is an essential source of information for understanding and explaining a person's behavioural responses.

However, for both the stimulus-analytical and the response-analytical approach to be applied successfully to the study of person–situation interactions, one needs to go beyond global measures of similarities and differences between situations. Such measures provide very little information about the underlying criteria of subjective definitions of situational similarity which could serve as a basis for predicting cross-situational coherence as well as establishing taxonomies of situations. Therefore, more fine-grained methods are required to clarify the nature of situational similarities at the perceptual as well as the behavioural level. Several inter-related tasks are involved in addressing this objective.

The first task consists in specifying the appropriate units of analysis for studying the 'psychological situation' (Pervin, 1978). Situations can be studied at different levels of complexity, depending on whether one is interested in the impact of single *stimuli*, for example, the mere presence or absence of a competent bystander in an emergency situation; the *situation as a whole*, comprising the dynamic chain of events in which the person under study, the bystander, the victim of the emergency and, possibly, still other people are involved, or the total *environment* in which the situation is embedded, for example, the emergency occurring at an isolated spot in the countryside as opposed to a busy office block. Closely related to this distinction is Magnusson's (1980) differentiation of within-situation and between-situation interactions. The first category refers to the interaction of the individual with various situational cues within the frame of reference of a certain situation, such as a seminar, a business lunch, etc. The second type of interaction refers to the way an individual distinguishes between situations and seeks to explain why he or she prefers certain situations and avoids others.

Clarifying different levels of analysis at which the psychological impact of situations on an individual's perceptions and responses should be studied is an important prerequisite for the systematic analysis of situations from an interactionist perspective. The empirical analysis of situations, however, is faced with another serious problem that has remained largely unaddressed in previous theorizing and research. This problem has to do with defining the temporal and spatial boundaries of a situation. How does a person, as subject or investigator, decide when a situation ends and a new one begins? Which single cues are included in or omitted from the person's subjective representation of an objective set of situational stimuli?

An empirical strategy to solve the first of these two questions can be derived from the work of Newtson and his colleagues (see, for example, Newtson, 1973; Newtson and Engquist, 1976; Newtson et al., 1987). They asked their subjects to break down a continuous videotape into distinct situational units, thereby arriving at a descriptive taxonomy of features which define the perceived boundaries of a situation (see also Deaux and Major, 1977). A theoretical answer from the perspective of goal-directed action theory is offered by Lantermann (1980) who claims that the beginning of a situation is marked by the instigation of an action directed at achieving a certain goal, and the end of the situation is reached with the attainment of that goal. However, the fact that the attainment of one goal may involve pursuing several other, subordinate goals, means that any attempt at arriving at an operational definition of the beginning and end of a situation on the basis of this approach is bound to prove problematic.

A second important task involved in gaining more specific information about the psychological meaning of situations is to identify the criteria on which individuals rely in their interpretation of situations. While some of these defining features will always be unique to particular types of situations (for example, stressful situations, interpersonal situations, achievement situations, etc.), there may also be more general criteria which allow one to compare situations from different categories with one another. Identification of the criteria for distinguishing between situations is required as a basis for establishing taxonomies or typologies of situations from which more precise hypotheses on the expected consistency or variability of behaviour can be derived. These typologies can either be categorical, with each situation being assigned to one of several clearly separated categories (a party situation, a situation involving physical harm, etc.) or continuous, with each situation being located at a certain point of a quantitative dimension (pleasant–unpleasant, formal–informal, etc.).

Despite Endler's (1983: 171) claim that 'ideally, a taxonomy of situations (or stimuli or environments) should be derived within a theoretical context and not be developed primarily on empirical grounds', it is the latter strategy that has been employed in most of the studies conducted so far. Price and Bouffard (1974) identified the dimension of *behavioural constraint* as a central aspect of distinguishing between situations. They showed that in certain situations, such as attending a church service or being in a job interview, very few behaviours are appropriate, while other situations, such as being in one's own room, are characterized by a wide range of acceptable behaviours.

King and Sorrentino (1983) discovered seven dimensions underlying the perception of interpersonal goal-oriented situations, three of which were identical with dimensions identified by other authors for different situational domains. These three dimensions, namely 'pleasant versus unpleasant', 'accidentally caused or involved versus intentionally caused or involved', and 'social versus non-social', can be regarded as general dimensions for describing the perception of situations in a variety of domains. Interestingly, when King and Sorrentino looked at the individual patterns of situation perception obtained for each subject, they found substantially higher degrees of interpersonal variability than interpersonal agreement. In a similar vein, Pervin (1976) collected open-ended descriptions from four participants of 'the situations of their current life' and subjected them to individual factor analyses. His results show that individuals differ not only with respect to the number and the content of the general factors which emerged from their descriptions but also with respect to their characteristic feelings and responses in objectively similar situations.

Another widely applicable dimension for distinguishing between situations is that of situations as *chosen* versus *imposed* (Emmons and Diener, 1986a, b; Magnusson, 1980; Snyder and Ickes, 1985). As highlighted in the concept of dynamic interaction, individuals are not only passively exposed to a variety of situations forced upon them; they also play an active role in choosing and influencing situations in their social environment. Emmons et al. (1985) present evidence in support of the assumption that people actively choose situations which are reflective of their personalities. They examined the relationship between different personality measures (for example, extroversion, sociability, impulsivity) and the frequency with which the individual engaged in various recreation activities. The overall pattern of their findings suggests that individuals tend to prefer those activities which are congruent with their personal dispositions (see Chapter 5 for a more detailed discussion).

A third essential task for a more adequate treatment of the psychological situation in the interactionist approach consists in the development of a theoretical conceptualization of situation cognition. A theoretical model is required to explain how objective situational information is processed and translated into specific cognitive representations. As even sympathetic critics have to admit, this task has not been properly addressed within the interactionist paradigm.

There are, however, developments in other areas of psychology, especially cognitive social psychology, where different conceptualizations of the cognitive representation of situations have been advanced. For instance, Abelson (1981; see also Schank and

Abelson, 1977) explore the organization of situational information in the form of *cognitive scripts* containing the characteristic events and appropriate action rules of a particular situation. Another line of theory and research has addressed the problem of how situations are organized into *cognitive categories*. In this work (see, for example, Cantor, 1981; Cantor et al., 1982), the prototype approach to natural language classification has been applied to the study of situation perception. It is proposed and empirically demonstrated that, like persons and physical objects, situations are categorized into 'fuzzy sets', with the prototype of a category consisting of that set of situational features which is shared by the majority of situations within the category while being less typical for situations in other categories.

While few attempts have been made to apply these approaches to the study of person–situation interactions, a study by Krahé (1990) illustrates the feasibility of such strategies. In this study, measures of situation cognition were derived from different theoretical models of situation cognition and then related to behavioural responses to different anxiety-provoking situations. The findings suggest that when the theory-based measures of situation cognition are applied to a representative sample of situations from the individual's personal experience, then there are systematic links between situation perception and behaviour at the intra-individual level. A more detailed description of this work will be given in Chapter 8 in the context of other recent developments towards a more systematic analysis of the situation in personality research.

So far, this chapter has reviewed the basic postulates and key concepts of the modern interactionist perspective on personality. In the first section, it was shown that the interactionist approach entails a definition of personality that places special emphasis on an intra-individual level of analysis where individual behaviour is explained as a joint function of internal mediating variables and situational stimuli. As far as the exact meaning of the term 'interaction' is concerned, it became clear that the majority of interactionist personality researchers advocate the understanding of 'interactions' as dynamic, reciprocal effects of latent person variables, situations and behavioural responses. In practice, however, research has been dominated by studies examining the less complex notion of the statistical interaction of two independent variables, namely, the personality characteristics and situational influences. The second section examined how the interactionist tenet that the subjective meaning of situations is crucial to the understanding of individual behaviour has been reflected in theorizing and research. It can be concluded that some progress has been achieved in the systematic description of situations and their defining properties. Yet, the central question of how subjective interpretations of situations are formed on the basis of objective situational properties and how situational knowledge is cognitively represented still needs to be addressed.

Before turning to a review of interactionist research in different personality domains in the next chapter, it is necessary to look at the interactionist reconceptualization of another general aspect of personality: the process of *personality development and change* over the life-span. Rather than regarding personality development as the result of maturation or adaptation to environmental pressures, the interactionist view stresses an individual's ability to shape his or her environment and to be actively involved in the process of creating a match between personal well-being and environmental demands.

Personality development from an interactionist perspective

The majority of research generated by the modern interactionist approach is based on what Magnusson (1990a) terms the 'current' perspective on the study of personality and social behaviour. From this perspective, the emphasis is on explaining individual thoughts, feelings, and actions within the temporal and spatial boundaries of a given situation or set of situations, without reference to the person's past history or future orientations. The complementary developmental perspective, on the other hand, is concerned with understanding the stability and change in personality and behaviour in relation to different phases in individual development from infancy to old age. The range of developmental issues addressed from an interactionist point of view is reflected in a growing body of literature (see, for example, Lerner and Busch-Rossnagel, 1981; Magnusson, 1988; Magnusson and Allen, 1983a; West and Graziano, 1989a). The general idea underlying this approach is described by Magnusson and Allen:

> From a developmental point of view, the person–environment interaction is regarded as a continuously emerging and ever-changing process over time as symbolized not by a circle but by a helix or spiral. (1983b: 7)

While any conception of personality development must, by definition, allow for a substantial amount of change or temporal instability, one would be mistaken to interpret these changes as reflections of inconsistency so long as they follow a systematic, reconstructible pattern. As we saw at the beginning of this chapter,

new job or getting married, into his or her existing knowledge structure in order to be able to approach and master it in an adequate way. The complementary process of accommodation would involve adjusting and differentiating the person's cognitive and behavioural repertoires so as to meet the demands of the new job or the new role as spouse. Thus, the two processes both presuppose and determine one another. Development can be conceived of as the continuous interaction between elements of the environment requiring to be assimilated, and, possibly, changed by the person, and his or her ability to accommodate existing cognitive and behavioural patterns to the changing demands of the environment.

While in Piaget's work these principles are linked primarily to the process of intellectual development, Flavell (1963: 43) points out that they are characteristics of biological functioning in general. Thus, assimilation and accommodation can be utilized from an interactionist point of view as basic principles in explaining the process of personality development in terms of the dynamic interaction of the person and the environment (Block, 1982).

The longitudinal studies of Caspi (1989; Elder and Caspi, 1988) and Magnusson (1988) illustrate the scope of an interactionist approach in explaining the development and consequences of maladaptive behaviour patterns. Central to these lines of research is the idea that development is not only determined by a 'biological clock' but also by a 'social clock' of environmental demands and affordances presented to the individual at different age levels.

In an ongoing longitudinal project reported by Magnusson (1988), the development of a large sample of individuals has been traced from early adolescence to their late 20s. He presents a rich body of findings that cannot be discussed fully in the present context. In one part of the research particularly pertinent to the process of person–situation interaction, he examined the implications of girls' early versus late biological maturation for the development of maladapted behaviours, such as alcohol consumption and norm-breaking. He found that early maturing girls (that is, below-average age at menarche) showed a significantly higher incidence of different norm-violations (for example, playing truant, getting drunk, or shoplifting) than average or late maturing girls. However, the link between early maturation and norm-breaking was found to be mediated by a powerful social factor. Girls in this group were much more likely to have older peers as friends than girls in the other two groups, and they expected older peers to react less negatively to their norm-violations. Thus, norm-breaking behaviours are condoned by the social environment of early maturing girls to a greater extent than experienced by girls with a later onset of biological maturation. As far as the long-term consequences of this particular interaction of biological maturation and social influence is concerned, Magnusson's findings reveal both transient and stable effects. For alcohol consumption, a short-term, transient effect was obtained. Early maturing girls reported higher frequencies of being drunk up to the age of 15, a difference that gradually disappeared with age. The same was true for the persistence of norm-breaking behaviour into adulthood. Again, the difference between early, average and late maturing girls was no longer discernible at the age of 25. However, more stable effects of the interaction of biological maturation and peer relationships were found on a number of broader life style variables. Thus, early maturing girls were more likely to have started a family at the age of 26 and less likely to have entered higher education, especially in comparison with late maturing girls. Altogether, these long-term data indicate that early maturing girls both aspired to and achieved a more traditional family-oriented life style than their average and late maturing counterparts.

Drawing upon archival data from a long-term project started in 1928, Caspi and his colleagues were able to follow the life courses of individuals in different cohorts, living under different historical circumstances (Caspi and Bem, 1990). They were particularly interested in the developmental implications of three personality characteristics denoting specific interactional styles of the child with his or her social environment: ill-temperedness, shyness, and dependency. Childhood interactional styles are regarded as influencing subsequent development through two distinct but complementary processes. The first is termed *cumulative continuity* and refers to the notion that 'an individual's interactional style channels him or her into environments that themselves reinforce that style, thereby sustaining the behavior pattern across the life course through the progressive accumulation of their own consequences' (Caspi et al., 1989: 375). An ill-tempered adolescent, for example, might leave school without proper qualifications and thereby channel him- or herself into a frustrating low-status work life that further promotes an ill-tempered way of interacting with his or her environment. The second process whereby continuity is created in individual development is called *interactional continuity*. It is assumed to operate through the individual's evoking 'reciprocal, sustained responses from others in ongoing interaction, thereby reinstating the behavioral pattern across the individual's life whenever their relevant interactive situation is replicated.' (Caspi et al., 1989: 375). The link between childhood ill-temperedness and frequency of job changes in adulthood reported by Caspi and Bem (1990) constitutes indirect evidence for the operation of inter-actional continuity by suggesting that occupational instability is a result of the persistence of ill-tempered responses to frustrating situations.

Following the life course of ill-tempered, shy, and dependent children over a period of thirty years, Caspi et al. (1989) identified conclusive links between childhood interactional styles and adult life course patterns. Thus, it was found that ill-tempered boys developed into men characterized as undercontrolled, irritable and moody, who were significantly more likely to experience downward social mobility, low ranks in the military and divorce. Ill-tempered girls showed a comparable pattern in that they tended to marry men with lower occupational status and were described as ill-tempered mothers by both their children and husbands. As far as the developmental consequences of shyness are concerned, Caspi et al. (1988) showed that men with a childhood history of shyness were generally reluctant to enter new and unfamiliar situations in adult life and were typically delayed in their transitions to age-graded roles, such as marriage and fatherhood. Women who were shy as children were more likely to adopt traditional female roles as mothers and homemakers, yet they did not show a pattern of delayed role transitions comparable to that observed for shy men. The findings for childhood dependency revealed that this inter-actional style generally has positive implications for the develop-ment of boys and negative implications for girls. Dependent boys grew up to be men who were 'on time' in their role transitions, described as warm, calm, and sympathetic and who were more likely to have stable marriages compared with the rest of the sample. The adult life of dependent girls, in contrast, was typically characterized by low aspiration levels, lack of personal meaning in life, moodiness and self-pity. In conclusion, Caspi (1989: 93) states that 'life-course patterns are related, importantly and coherently, to interactional styles observed in late childhood. Invariant patterns do not emerge in the findings, but a predictable way of approaching and responding to the environment in different social settings is clearly indicated by the results' (see also Caspi and Moffitt, 1991).

This conclusion is clearly backed by Stokes et al.'s (1989; see also Mumford et al., 1990) research on life history prototypes. They proposed that individuals with similar biographical experiences at one point in time, who are grouped into the same 'prototype', should continue to show similar developmental patterns in the future due to their preference for and selection of comparable activities and environments. On the basis of a wide range of biographical information, different personality prototypes, containing similar patterns of activities and experiences, were identified for a large sample of adolescents. The same individuals were approached again six to eight years later, and prototypes were again formed on the basis of the young adults' responses to a life history questionnaire. The central question underlying this research was whether a person's membership in a particular life history subgroup in adolescence predisposes him or her to membership in a certain life history subgroup in young adulthood. Thus, the aim was to identify 'pathways' of development, that is, predictable directions in which young persons' experiences and behaviours developed over the period of six to eight years. Supporting the idea of continuity in life history prototypes, Stokes et al. (1989) report, for example, that male adolescents in the subgroups labelled 'competent independent aesthetes' and 'athletically oriented science majors' showed a strong pathway into the category of 'enterprising intellectuals'. A pathway was identified if the percentage of subjects in an adolescent subgroup who entered a particular adult subgroup was greater than expected under the assumption of an equal distribution of adolescent subgroups into adult subgroups. For the female participants, the strongest pathways emerged from the adolescent prototype of the 'cognitively complex achiever' to the adult prototype of the 'adapted conventionalist' and from the 'unconventional achiever' to the 'underemployed intellectual'. While the identification of continuous pathways of individual development clearly underline the temporal coherence of personality, it is equally interesting to look at those individuals who *did not* follow consistent paths. Apart from revealing a number of specific biographical differences between 'path followers' and 'non-followers', the findings reported by Stokes et al. (1989) permit the overall conclusion that non-followers are characterized by lower levels of general adaptation and self-esteem.

Another extensive research programme committed to an interactionist perspective on personality development has been developed by R.M. Lerner (1983; Lerner and Lerner, 1987). Building on the Piagetian principles of accommodation and assimilation, a 'goodness of fit model' is suggested to conceptualize the reciprocal influence of individual temperament factors and environmental factors on development. According to the model, adaptive personality development and change are a function of the extent to which an individual succeeds in meeting the differential demands of the various social settings in which he or she participates. Thus, problems of adjustment can result, for example, if the child's level of motor activity is not matched by the spaciousness of his or her home environment or if irregular sleep and eating patterns conflict with the demand for regularity imposed by the family routine. By implication, parental intervention and feedback designed to change a child's ill-matched behaviour patterns in a certain domain is regarded as instrumental to the development of a well-adjusted personality.

In a series of empirical studies, R.M. Lerner and his associates found support for the proposed relationship between person–environment match and level of adjustment. They used a multi-dimensional measure of temperament to represent the 'person' side of the interaction and related the different temperament dimensions (for example, activity level, distractability, and approach versus withdrawal tendencies) to corresponding situational demands. In one of these studies, J.V. Lerner (1983) studied the relationship between the temperament scores of eighth-grade students and the behavioural demands placed upon them by their teachers and peers in the classroom setting. In line with the predictions of the goodness of fit model, she found that those students whose temperament scores corresponded most closely to the environmental demands were rated more favourably by their teachers with regard to ability and adjustment. They also obtained better grades, had more positive relations with their peers and were generally characterized by higher levels of self-esteem than the less well-matched students.

Further support for the model was obtained in a number of similar studies summarized by Lerner and Lerner (1987). Altogether, the findings suggest that the better the match between individual characteristics and the demands of different environmental contexts, the more favourable the conditions are for personality development, subjective well-being and the maintenance of positive as well as lasting interpersonal relationships. However, in bringing about a 'good fit' the decisive part is clearly played by the person, not by the social environment, as R.M. Lerner's (1983: 282) use of the terms 'mismatched people' and 'adaptive person' reveals. Personality development is treated first and foremost as an accommodation task, consisting in children's learning of how best to alter their behavioural styles to meet the changing demands of different environments and how to select environments that match their characteristics (a process called 'niche picking') while avoiding non-corresponding contexts. The reverse process, namely the modification of environmental demands to assimilate them to the child's characteristic patterns of response is given less attention by the model. When the possibility of modifying context demands through specific intervention is acknowledged, it is clear that the impulse for any such change at the physical as well as social level will come from some kind of expert, that is, from a source other than the person himself or herself. In short, therefore, the context or environment is treated in the goodness of fit model as an entity functioning largely independent of the person's own activities (Lerner and Lerner, 1987: 385). The developing person's role in shaping his or her environment is mainly that of a stimulus eliciting specific responses from others, which then act back onto the person and shape his or her subsequent responses.

Wohlwill's (1983) analysis of the relationship between individual development and environment assigns a more active, instrumental role to the person in influencing the contexts of his or her development. He begins by noting that the traditional view of the child as an essentially reactive respondent to environmental stimulation has gradually begun to give way to a dynamic or reciprocal understanding. There, it is recognized that children also have a powerful influence on their environment through their own actions from a very early age. In order to capture the nature of this reciprocal influence process, Wohlwill introduces the concept of 'environmental modes'. Environmental modes refer to different interaction types or strategies whose effectiveness is determined jointly by the behaviour of the child and the features of the situation:

1 In the 'responsive-interactive' mode, the influence of environmental stimuli on the child depends at least partially on the child's previous behaviour, such as pushing a mobile or dropping an object to attract the mother's attention.
2 In the 'affordant' mode, the emphasis is on the potential inherent in an environmental stimulus for facilitating certain behavioural responses. Affordances may thus be defined as properties of the stimulus which, while influencing the person's behaviour, are not influenced by it (Gibson, 1979). For instance, roller skates would 'afford' the child's pleasure at moving at high speed or the father's arm would afford the baby's resting on it.
3 In the 'ambient' mode, environmental stimuli impinge on the child in a more remote fashion without having a direct link to his or her behaviour. In this mode, a further distinction is made between 'focal' and 'background' stimuli. The child's watching a television programme would be an instance of the focal ambient mode whereas the diffuse sounds and voices coming from a nearby playground would represent the background ambient mode.

It should be noted that this categorization of person–environment interactions supersedes and, at the same time, integrates the distinction between the social and the physical environment. But how is this classification related to the process of individual development? Wohlwill suggests that three major principles are involved in developmental change which affect the various environmental modes in a differential way:

1   There is the growing capacity of the child to exert control over his or her environment by exploring it through spontaneous activity and selecting certain sections at the expense of others. In the course of this process, the 'focal ambient' mode becomes more and more important as compared to the background mode, since focal stimuli are more powerful in determining the child's environmental choices.

2   The child becomes increasingly able to pay selective attention to certain aspects or stimuli in the environment. This developmental process is closely linked to the preceding one in that it enables the child to differentiate the global perceptual field into more fine-grained units. This, in turn, involves the capacity to distinguish between functionally relevant and irrelevant stimuli with respect to achieving a particular aim, such as identifying a milk bottle among a range of objects placed on a table.

3   Another principle prominently involved in the process of development refers to the increasing role of language and non-verbal symbols in the child's exchanges with the environment. Obviously, the major impact of this developmental principle is on the 'responsive-interactive' environmental mode. The more elaborate the child's command of verbal as well as non-verbal forms of communication, the more specific and powerful their influence will be on the social environment. The result is that the behaviour of others towards the child becomes more and more contingent upon the child's own activity.

Wohlwill himself acknowledges that evidence in support of this reasoning is still due to be gathered systematically. Yet, he presents a promising framework for conceptualizing development in terms of the interaction between the increasing complexity as well as flexibility of the child's perceptual, cognitive, and motoric abilities and the forces in his or her social and physical environment. In particular, he emphasizes the fact that environmental stimuli – including the behaviour of social interaction partners such as parents and peers – are themselves shaped and modified by the child's activities. In so doing, he sketches a possible perspective for implementing the dynamic version of modern interactionism.

Due to the multiplicity and diversity of both environmental challenges and the person's internal states (emotions, cognitions, etc.), the match of person and environment must inevitably be seen as a fragile equilibrium in constant danger of being overthrown by new situational demands and/or internal states. Accordingly, the question arises whether it is possible to promote and stabilize the goodness of fit between person and environment through psychological intervention in those instances where the person is overtaxed by the requirements of the environment. Sarason and Sarason (1983) offer an affirmative answer to this question in what may be described as their 'coping approach' to person–environment interaction. They use the term of 'coping' to denote the individual's ability to respond effectively to the environment so that the smoothness and progress of personality development may be regarded as a function of the individual's coping competencies. These can be broken down into more specific components:

1 The ability to perceive and assess the environment accurately.
2 The acquisition of the necessary skills to deal with the environmental challenges.
3 The confidence to use these skills.

To the extent that an individual has acquired each of these interlocking competencies up to the level required in a particular stage of development, he or she will be able to respond to environmental demands in a successful way. However, when coping competencies are inadequate, the individual's potential for development is curtailed. It is here that intervention aimed to promote coping skills has to step in. Developmental problems are particularly likely to occur at those points in life which involve the transition from a familiar social setting to a new one and/or confront the person with certain critical tasks or events. These will often go hand in hand with an increased awareness on the part of the person of the need to change his or her behaviour so as to match the requirements of the new situation. Thus, intervention would appear to be most usefully timed to coincide with transition points in the individual's life which typically pose a particular challenge to the person's coping skills.

Sarason and Sarason (1983) describe two intervention studies aimed at improving cognitive coping skills, in particular the accuracy with which the person perceives the central features of the environment. As an operational definition of inaccuracy, they regard those perceptions as inaccurate which deviate from the consensual interpretation held by the relevant reference group. Deviation of the individual's perception of the situation from the predominant view of the reference group constitutes a major source of misunderstanding and maladjusted behaviour. Depending on the origin of inaccurate situation perceptions, intervention is directed at different objectives. If inaccuracy results from a lack of knowledge about what features of the environment are critical for framing an appropriate response, then the aim of intervention is to supply this knowledge. This is done, for example, by helping the person to identify correctly the rules and behavioural expectations pertinent to the situation. On the other hand, inaccuracy can be the result of the person's lack of attention to the relevant features due to some internal distraction or preoccupation. In this case, intervention would be aimed at training the individual to shift attention from ineffective cognitions in such a way as to enable him or her to use existing skills in an adaptive way.

In the first empirical example, this reasoning was applied to the task of improving the problem-solving skills of low achieving high school students. Participants in the intervention programme were exposed to a series of either live or televised modellings of group discussions in which optimal strategies for planning and decision making were illustrated. Compared with a control group, students in the two intervention conditions subsequently showed more adaptive problem-solving patterns (as measured by a test where they were given a problem situation as well as its solution and had to supply the intermediate steps required to reach the solution). Furthermore, subjects in the two treatment conditions were able to come up with a significantly higher number of alternative solutions to a given problem situation than the control subjects.

In another study, marine recruits during their first days of training were shown a film specifically geared towards highlighting the coping skills required by life in the naval forces (such as controlling the expression of emotions and maintaining a sense of self-efficacy). The film helped to promote these skills in the participants and even had more long-term positive effects on drop-out or attrition rates. Thus, it may be concluded that psychological intervention specifically directed at creating congruence between environmental demands and the personal skills required to master them is a viable strategy for facilitating personality development. This is true especially at those points where new and more challenging demands are placed on the individual.

The research discussed in this section illustrates that the study of personality development and change is by no means incompatible with the search for stability and consistency. Evidence that individual behaviour shows some degree of regularity attributable to characteristic features of the person is an essential requirement for any conceptualization of personality. At the same time, systematic changes in that regularity caused by the person's responsiveness to environmental challenges and affordances at different stages of development have an equally important place in the theoretical understanding of personality.

Summary

The idea that individual behaviour is determined by the joint, interactive influence of personal characteristics and situational features sounds very much like a platitude in the ears of most personality psychologists today. However, as demonstrated at the beginning of this chapter, this has not always been the case. About fifteen years ago, conceptions of personality in terms of person–situation interactions had to be reactivated after earlier theorizing along these lines had lain dormant throughout most of the consistency controversy. In order to implement a view of personality that embraces the impact of situational influences, modern interactionism has been faced with two major tasks:

1 To state explicitly how the proposed interaction between person and situation should be defined both conceptually and operationally.
2 To incorporate the study of situations into the envisaged new paradigm for the study of personality.

The first section of this chapter discussed the different meanings with which the term 'interaction' is used in the interactionist approach, each being linked to a particular measurement model. It was shown that most empirical studies carried out so far have been based on a mechanistic or statistical understanding of interactions. This approach is aimed at quantifying the effect of the interaction between personal and situational variables on behaviour relative to the effects of person and situation factors taken individually. At the level of measurement devices, S–R inventories were described as a form of data collection particularly pertinent to the assessment of statistical interactions. At the level of data analysis, analysis of variance designs have been most prominent in identifying the strength of person and situation effects as well as their interactions. Despite the predominance of research directed at the study of statistical interactions, another meaning of interaction is clearly more central to the theoretical framework of modern interactionism. This meaning refers to dynamic, reciprocal interactions or 'transactions' between person and environment which render the traditional distinction between dependent and independent variables obsolete. From the paucity of empirical research, two examples were quoted to illustrate feasible ways of showing how characteristics of the person and those of the situation mutually affect each other in shaping a person's behaviour and how the behaviour itself then acts back on both latent person variables and the situational context.

The second section examined the extent to which a systematic analysis of the 'psychological situation', that is, the subjective meaning of situational influences, has been offered by modern interactionism. Here, it became clear that the programmatic emphasis on the psychological meaning of situations has been slow to be translated into corresponding empirical endeavours. Research efforts have concentrated on the task of developing systematic classifications of situations and their central descriptive dimensions, while a systematic analysis of the process by which objective situational properties are translated into subjective meaning is yet to be undertaken. Another unresolved but fundamental problem concerns the units of analysis on which the study of situations should be based. In particular, there is a need for a clearer understanding of the criteria whereby the beginning and the end of a situation are defined, either by the investigator or by the respondent.

Finally, before turning to a review of interactionist research in specific personality domains in the next chapter, the central issue was addressed of how personality development and change are conceptualized from an interactionist point of view. Here, some promising approaches were identified. They were based on the general idea that personality development is a function of the match between a person's cognitive and behavioural repertoire at a given developmental stage and the extent to which the different sections of the person's environment provide opportunities as well as challenges for applying this repertoire. In line with a reciprocal view of the interaction process, it has been stressed that from a very early age children have an active role as 'stimuli' for producing changes in their environment instead of being only passive recipients of environmental stimulation. As a further aspect of the interactionist view of personality development, evidence was reviewed showing that the match between the person's coping skills and environmental demands can be improved through systematic psychological intervention.

Note

1   It should be pointed out that in this and the next figure (Figure 4.2) 'P' stands for (latent) personal characteristics which have the status of hypothetical constructs in the interactionist model. In any other sense, the separation of P, S, and B would not be meaningful, since it is, of course, the Person who shows the Behaviour on the basis of an internal representation of the Situation (see Hyland, 1984; Krauskopf, 1978).

5

Implementing the Interactionist Programme: Three Exemplary Areas of Research

The commitment to an interactionist view of personality and social behaviour has far-reaching implications for theorizing and research in virtually every domain to which personality theorists have traditionally contributed. It also offers a new outlook on all those areas of *social psychology* where the reliance on situationist explanations derived from experimental evidence has turned out to be insufficient for a proper understanding of individual behaviour.

A good example to illustrate this point is the domain of group leadership. The central problem confronting researchers in this area has been to identify the determinants of effective leadership. From a traditional trait-oriented perspective, the answer that offered itself was to look for certain qualities characterizing a successful leader. Although a large amount of evidence was generated in this vein up to the 1940s, no reliable pattern of leader traits emerged. The only exceptions are some weak generalizations suggesting that, on average, group leaders tend to score somewhat higher than ordinary group members on measures of ability, such as intelligence and verbal fluency, as well as measures of motivation, such as persistence and initiative (see Shaw, 1976). From a traditional social psychological perspective, on the other hand, the strategy of choice was to try and isolate certain features of the situation to account for differences in leadership effectiveness. Among the features thought to be influential were the nature and difficulty of the task at hand, the complexity of the network through which the group could communicate as well as the position of the leader within that network. While it turned out that some of these factors were related to leadership effectiveness in some situations, again no pervasive picture emerged which would hold across different types of groups as well as tasks.

Looking at the issue of leadership effectiveness from an interactionist point of view, the central question is phrased in a different way: what features of the situation *in combination with* what characteristics of the leader produce the most effective group results? A prominent approach designed to address precisely this question is Fiedler's contingency model of leadership (see, for example, Fiedler, 1977; Fiedler et al., 1976). The contingency model suggests that the effectiveness of a leader in cooperating with a group to solve a given task is dependent on two main factors:

1   The personal style of the leader as being either concerned mainly about the successful accomplishment of the task (task-motivated leader) or about maintaining close personal relations among the group (relationship-motivated leader).

2   The favourableness of the situation as determining the degree of control and influence the leader has over the course of the problem-solving process. Situational favourableness is seen as a function of three factors: good leader–member relations, clear structure of the task, and high position power in the sense of the leader's institutionalized power to distribute rewards and punishments to the members of the group.

According to this model, effective group leadership results from the interaction between leadership style and situational favourableness. This means that the impact of leadership style on leadership effectiveness is contingent upon certain specified situational conditions and vice versa.

In a similar way, interactionist reformulations of a number of essential problems have been offered and empirically examined since the mid-1970s. Aggression and hostility (for example, Olweus, 1980; Pervin, 1984c), leisure behaviour (Bishop and Witt, 1970), Machiavellianism (Vleeming, 1981), person perception (Zuroff, 1982) self-disclosure (Miller et al., 1983), jealousy (Bringle et al., 1983), and emotional adaptation to life changes (Stewart, 1982) are but a few examples. Some recent contributions have highlighted the relevance of the interactionist perspective for organizational psychology (Chatman, 1989; Spokane, 1987). A comprehensive coverage of the early years of modern interactionism can be found in Endler and Magnusson (1976a), Magnusson and Endler (1977a) and Pervin and Lewis (1978).

The present chapter will take a closer look at three lines of empirical research which have originated from an explicit commitment to the modern interactionist model of personality. Of necessity, this review will be selective, guided by the aim of clarifying the principal objectives as well as problems in substantiating the interactionist view of personality in each of the three domains. To begin with, research exploring the interactive effect of person and situation variables in the domain of *anxiety* will be discussed. The major part of this work has been carried out by Magnusson, Endler, and their co-workers, and it represents by far the most extensive effort of putting the interactionist model into practice. Therefore, the domain of anxiety-provoking situations can almost be regarded as the paradigmatic field of application for modern interactionism. In the second section, recent work on the role and functioning of *emotions* in relation to situations and responses will be presented. Located at the level of latent person variables, this research lends itself most readily to demonstrating the intimate link between internal and external determinants of behaviour. Finally, the field of *prosocial behaviour* is selected to demonstrate that modern interactionism can shed new light not only on issues traditionally belonging to the realm of personality psychology. It also offers a new perspective on specific kinds of interpersonal behaviour whose explanation and prediction has been a challenge to social psychologists for quite some time.

Anxiety: a multidimensional approach

Like previous cognitive theories of anxiety, especially Spielberger's two-factor theory (1966, 1972), the interaction model of anxiety is based on the distinction between trait anxiety (A-trait) and state anxiety (A-state). State anxiety is defined as a transient emotional condition which is accompanied by physiological arousal. Its actualization is a function of the cognitive evaluation of external stimulus conditions which, in turn, depends on the individual's enduring disposition towards anxiety. The relationship between A-trait and A-state is conceptualized in probabilistic terms:

> The stronger a particular personality trait, the more probable it is that an individual will experience the emotional state that corresponds to this trait, and the greater the probability that behaviors associated with the trait will be manifested in a variety of situations. (Spielberger, 1972: 31)

In order to examine the correspondence between trait and state anxiety, Spielberger et al. (1970) developed the 'State-Trait-Anxiety Inventory' (STAI). The STAI consists of two partly overlapping sets of reaction scales comprising both physiological symptoms (such as feeling jittery) and affective responses (such as feeling upset) to anxiety-provoking situations. In completing the STAI, subjects are requested to indicate, on the first set of scales, the extent to which they experience each response at that particular moment in time (state measure). On the second set, they indicate the extent to which each of the responses is typically characteristic for them in reacting to anxiety-provoking situations in general (trait measure).

The Spielberger model acknowledges that cognitive processes

mediate between anxiety-provoking stimuli and individual responses. Nevertheless, it is clear from both the theoretical formulation of the relationship between trait and state anxiety and the format of the STAI that this approach remains committed to the traditional trait model. The emphasis is on explaining individual differences in responding to anxiety-provoking stimuli as a function of individual differences in the strength of an underlying disposition, namely A-trait. This view implies that trait anxiety is treated as a unidimensional construct and no allowance is made for the differential effect of particular types of anxiety-provoking situations on the link between A-trait and A-state.

It was precisely this assumption of a unidimensional A-trait which prompted the interactionist critique of Spielberger's model and the subsequent development of a multidimensional interaction model of anxiety (Endler, 1975, 1980). The empirical basis for criticizing the state–trait theory was furnished by a number of studies showing that individual differences in A-trait predicted corresponding differences in A-state only for certain types of anxiety-provoking situations. Primarily, these were situations involving threats to self-esteem and interpersonal threats. For other types of situations, in particular those involving physical danger, A-trait levels failed to predict the intensity of A-state reactions.

What this evidence suggested, then, was to think of A-trait not as a global disposition but as a multidimensional concept, with different dimensions of A-trait pertaining to different types or classes of stressful situations. In the interaction model of anxiety, five dimensions or facets of trait anxiety are distinguished which have emerged from factor analyses of different samples of anxiety-provoking situations in a series of studies (see Endler, 1975, 1983). The five facets are labelled

- *Interpersonal* A-trait, referring to situations which involve interactions with other people that are perceived as anxiety-provoking.
- *Physical danger* A-trait, activated by situations in which the person faces the probability of physical injury.
- *Ambiguous* A-trait, referring to threats posed by situations in which the person does not know what is going to happen to him or her.
- *Social evaluation* A-trait, pertaining to situations which involve threats to the person's self-esteem as a result of being evaluated by other people.
- *Daily routines* A-trait referring to anxiety-provoking circumstances encountered in everyday and routine situations. The

exact meaning of this facet, however, remains somewhat obscure, since no clear definition is given of the anxiety-provoking nature of these situations.

Introducing different facets of A-trait referring to different classes of anxiety-provoking situations allows one to predict specific interactions between A-trait and the situation in producing individual differences. In general terms, the model holds that individual differences with respect to one facet of A-trait are predictive of corresponding differences in A-state *only in those situations* which are congruent with the respective A-trait facet. For example, persons differing in 'social evaluation' A-trait are expected to respond with different levels of A-state to situations involving evaluation by others but not necessarily respond differently to situations involving physical danger or ambiguity. In the same way, intra-individual changes in A-state may be predicted. Increases in A-state as a result of changing from a non-stressful situation to a stressful one are no longer assumed to be a function of the person's overall level of trait anxiety. Instead, predictions are based on the person's standing on that facet of A-trait which is congruent with the type of anxiety-provoking stimuli involved in the respective situation.

As far as the dimensionality of *A-state* is concerned, a study by Endler et al. (1976) suggests that state anxiety should not be understood as a unidimensional construct either. According to their findings, it can be differentiated into at least two dimensions interpreted as 'psychic' and 'physiological' state anxiety. This distinction is reflected in more recent measures of A-state, such as the 'Present Affect Reactions Questionnaire' (PARQ) (Endler, 1980) and the Endler Multidimensional Anxiety Scales (EMAS) (Endler et al., 1991). The PARQ consists of ten 'autonomic arousal' items (for example, perspire, hands feel unsteady) and ten 'cognitive worry' items (for example, feel self-conscious, unable to concentrate). However, no specific hypotheses have as yet been formulated about the interaction between the two dimensions of A-state and particular types of anxiety-provoking situations.

In a large number of empirical studies, support was obtained for the interactionist model of anxiety and its major hypotheses that, instead of being characterized by a general trait of anxiety, individuals may show high levels on certain facets of A-trait while scoring low on other facets; and only those facets of A-trait which are congruent with the specific threats inherent in particular situations are predictive of A-state responses in those situations. A summary of this research is provided by Endler (1983: 184f.). Rather than attempting a comprehensive review, this section will concentrate on a select sample of studies pertaining to the five facets of A-trait and their differential effect on A-state responses in different types of situations.

There are only a few investigations that allow an immediate comparison between unidimensional and multidimensional conceptualizations of A-trait. Among these, a study by Kendall (1978), addressing physical danger and social evaluation situations, offers conclusive support for the proposed multidimensional nature of dispositional anxiousness. Participants were sampled on the basis of their scores on three measures of A-trait administered some time prior to the actual study: the A-trait scale of Spielberger's STAI as a global measure of A-trait, and the 'physical danger' and 'social evaluation' subscales of the revised S–R GTA (see Endler (1980: 262) and Table 4.1, above). Subjects were included in the sample if they scored either high (upper 40 per cent) or low (lower 40 per cent) on the trait measures. In order to allow for a conclusive decision between the two models, an additional requirement was introduced: subjects scoring high (or low) on 'physical danger' A-trait should not score high (or low) on the STAI and 'social evaluation' A-trait measures and vice versa.

In the actual experiment, subjects were exposed to two types of anxiety-provoking situations: in the 'physical danger' situation, they were shown a film depicting vivid scenes of car crash tests; in the 'social evaluation' situation, they were asked to complete a word decoding task which was construed in such a way that it could not be completed within the available time. A-state was measured three times: first after the subjects had arrived for the experiment to obtain a base rate level of A-state and then again immediately after the film and after the word coding task. The increase in A-state from the base rate scores to the two post-treatment levels constituted the dependent variable in this study. Two competing hypotheses about the relationship between A-trait and A-state as well as the proposed increase in A-state following the experimental treatments derive from the unidimensional and multidimensional models of anxiety, respectively:

1 According to the *unidimensional* model, subjects scoring high on general A-trait as measured by the STAI should show higher increases in A-state than low scoring subjects in both the physical danger and the social evaluation situation.

2 According to the *multidimensional* model, dimensional A-trait and type of situation are expected to show an interactive effect on the increase in A-state. Subjects scoring high on the physical

danger A-trait measure should show higher increases than low scoring subjects only after being exposed to the physical danger situation. Subjects scoring high on social evaluation A-trait are expected to respond with higher increases in A-state than their low anxiety counterparts only after failing in the social evaluation situation.

Kendall's findings strongly support the second set of hypotheses derived from the interactionist model. Following the crash film, subjects with high A-trait levels on the physical danger facet showed a significantly higher rise in A-state levels than low scorers while no difference emerged between the two groups in response to the social evaluation situation. Similarly, after failing to complete the word coding task subjects with high scores on social evaluation A-trait showed a significantly higher A-state increase than subjects scoring low on this anxiety facet, while no such pattern was found following the crash film.

Thus, the results of Kendall's study along with findings from similar investigations (for example, Donat, 1983) speak in favour of the multidimensional conceptualization of A-trait compared with the assumption of a general anxiety trait. They underline the need to predict an individual's acute anxiety responses with respect to specific types or classes of anxiety-provoking situations.

The validity of the interaction model of anxiety was further supported in a field study by Flood and Endler (1980). There, the relationship between the interpersonal and social evaluation facets of A-trait and A-state levels was explored in an athletic competition situation. Participants in a running contest were asked to complete a measure of A-state, the Behavioural Reactions Questionnaire (BRQ) (Hoy and Endler, 1969), shortly before the start of the competition. Immediately after the race, subjects completed another measure tapping their subjective interpretation of the situation. This 'Perception of Competitive Events Questionnaire', reflected the interactionist tenet that the meaning of a situation is a crucial factor in explaining individual behaviour. Subjects were asked to indicate the extent to which they perceived the contest as being an 'interpersonal situation', a 'physical danger situation', 'an ambiguous situation' and a 'social evaluation situation'. Base rates of A-state in a non-competitive situation as well as measures of A-trait using the S–R GTA had been collected as part of a training session two weeks prior to the race. On the basis of these data, the following hypotheses were tested:

1   Participants with high levels of interpersonal A-trait and social evaluation A-trait will show a higher increase in state anxiety

from the neutral situation to the contest situation than those who score lower on the two A-trait facets.

2 No corresponding interaction between A-trait and situation will emerge with respect to the remaining facets of A-trait, namely physical danger, ambiguous, and daily routines.

The analysis of the situation perception questionnaire confirms, first of all, that the situation was perceived predominantly as a 'social evaluation situation'. The category of 'interpersonal situations' received the second highest ratings and was not significantly different from the social evaluation category. However, the two differed significantly from the remaining situation categories. An interaction of dimensional A-trait and situation could be demonstrated only for social evaluation A-trait but not for the interpersonal facet of A-trait. Thus, the hypotheses were only confirmed for one of the two A-trait facets thought to be involved in the athletic contest situation – that facet, however, which corresponded most closely to the subjective interpretation of the situations by the participants.

A similar study by Phillips and Endler (1982), carried out in a real-life exam situation, also demonstrates the proposed interaction between the situation and the congruent dimension of A-trait for the social evaluation facet but not for the interpersonal facet. In this study, the subjective interpretation of the situation was incorporated as a separate factor in the analysis. When subjects were classified on the basis of whether or not they perceived the exam situation primarily as a social evaluation situation, significant differences between A-state levels in the stress and non-stress situations emerged only for one group of subjects: those who scored high on social evaluation A-trait and, at the same time, interpreted the exam primarily as a social evaluation situation. Additional analyses revealed that the extent to which the situation was perceived as being a social evaluation, interpersonal, ambiguous or physical danger type of situation, respectively, was not significantly related to the level of A-trait on the corresponding facets. This suggests that the subjective interpretation of anxiety-provoking situations is an additional, independent factor determining an individual's anxiety responses.

Yet, what exactly is the impact of situation perception on the level of A-state experienced in a given situation and on the link between A-trait facets and A-state? At present, research within the framework of the interaction model of anxiety fails to provide a conclusive answer to this question. This point is illustrated in two studies reported by Endler et al. (1983). They studied subjects' responses in an academic examination and in a demanding occupational situation, both representing situations congruent with the social evaluation facet of A-trait. In line with their predictions, changes in A-state levels from a non-stress situation to either of the two stress situations were significantly higher for subjects scoring high as opposed to low on the social evaluation facet of A-trait. High versus low scorers on the remaining facets of A-trait showed no corresponding differences in their patterns of A-state change. Even though these findings confirmed the authors' hypotheses, disturbing evidence came to light when the subjects' interpretations of the two situations were analysed. These data revealed that, in general, the participants had not considered the situations as being significantly more of a social evaluative than an interpersonal, ambiguous, physical danger or daily routine nature, thus failing to share the authors' a priori classification.

Equally problematic patterns of results were found with regard to the 'ambiguous' A-trait facet by Ackerman and Endler (1985) and also by King and Endler (1982) who studied patients undergoing medical treatment. In each of these studies, the interaction model was confirmed *in spite of the fact* that the stipulated correspondence between perceived situational threat and the activation of a particular facet of A-trait failed to emerge. As a post hoc explanation, King and Endler speculate that A-trait dimensions may differ with regard to the strength of situational features or prompts they require to be activated. They argue that few situational cues or low levels of situational threat may be sufficient to arouse the social evaluation or physical danger facets of A-trait, while comparatively stronger cues indicating ambiguity or interpersonal threat may be required before the corresponding A-trait facets are activated. However, this explanation is not altogether convincing, as one would assume the proposed differences in the anxiety thresholds of different types of situations to affect the activation of A-trait and the subjective interpretation of the situation in the same way. If a situation is not perceived as being particularly ambiguous by the person, then why – and, more importantly, how – should the ambiguous facet of A-trait be activated at all?

It seems, therefore, that more complex theoretical assumptions as well as empirical measures are required to explain the impact of situation perception on the state–trait relationship (King and Endler, 1989). An illustrative example of how this task can be approached was offered by Dobson (1983). He examined the relationship between A-trait and A-state for the two facets of physical danger and interpersonal threat. In his analysis, he drew on the cognitive theory of emotion by Lazarus and Launier (1978) where two types of cognitive appraisal are distinguished as influencing an individual's response to stressful situations. The first type or 'primary appraisal' refers to the person's subjective evaluation of the situational cues in terms of whether they have any negative significance for his or her well-being. As an operational definition, the perceived difficulty of different situations involving physical danger and interpersonal threat was measured in Dobson's study. The second type, 'secondary appraisal', refers to the perceived ability of the individual to cope with the situation, that is, to handle the difficulties inherent in that situation.

Both types of cognitive appraisals are regarded by Dobson as mediating between the situation-congruent facets of A-trait and the amount of anxiety experienced in the situation in a two-step process: 'In the context of a given situation, the situationally specific traits of the person would predispose certain appraisals of the situation. The situational appraisals would, in turn, predict a rating of stress in that situation' (Dobson, 1983: 165). After completing the S–R GTA as a measure of A-trait, participants in his study were instructed to imagine themselves being in four different anxiety-provoking situations, two involving physical danger and two involving interpersonal threat. They were then asked to rate the perceived difficulty of each situation, the ease of coping with the situation and the extent to which they would find the situation stressful. Results from this study support the proposed influence of cognitive appraisals as mediators between situation-specific A-trait and A-state. It was found that the only significant predictors of both situation difficulty and ease of coping were the respective situation-congruent facets of A-trait. When A-state was considered as the dependent variable, situation difficulty turned out to be a highly significant predictor of the stress ratings for each of the four situations, while ease of coping failed to produce any significant effects. Unexpectedly, physical danger A-trait was found also to have a direct, unmediated effect on A-state levels in the two congruent situations.

The studies discussed in this section support the conclusion that increases in the level of A-state as a function of encountering anxiety-provoking situations are predicted more accurately on the basis of situation-specific measures of A-trait than on the basis of a global, unidimensional measure of dispositional anxiousness. In addition to the clear-cut effects obtained for physical danger situations, the social evaluation dimensions appears to be a particularly powerful component of A-trait. Support for the interpersonal and ambiguous facets of A-trait has been far less conclusive, suggesting that the present version of the interaction model of anxiety may have to be revised in the light of these recent findings (see also Mothersill et al., 1986).

Taken together, the present examples originating from an inter-actionist approach to the study of anxiety have demonstrated how the theoretical assumptions concerning the interaction of personal and situational determinants of behaviour may be translated into empirical research strategies. They illustrate how specific hypotheses are derived from the general postulate of person–situation interactions and present a methodological approach which facilitates the measurement of personality variables contingent upon particular types of situational characteristics. Additional credit derives from the fact that the majority of studies have been carried out in natural settings where individual responses to anxiety-provoking situations could be measured in an ecologically valid way.

There are, however, problems with this research that limit its contribution to an interactionist reformulation of personality. One such problem refers to the reliance of the interaction model on the distinction between anxiety traits and states. A second problem concerns the prominence of an individual difference approach in studying the interactive effect of A-trait and situation perception on behaviour.

As a general feature of the state–trait distinction, the temporal stability of traits as opposed to the short-term and variable nature of states is of central importance. For the state–trait distinction to be validated, therefore, evidence is required that while state measures vary substantially from non-stressful situations to stressful situations, corresponding trait measures remain stable across situations (see Allen and Potkay, 1981, 1983). However, the design of most empirical studies testing the interaction model of anxiety fails to provide this evidence. Generally, base rates of A-state are obtained in non-stressful situations and then compared with A-state levels in stressful situations. A-trait, on the other hand, is only measured once in the non-stressful situation. Thus, no information is available on whether A-trait levels do, in fact, remain stable across situations which differ in terms of their anxiety-provoking nature. Without such information, it is hard to challenge critical voices denouncing the 'arbitrary' nature of the state–trait distinction (Allen and Potkay, 1981).

A second problem results from the close association between the interaction model of anxiety and the trait concept which highlights its limitations with respect to the issue of cross-situational consistency: the strategy of investigating individual differences in A-state as a function of corresponding differences in dimensional A-trait continues to be committed to the concept of 'relative consistency', a basis which has been rejected as inadequate by the advocates of modern interactionism for a long time. In its current form, the model has little to offer towards the analysis of *intra-individual* patterns of regularity and change across different categories of anxiety-provoking situations. However, it is precisely this type of analysis that is needed to establish the concept of coherence as an alternative way of approaching the consistency problem.

Emotions and person–situation congruence

As the research discussed in the previous section has shown, it would be simplistic to assume that a person's latent characteristics find a direct expression in overt behaviour if only those characteristics are defined as well as measured with reference to a corresponding class of situations. Rather, it became obvious that the relationship between personality and behaviour is a more complex one, influenced in various ways by different mediating variables, such as the cognitive appraisal of the situation. Among the variables that affect the link between latent characteristics and overt responses, the person's momentary emotional states are of primary significance. Emotions, more than most other psychological states, can be viewed as the immediate result of the reciprocal interaction between internal dispositions (including attributional styles, attitudes, abilities, etc.), behaviour and the situational context. Accordingly, the study of emotions from an interactionist point of view has begun to develop into a line of research in its own right. A cross-section of this research will be discussed in this part of the chapter, focusing on representative efforts to clarify the significance of emotional states for the study of personality and social behaviour (see also Pervin, 1984c: ch. 5).

The general issue concerning the role of emotions in the process of person–situation interactions can be subdivided into two more specific questions:

1   What is the relationship between personal dispositions and emotions?
2   How are emotions related to overt behaviour?

Research directed at the first question starts from the idea that personality traits and emotions are related to one another in such a way that traits may be defined in terms of an individual's disposition to react to situations with certain emotional responses (Plutchik, 1980). While theoretical work on the interdependence of personality dimensions, situations, and emotions is still in its beginnings, one approach is gaining prominence which looks at the congruence or goodness of fit between individual characteristics and environmental features on emotional states (see, for example, Diener et al., 1984; Kulka, 1979; Snyder and Ickes, 1985: 922ff.). As in the developmental work discussed in the previous section, the congruence model assumes that the mismatch between personal qualities, needs and expectations on the one hand and the opportunities, demands and constraints presented by the environment on the other leads to psychological strain and poor adjustment. Kulka (1979: 58) quotes evidence that depression among workers was lowest when the amount of job complexity preferred by the individual was matched by the level of complexity involved in his or her current job. However, depression increased if job complexity was either lower or higher than the preferred level.

The psychological implications of the congruence versus incongruence of personality and situations were addressed in a series of studies by Diener and his colleagues. Emmons and Diener (1986a) conducted an in-depth study of the effects of person–situation congruence versus incongruence on emotional states in everyday life situations. As a first step, they asked their nineteen subjects to generate a list of twenty situations from their current lives and classify each situation into one of four categories: 'social', 'alone', 'work' and 'recreation'. Over a period of one month, subjects then completed daily ratings of the extent to which they experienced different emotions (happy, depressed, angry) in up to five situations from their initial list that they had encountered in the course of the day. In addition, they indicated for each situation whether they had chosen to be in that situation or whether it had been imposed on them. Finally, all subjects completed two standard personality inventories tapping a variety of personality dimensions, such as extroversion, aggression, and need for achievement.

Based on this information, the following questions were examined:

1 Is there a systematic relationship between personality dimensions and the intensity as well as frequency with which certain emotions are experienced in various real-life situations?
2 Do individuals experience more positive affect in situations that are congruent with their personalities, especially when the situations are chosen rather than imposed?

To answer these questions, average levels of the different emotions as well as correlations between intensity of emotions and personality scores were established separately for chosen and imposed situations in each of the four categories of social, alone, work, and recreation situations. As far as the proposed consistency between personality dimensions and emotions is concerned, the obtained data by and large confirm the assumption that in their everyday lives people typically experience emotions which are in accord with their personalities. So, for instance, highly significant correlations were found between personality measures of aggression and need for order and the extent to which emotions such as 'angry' and 'hostile' as well as 'peaceful' and 'docile' were experienced in the course of the month-long recording period. Looking at the correspondence between personality scores and emotional intensity in the four situation categories separately, further support for the congruence model was obtained, especially in the work and recreation situations. Here, need for achievement was found to be positively correlated with feeling productive in work situations, while feelings of productivity were negatively correlated with need for achievement in recreation situations. An unexpected finding emerged with respect to the link between extroversion and joyful emotions which turned out to be significantly positive in both (congruent) social and (non-congruent) alone situations. However, in accordance with the congruence model correlations were higher in the social than in the alone situations.

When the voluntary nature of the situations was considered as an additional factor, it became apparent that the fit between personality measures and corresponding emotions in situations congruent with those personality dimensions was generally better for chosen than for imposed situations. Feeling joyful, for example, was found to correlate substantially higher with extroversion in social situations chosen by the individual than in social situations that were imposed on him or her.

In summary, therefore, the findings of Emmons and Diener (1986a) underline the significance of emotional responses as referents for certain personality dimensions as well as their dependence on the fit between personality and situation. Furthermore, the fact that the match between stable personality traits and more short-term, transient emotional states is generally better in chosen than in imposed situations highlights the role of the person as an active and intentional agent in the interaction process.

The second crucial issue involved in studying the role of emotions in the process of person–situation interaction refers to the relationship between emotions and behaviour. This aspect is addressed as part of Staats's (1980) 'behavioural interaction approach'. In this approach, it is suggested that social behaviour results from the interaction of situational features with the 'personality repertoires' acquired by the individual in the course of socialization. One of these repertoires or 'systems' is the 'emotional–motivational personality system', containing the individual's knowledge of how and when to respond with positive or negative emotions to persons, objects, and events in his or her environment. This knowledge, which is based on the person's previous social experiences and acquired primarily through classical conditioning, is unique to the person to the extent that his or her social experiences are distinct from those of other people. Thus, it is held that individuals learn to associate positive or negative emotions with a certain stimulus and these emotions, in turn, determine subsequent behaviour. If a stimulus elicits negative emotions, this will lead to avoidance or escape reactions. If, on the other hand, the stimulus elicits positive emotions, approach responses are likely to result.

In a study by Staats and Burns (1982), the proposed link between situational stimuli, emotions, and approach versus avoidance behaviour was examined with regard to the personality dimension of religiosity. Subjects were classified as either high or low in religiosity on the basis of their responses to the 'religious values' subtest of the Allport–Vernon–Lindzey *Study of Values* Inventory. Several weeks later, the actual experiment took place. Then, the subjects' task consisted of responding to a number of different words presented in the display frame of a word presentation apparatus by either pulling a handle towards themselves or pushing it away. Two sets of words were used, one including six religious terms, the other including six stimulus words that were irrelevant to the dimension of religiosity. Depending on their experimental condition, subjects were instructed either to pull the handle of the word presentation apparatus towards them after the exposure of a religious word and pushing it away from them after the exposure of an irrelevant term or vice versa. Response latency in pushing or pulling the handle was the major dependent variable with ratings of the pleasantness versus the unpleasantness of each stimulus word being obtained as additional information.

In accordance with the model outlined above, a three-way interaction of religiosity, word type, and direction of movement was predicted on response latencies. More specifically, the following predictions were tested:

1 When exposed to the religious words, highly religious persons should pull the handle towards themselves faster and push it back more slowly than non-religious persons.
2 Highly religious persons should pull the handle towards them-selves faster and push it away from themselves more slowly when presented with religious as opposed to irrelevant words.
3 Non-religious persons should pull the handle towards them-

selves faster and push it away more slowly when presented with irrelevant as opposed to religious words.

These predictions were clearly confirmed by the data. Analyses of evaluative ratings of each stimulus word on the pleasant–unpleasant scale showed that highly religious persons perceived the religious words as being significantly more pleasant than the irrelevant words while the reverse was true for the non-religious group. Thus, findings from this study lend convincing support to the behavioural interaction approach. They suggest that emotional personality repertoires, in this case referring to the domain of religiosity, determine the extent to which the individual responds with positive or negative emotions to relevant stimuli which, in turn, leads to corresponding patterns of approach and avoidance reactions.

While Staats and Burns (1982) examined behavioural responses on a molecular level (such as, pulling or pushing a handle), the question remains as to whether similar relationships between emotional states and behaviour would also be found at the level of more complex behavioural responses. Here, the available evidence, while generally supportive of that claim, is somewhat less conclusive. Using a global behavioural criterion, namely the percentage of time spent in a situation, Diener et al. (1984) found no support for the hypothesis that individuals spend more time in situations in which they experience positive affect than in situations associated with negative emotional states. However, two interrelated features of the design of their study render these findings ambiguous. Firstly, subjects were prompted by an alarm to complete mood and activity protocols twice a day at times controlled by the investigators on the basis of a random time sampling procedure. Secondly, no information was obtained on whether the situations in which the participants were involved at the time the alarm went off were freely chosen or imposed on them. Thus, it may be the case that the relationship between the percentage of time spent in a situation and the positive versus negative affect experienced in that situation was confounded by differential base rates for pleasant and unpleasant situations in conjunction with the failure to distinguish between chosen and imposed situations. This reasoning receives support from another study by Emmons and Diener (1986b). They found that the *consistency of emotional states* across a heterogeneous range of situations was significantly higher for chosen than for imposed situations, while *behavioural consistency* was higher across imposed than across chosen situations (see also Emmons et al., 1986).

More conclusive support for the proposed link between emotions and behaviour is offered in a study by Epstein (1983c) in which two aspects of behavioural responses were examined: (a) the behavioural impulses elicited as a function of positive or negative emotions and (b) the expression of these impulses in actual behaviour. He asked a group of thirty subjects to keep records, over a period of twenty-eight days, of the single most pleasant and most unpleasant emotional experience encountered in the course of each day. The recorded emotional experiences then had to be described, among other aspects, in terms of more specific affective states associated with them and the extent to which they elicited different behavioural impulses. For each of these impulses, subjects also indicated whether they had actually carried it out in their overt behaviour. Epstein's findings clearly suggest that positive emotional experiences give rise to approach responses or positive behavioural impulses, such as being nurturant, affiliative and exuberant, while negative emotional experiences evoke avoidance responses or negative impulses, such as mental escape, counteraction and aggression. Inspection of the percentage of these behavioural impulses actually expressed in overt action, however, reveals a somewhat different pattern. Positive impulses are more frequently expressed in behaviour than negative impulses. An obvious explanation is, of course, that many negative impulses are socially unacceptable and are therefore likely to be suppressed in overt behaviour.

Most of the studies discussed in this section examined the role of emotions in naturally occurring everyday situations, allowing an immediate test of the proposed congruence model of personality, situation, and emotions. Despite the handicap of small sample sizes, incurred due to the complex and time-consuming data collection process, they provide essential support for the validity of the interactionist perspective: individuals show a clear tendency to choose situations that are congruent with their personalities and experience more positive emotions in congruent than in incongruent situations. At the same time, they are subjected to environmental constraints, including general social norms, that may force them into incongruent situations and also prevent them from expressing their emotional feelings in overt behaviour. Therefore, to understand the function of emotions in relation to personality variables and behaviour, it is essential to study simultaneously both the person and the context in which his or her behaviour takes place.

Prosocial behaviour

The complex effects of emotional states as determinants of social behaviour have also been a central issue in the third domain of interactionist research to be looked at in this chapter: prosocial or helping behaviour. Therefore, let us remain for a while with the topic of emotions before turning to other aspects of the interaction of personal and situational factors on helping behaviour. In analysing the effect of emotions, the central question for research on prosocial behaviour is whether being in a good or bad mood has any systematic influence on people's readiness to help others. Reviews of the evidence on mood states and helping (for example, Carlson and Miller, 1987; Carlson et al., 1988; Salovey et al., 1991) suggest that a person's momentary emotional state is a powerful determinant of the willingness to perform altruistic behaviour. However, the exact nature of the link between emotions, in particular as far as negative emotional states are concerned, is as yet not fully understood.

Being in a *positive* emotional state – induced, for instance, by the experience of success, the recall of positive events, small gifts or unexpected finds of trivial sums of money – has consistently been found to make people more willing to engage in helping behaviour (Carlson et al., 1988). Helping rates tend to increase not only towards the person who was responsible for the positive mood in the first place but equally towards an uninvolved third party. Studies on children's helping behaviour also confirm the link between positive emotions and increased readiness to show a variety of prosocial behaviours (see Marcus, 1986).

Findings pertaining to the role of *negative* emotional states are far less conclusive, possibly due to the greater diversity of emotions comprised by that category. The likelihood of the person performing a prosocial act has generally been found to increase following a social transgression or harm doing that produces feelings of guilt in the transgressor. This was true for various kinds of transgressions (intentional and unintentional, public and private) as well as various forms of prosocial behaviour in both natural and laboratory settings from volunteering for an experiment to donating blood. Again, helping rate increased not only towards the initial target of the transgression but extended to other, uninvolved persons as well.

One explanation for these findings is advanced in the 'negative state relief model' by Cialdini et al. (1982; Manucia et al., 1984; Schaller and Cialdini, 1988) which suggests that performing a prosocial act serves to alleviate or compensate the feeling of guilt and re-establish positive self-esteem. In this sense, prosocial behaviour operates as a kind of therapeutic strategy aimed at making the person 'feel good' again. Cialdini et al. propose that there is a systematic difference in the link between emotions and helping for children and adults: children show a linear increase in helping behaviour from negative over neutral to positive affective states. For adults, the relationship is more adequately described by a U-shaped curve, with both positive and negative affective states leading to more prosocial behaviour than neutral states. However, helping as a therapeutic strategy – and, with it, the negative state relief model – does not appear to be generally viable. It was found that other types of negative emotions, such as sense of failure and fear of rejection, either decreased or left unaffected the likelihood of engaging in prosocial behaviour. To reconcile the two conflicting sets of evidence on negative mood and helping, it has been suggested that a critical factor is the focus of the person's attention during the emotional state. When the focus of the emotion is on the person himself or herself (as with fear of rejection or sense of failure), then the likelihood of helping is supposed to decrease. In contrast, emotions that are focused on others (such as feeling guilty as a consequence of causing harm or mishap to another person) are thought to lead to an increase in helping behaviour (see Thompson et al., 1980).

From a different theoretical perspective, it has been argued that the negative emotions of guilt and shame – implying the acceptance of personal responsibility for one's bad mood – induce a state of 'objective self-awareness' characterized by a salient discrepancy between a person's ideal standards and his or her actual behaviour (see, for example, Gibbons and Wicklund, 1982). To the extent that helping norms are salient in the situation and no other means of diverting attention away from the discrepancy is readily available, helping takes the function of alleviating the aversive tension experienced as a result of not living up to one's internal standards.

In their expanded meta-analysis of the literature on negative mood and helping, Carlson and Miller (1987) failed to confirm the negative state relief model as a general explanation of the relationship between negative mood and helping. However, they did find support for both the attentional focus and the objective self-awareness (or personal responsibility) explanations. Both models are specifically addressed to certain categories of negative emotions, whereby feelings of personal inadequacy which give rise to guilt and shame are found to be most clearly related to helping behaviour.

So far, we have been dealing with emotional states originating from a source that is not related in any way to the specific circumstances in which a prosocial intervention is called for. If one looks at emotions experienced as an immediate result of witnessing a situation where help is required, an even more complicated picture emerges. Batson and Coke (1981) suggest that emotional responses elicited by the perception of a person in need of help fall into two distinct categories: personal distress and empathic concern. Personal distress refers to the unease and discomfort experienced by the individual as a result of observing another person's predicament. It gives rise to an egoistic motivation for engaging in helping behaviour, namely to reduce the person's own discomfort by means of helpful intervention. Empathic concern, on the other hand, is a sympathetic response to the other person's lot, and helping behaviour results from the prosocial motivation to promote the other's well-being. In line with an interactionist understanding of helping behaviour, the differential impact of these two types of emotions on actual helping behaviour becomes clear only when the perceived costs of not helping – or, conversely, the ease with which the person may escape from the situation – is taken into consideration as a critical situational feature. Here, the prediction is that empathic concern is likely to result in helping intervention irrespective of whether escape from the situation is easy or difficult. Personal distress, on the other hand, will only lead to helping if the situation is difficult to escape and there is no other way through which the person may alleviate his or her negative emotional arousal. This prediction has, in fact, been confirmed in studies by Batson et al. (1981) as well as Toi and Batson (1982). They demonstrated that the ease with which a help-requiring situation could be escaped without the threat of shame or guilt systematically influenced the likelihood of help from people under high versus low personal distress. No such differences were found for people experiencing high versus low levels of empathic concern. In a recent series of studies, Batson et al. (1989) showed that high empathic concern for the plight of another person leads to higher helping rates than low empathy, irrespective of whether subjects expected imminent mood enhancement (exposure to a video that would cause 'strong feelings of happiness and pleasure'). These findings speak against the negative-state-relief model and its core assumption that helping following the experience of high empathy is motivated primarily by the desire to enhance one's own mood. Those high-empathy subjects who were led to anticipate imminent mood enhancement did not show less helping than subjects not expecting such a mood change. Instead, the results support the alternative view that high empathy with a person in need of help activates the altruistic motivation to relieve the victim's distress.

In the work of Batson and his colleagues, empathy has been conceived of as a particular form of (momentary) emotional arousal elicited by the features of a specific help-relevant situation. However, it has also been suggested that the capacity to show empathy for a person in need of help is an enduring personal disposition acquired early on in the process of socialization and moral development (see, for example, Hoffman, 1981; Rushton, 1981, 1984). Davis (1983) demonstrated that individuals with strong dispositional empathy experienced significantly higher levels of empathic arousal than individuals characterized by low dispositional empathy in a specific situation. As a consequence, they helped the person in distress more frequently across both easy- and difficult-to-escape situations. In his study, these individual differences in dispositional empathy were much more powerful predictors of helping behaviour than experimentally induced differences in empathic arousal through explicitly instructing half of the subjects to evaluate the situation from the perspective of the person requiring help. In contrast, results by Batson et al. (1986) showed that dispositional empathy was related to helping only when escape from the situation was difficult. Thus, there seems to be no conclusive evidence as yet in support of empathy as a stable dispositional predictor of prosocial behaviour.

Altogether, there is a large body of empirical evidence suggesting a positive link between empathic emotional arousal and the readiness to perform a variety of helping behaviours. But, as the findings discussed above illustrate, there is some doubt as to whether or not empathic concern should be seen as an unambiguous reflection of an altruistic, non-selfish motive to help others in distress. Thus, the precise nature of the link between empathy and helping needs to be further explored.

This issue is addressed as part of Staub's (1980, 1984) approach to the study of prosocial behaviour which is located within the broader framework of a general model of social behaviour. At the core of this general model is the concept of *personal goals*. Personal goals are understood as motivational tendencies directing the person's behaviour towards the achievement of certain preferred aims or psychological states. In this sense, the nature of prosocial goals is such as to motivate the person to engage in behaviours which lead to enhancing another person's well-being. Prosocial goals are formed through the internalization of social norms and values, and, accordingly, can be described as broad value orientations. Personal goals in general are characterized by three major defining features: (a) they contain specifications of what outcomes, or classes of outcomes, are desirable; (b) they have an energetic component in that they involve the arousal of tension; and (c) they consist of a network of cognitions which facilitate the interpretation of situational stimuli as relevant or irrelevant to the goal. In this sense, empathic concern can be regarded as the energetic component of a prosocial goal.

Personal goals, and prosocial goals in particular, represent internal potentials for responding in a certain way to situational demands. In order to become effective determinants of the individual's behaviour, they have to be activated by relevant stimuli in the external environment. In any one situation, more than one personal goal may be activated at the same time and, to the extent that the respective goals are incompatible, a motivational conflict will ensue. How this conflict will be resolved is a function of both the strength of the personal goals involved and the strength of the activating potential of the situation with respect to that goal. Consider, for example, a situation where a person is working on a task when suddenly faced with a request for help. Whether the person will meet the request or continue to work on the task will depend on, first, the relative strength of the person's prosocial goal as compared to his or her achievement-related goals and, secondly, the relative strength of the activating potential with which different situational cues are charged in relation to the two goals, such as the urgency of the request as compared to the importance of the task.

Staub suggests that the relationship between these two potentials should be conceived of as a multiplicative function: if either potential is zero, then that goal is considered as irrelevant to the person's behavioural decisions. Such a view of the link between external situations and internal motivations highlights the need for a 'relational' classification of situations. The meaning of situations is defined in terms of their relationship to certain personal goals, and situation categories comprise situations that pertain to the same or similar personal goals. By implication, this involves the development of a common metric in which personal and situational features are captured in corresponding units of analysis.

Thus, Staub regards prosocial behaviour as the result of the correspondence between a prosocial goal and the activating potential of the situation, modified in significant ways by different mediating variables on the person and the situation side (see Staub, 1980: 272ff.). The multiplicity of ways in which these sets of variables may interact to produce a particular behaviour in a given situation poses problems for a comprehensive test of the complete model. This is true, in particular, for the crucial issue of predicting whether or not a person will help under a given set of circumstances. Therefore, empirical work aimed to test the Staub model has concentrated on examining specific aspects of this interactionist perspective on helping behaviour. Considered in combination, findings from these studies furnish conclusions on the validity of the model as a whole.

In a study by Erkut et al. (1981), prosocial behaviour was predicted on the basis of the interaction between moral development and the social appropriateness of the helping act. Starting from Kohlberg's theory of moral development in which six increasingly differentiated stages of moral judgement are distinguished (Kohlberg, 1981), they postulated that neither knowledge of a person's moral stage nor knowledge of the situation alone are sufficient to predict prosocial behaviour. Therefore, they used a design that allowed them to examine the interactive effect of moral awareness and situational constraints on helping a person in distress. Subjects at different levels of moral development were asked to complete an experimental task in the course of which they overheard sounds of distress coming from an 'ailing' confederate in an adjacent room. The nature of the contract between the subject and the experimenter was systematically varied: subjects were either told that they were free to interrupt their work to get some coffee (permission condition), that the task had to be completed as quickly as possible (prohibition condition) or received no such information at all. The prediction was that subjects in the most advanced stage of moral development would be most strongly aware of a conflict of norms between observing the experimental instructions and helping the person in distress. As a consequence, they were expected to be more likely to help in the permission condition – where they felt free to stop work on the task without violating their contract with the experimenter – than in the prohibition and no information conditions. Subjects in the lower stages of moral development would have a less differentiated awareness of a conflict of norms. They would stick to a more literal interpretation of the 'permission' condition as being limited only to the stated reason for interrupting the task. Accordingly, their rate of helping behaviour should not be affected by the nature of the experimental instruction.

The findings obtained by Erkut et al. clearly confirm these hypotheses. At the most advanced level of moral development, subjects assigned to the permission condition offered significantly more help than subjects in the prohibition and no information conditions. They also helped significantly more than subjects at the lower stages of moral development across all three experimental situations. The authors conclude that there is no general relationship between moral judgement and prosocial action that predicts how a person of a given stage of moral development will act in any one situation. None the less, moral development can be predictive of prosocial behaviour if considered in conjunction with relevant situational information, among which the extent of normative ambiguity inherent in the situation appears to be of primary significance.

In a related vein, the interaction of different types of prosocial goals and corresponding situational features on helping behaviour was examined in a study by Romer et al. (1986). Like Batson and his colleagues whose work was presented earlier in this section, Romer et al. start from the general idea that helping behaviour can be the result of either altruistic or egoistic motives. Egoistic motives underlying helping behaviour lead to helping only if the person expects some form of reward or compensation (such as enhancing his or her negative mood) in return. In contrast, an altruistic helper is concerned entirely about improving the fate of the person in need of help. These differences in motivation for helping behaviour are conceived of as relatively stable dispositions, so that individuals can be categorized as either altruists or non-altruists, that is, receptive givers. While both types are expected to show help under certain conditions, a third category of people, namely selfish individuals, is included who are seen as being interested primarily in obtaining help from others rather than providing help themselves.

Whether altruists and receptive givers will actually offer help in a particular situation depends on whether or not the situation is favourable to the satisfaction of their respective motives. Romer et al. first classified their subjects as altruists, receptive givers and selfish individuals on the basis of a 'Helping Orientation Questionnaire'. Subsequently, they examined the extent to which each group responded to a request (participating in an experiment) where compensation in return for their help in the form of course credit was either offered or explicitly denied. In line with the interactionist understanding of personality dispositions, a significantly higher percentage of altruists helped in the non-compensation condition as compared with the compensation condition. Conversely, receptive givers offered help to a significantly greater extent when they expected to be compensated than when no compensation was expected. Selfish people showed substantially lower rates of helping than both altruists and receptive givers in each of the two experimental conditions. Thus, the findings of Romer et al. further challenge the idea that willingness to help is rooted in a single, unified trait or value orientation of altruism. Instead, they suggest that several types of personal orientations relevant to helping need to be distinguished which have a differential impact on actual helping behaviour contingent upon the specific features of the situation where help is required.

This selective review of the evidence supporting an interactionist understanding of prosocial behaviour concludes our discussion of three domains of personality and social behaviour. Anxiety, emotions, and prosocial behaviour were chosen to illustrate the characteristic approach adopted by modern interactionism to establish a new perspective on personality in theoretical terms as well as empirical research. In each domain, the presentation of the evidence was guided by the aim of highlighting the distinctive features of the interactionist orientation compared with traditional trait-oriented and situationist explanations. While many more domains of personality functioning and social behaviour have been subjected to an interactionist reformulation since the mid-1970s, it is fair to say that the three domains examined more closely in this chapter are among the most advanced and comprehensive of these endeavours. To complete the discussion of the modern interactionist approach, the final section is devoted to a review of the critical appraisals the interactionist approach has received from the ranks of personality psychologists.

Has interactionism come of age: critical voices

To evaluate the progress achieved by modern interactionism in implementing a new framework for the study of personality and social behaviour, the judgement of one of its major representatives provides a fitting point of departure. In 1982, Endler confidently claimed in the title of a paper that 'interactionism comes of age'. A year later, he qualified this view, admitting that at present modern interactionism is a model but not yet a fully fledged theory of personality (Endler, 1983). In particular, he pointed to the following shortcomings of interactionism precluding its claim to the status of a comprehensive theory.

The first shortcoming is seen in the fact that most empirical work has been limited to the study of mechanistic interactions of two independent variables, that is, a personal characteristic and a situational manipulation, on individual behaviour as the dependent variable. What has been largely neglected is the study of sequences of behaviour which reflect the proposed dynamic and bidirectional exchange between person and situation.

However, this is not to suggest that no further studies are needed to investigate the mechanistic interaction of personal dispositions and environment. On the contrary, the renewed concern with separating the genetic bases of personality differences from the effects of environmental sources (see Chapter 3) is intimately linked to the concept of mechanistic interaction. This work reflects the sustained interest in identifying the stable hereditary characteristics of personality in relation to the environmenal influences confronting the person in the course of development. Here, specific methods have been used, such as the study of adopted children and the comparison of monozygotic and dizygotic twins raised together or apart (Plomin, 1986), to establish the relative impact of genetic and environmental influences on individual behaviour.

A second problem consists in the lack of progress in investigating the process whereby persons select and influence the situations in which they act. Currently, we do not know very much about those properties of situations that are most influential in shaping the person's affective and behavioural responses. Here, Endler suggests that the answer lies in the development of systematic taxonomies of situations. These should be geared not so much towards describing the content of different situations as towards emphasizing the rules and norms inherent in different situations that provide a kind of structural and functional framework within which actual behaviour takes place (see also Argyle et al., 1981). In this way, the ground could be prepared for the development of a comprehensive theoretical treatment of the 'psychological situation' which would go beyond the basically piecemeal way of dealing with situational variables that is characteristic of the interactionist work carried out so far. This state of affairs is reflected not least in the fact that one would generally look in vain for an explicit definition of the meaning with which the term 'situation' is used in a specific research context.

Taken together, these two lacunae highlight the need to advance a more elaborate version of interactionism extending to the explanation of the process of interaction. An essential requirement for achieving this aim is the development of a methodology for investigating the dynamic, continuous interplay between persons on the one hand and situational properties, their cognitive representation as well as their relationship to overt behaviour on the other (see also Aronoff and Wilson, 1985). Potential avenues for addressing this task illustrated by the work of Peterson (1979) and Malloy and Kenny (1986) were briefly mentioned in the previous chapter. But modern interactionism is still a far cry from providing a comprehensive answer to the question of how the process of person–environment interaction is properly understood. As Mischel (1990: 116) summarized it: 'Going beyond lip service about the importance of person–situation interactions to generate and test theory-based predictions of those interactions became and remains high on the agenda for personality psychology.'

Hyland (1984) also takes a critical view of modern interactionism as a theoretical alternative to the situationist and trait positions, respectively. In his view, the impact of the modern interactionist

approach is limited largely to the level of methodological developments and fails to contribute to a new theoretical understanding of
personality. He also denies that situationism and the trait approach
have ever been presented as competing theoretical approaches,
seeing their main difference in terms of the preferred strategies for
measuring individual behaviour. Whereas Hyland's criticism of the
lack of a comprehensive theoretical network of modern interactionism is certainly valid, his comments on how the model deals
with the concept of the 'psychological situation' cannot be accepted
without qualification. When he states that 'certainly from a
methodological point of view there has never been any suggestion
that the situation which appears in the ANOVA paradigm is
anything other than an objective reality' (Hyland, 1984: 319), then
this is clearly not true for the large number of studies which are
based on S–R inventories. When the different measurement models
underlying the interactionist approach were discussed in the previous chapter, it became clear that S–R inventories, such as the S–R
GTA, relied exclusively on the person's subjective interpretations
of different anxiety-provoking situations and their relationship to
individual behaviour (see Table 4.1). Despite his generally critical
attitude, however, Hyland credits the modern interactionist
perspective with pressing the view that for the prediction of
behaviour to become more successful, it is essential to define
explicitly those classes of situations and behaviours for which
predictions are made (see also Peake, 1984: 336). This view is
shared by Pervin who sees the major contribution of modern
interactionism in its emphasis on the variability and discriminativeness of behaviour to counterbalance the preoccupation with consistency that has hampered the resolution of the person–situation
debate for a long time: 'The real significance of the person–situation
debate may be in calling attention to the critical issue of understanding patterns of stability and change.' (Pervin, 1984b: 344).

A far more radical criticism of modern interactionism is advanced
by Gadlin and Rubin (1979). They already make it clear in the title
of their paper that they consider the interactionist approach to be a
'non-resolution of the person–situation controversy'. Their critique
is not primarily directed against the theoretical postulates or
methodological strategies of the interactionist model but against
what they identify as its *ideological foundations*. Gadlin and Rubin
argue that the conflict underlying the entire person–situation debate
is essentially a conflict between psychological explanations of
human behaviour on the one hand and sociohistorical realities on
the other. The focal point of their critique is once again the way in
which the concept of 'situation' is treated in the interactionist

model. In particular, they take exception to the conceptualization of situations in terms of subjective representations of objective stimulus conditions that they consider to be ahistorical and asocial. The view of adaptive social behaviour as resulting from the perfect integration of person and situation – which is reflected, for example, in the 'goodness of fit' and congruence models discussed above – is criticized as an essentially ideological notion. It is seen as tantamount to abolishing the independence of person and situation as analytical units, motivated by the attempt to salvage 'the continued social cohesion of a failing system' (Gadlin and Rubin, 1979: 235). In historical reality, they argue, disjunction rather than congruence between persons and situations is the rule, resulting from the constraints imposed by certain sociohistorical conditions upon the person's choice of situations and social settings. Accordingly, Gadlin and Rubin argue that the only way in which situational factors can become meaningful elements of any psychological theory of human behaviour is by acknowledging explicitly the historical and societal determination of individual action:

> People do not act in situations; they act in specific historical circumstances that they interpret in certain ways and that constrain and compel them in certain ways; and it is the particular features of those circumstances we must understand to understand why they act as they do. (Gadlin and Rubin, 1979: 225)

Undoubtedly, it is a legitimate challenge to the advocates of modern interactionism to be more aware of the political and historical premises and implications of their research. Gadlin and Rubin's criticism, however, can hardly be accepted as an overall rejection of the interactionist perspective and its research output. Instead, by demanding greater recognition of behavioural determinants beyond the boundaries of a psychological perspective, they add an important level of analysis to the study of personality and social behaviour which future developments within the interactionist framework need to take into account.

Summary

The present chapter has been devoted to a review of empirical research generated by the interactionist approach in three representative domains of personality. First, the domain of anxiety-provoking situations was considered. The majority of research in this area is based on the multidimensional model of anxiety advanced by Endler. This model predicts behavioural responses, that is, anxiety 'state' reactions, on the basis of the interaction between a particular dimension of dispositional or 'trait' anxiety and the specific features of a situation pertinent to that dimension. Various studies have shown that people scoring high on a particular facet of A-trait, such as physical danger, respond with increased levels of A-state only in those situations that correspond to the A-trait facet in terms of their anxiety-arousing nature (for example, situations involving the risk of bodily harm). Secondly, the domain of emotions was examined by looking at recent research based on a 'congruence model' of the relationship between personal dispositions, situations and emotional states. In accordance with this model, evidence has been presented by Diener and his associates, among others, that individuals prefer and experience more positive emotions in situations that are congruent with their personalities. Conversely, they tend to avoid situations which are discordant to their personality traits. Thirdly, research on person–situation interactions in the field of prosocial behaviour was examined. One line of evidence focused on the notion that helping another person may serve to compensate or alleviate negative emotional feelings. This was found to be true especially in those situations where the escape from the situation is difficult and the costs involved in not helping are high. Furthermore, Staub's model of (pro)social behaviour was discussed in which helping behaviour is conceptualized as a function of the interaction between the person's generalized prosocial goals or motives on the one hand and the potential of a given situation for activating those goals on the other hand.

In the concluding section, critical appraisals of the modern interactionist model of personality and social behaviour were presented. There appears to be a general consensus that the major shortcoming of this approach in its current form lies in the lack of appropriate methods for analysing dynamic, reciprocal interactions between the person and the environment. It is thus fair to say that modern interactionism is underdeveloped as far as the methodological side is concerned.

In recent years, however, new strategies of personality measurement have been developed at the fringes or outside the interactionist mainstream to facilitate better predictions of behaviour and to obtain more sophisticated evidence on the issue of behavioural consistency over time and across situations. The next two chapters will look in detail at these methodological developments which, again, have been encumbered by a fundamental controversy. In this case, the controversy has involved the proponents of a nomothetic rationale for personality measurement and a growing minority of personality researchers who advocate a greater idiographic orientation in the study of personality.

6

Improving Personality Measurement: The Nomothetic Road to the Study of Consistency

Throughout the previous chapters, it has been evident that theoretical controversies in personality psychology as well as the efforts to resolve them are inextricably linked to issues of personality measurement. In the course of the consistency controversy, experimental and correlational research methods have been pitted against each other in the attempt to declare either the situationist or the trait-based model superior in explaining personality functioning. In his introduction to a collection of papers on methodological developments in personality research, West (1986b) still described the state of the field by stating: 'The consistency debate continues, reflecting the field's failure to reach consensus on several basic units of analysis and conceptual issues' (West 1986b: 2f.). At the same time, the proponents of the interactionist approach have stressed that any progress of personality psychology is conditional upon the development of improved methodologies capable of tapping the complex process of dynamic interactions between the person and the environment. Thus, despite the methodological pluralism identified by Craik (1986) as a characteristic feature of personality research today, there can be no doubt about the pressing need to develop empirical strategies that correspond more closely to the theoretical constructs they want to address.

For much of this century, personality psychologists have shown fundamental disagreement over the methodological orientation of their discipline. Should the aim be to discover general patterns or even 'laws' of personality functioning applicable to as many people as possible, or should one concentrate on the intensive analysis of individual personalities to understand the unique life course of a person? The first of these two approaches is commonly referred to as the *nomothetic* perspective and has been the majority position among personality researchers throughout the history of the field. The second approach refers to the *idiographic* understanding of the aims and principles of personality measurement which has always been present as a minority viewpoint but has become more accepted in recent years.

Following Mischel's (1968) attack on the notions of trait and consistency, a variety of methodological approaches have been introduced with a view to overcoming the limitations of traditional research strategies and enhancing the validity and reliability of personality measurement. These developments will be reviewed in this and the next chapter, whereby the nomothetic–idiographic distinction is used as an organizing principle. It should be noted at the outset, however, that no attempt will be made to present a comprehensive coverage of the diverse issues addressed in the recent literature on personality measurement (see for example, Rorer, 1990; West, 1986a), including critical assessments of personality inventories (for example, Hogan et al., 1983; Nicholls et al., 1982; Werner and Pervin, 1986). Instead, the emphasis will be on those lines of development that are particularly relevant to the issues raised in the course of our discussion of the consistency controversy and the interactionist model of personality.

There are good reasons to discuss the range of recent methodological developments in two special chapters rather than describe them only in the context of individual models or empirical studies. It is easier to assess the strengths and weaknesses of each strategy if methodological issues are at the focus of attention rather than being subordinated to the assessment of specific content-bound hypotheses. Furthermore, such a perspective allows one to examine the range of applicability of each strategy by collecting empirical evidence from a wide spectrum of content domains. Last but not least, the general issue of whether a nomothetic or an idiographic approach is more likely to promote constructive development in personality research can also be more clearly addressed by looking in detail at the different strategies in their own right.

The present chapter will discuss three broad strategies based on a *nomothetic* understanding of the goals of personality measurement. According to this understanding, measurement strategies should be designed such as to facilitate the discovery of general principles of personality functioning which would hold – in a probabilistic sense – for the majority of individuals in the majority of personality domains. In terms of a popular rhetorical phrase, these strategies should yield explanations and predictions that are true for 'most of the people most of the time'.

In Chapter 7 the methodological perspective will be extended to include research based on an *idiographic* commitment to personality measurement. In this work, the aim is to explain the personality and behaviour of 'individual persons most of the time', that is, to grasp as comprehensively as possible the dispositions, feelings, cognitions, and behaviours of a particular individual. The search for general principles of personality functioning is thus replaced by the aim of capturing the uniqueness of the individual person. In addition to a limited range of strictly idiographic contributions, there is a small but distinct group of studies aimed at reconciling nomothetic and idiographic objectives. Here, the focus is on developing empirical procedures that lend themselves both to the (nomothetic) study of individual differences and to the (idiographic) exploration of individual patterns of consistency and stability.

Since the distinction between nomothetic and idiographic object-ives in personality measurement is the central organizing principle for the material to be presented in the two chapters, we should start by looking briefly at the meaning and history of these terms. The two contrasting terms 'nomothetic' and 'idiographic' were first coined by the German philosopher Windelband (1894) and subse-quently introduced into psychology by Stern (1921) and Allport (1937). In their original meaning, they served to denote the different aims and objectives of the natural sciences and the humanities, respectively. Research in the humanities, such as history or literary criticism, is considered idiographic inasmuch as its main concern is with arriving at conclusions about individual persons, events or works of art, not necessarily with the aim of combining or extrapolating such conclusions into generalized infer-ences. The natural sciences, on the other hand, are nomothetically oriented in the sense that they are concerned primarily with establishing general laws, whereby single observations are relevant only to the extent that they confirm or contradict the postulated laws. Within this classification, psychology as an empirical discipline is assigned a status similar to the natural sciences.

The exclusive frame of reference for idiographic measurement is the individual person, and the obtained data are interpreted as samples from the individual's total population of the characteristics in question (for example, emotions, cognitions, manifestations of traits in overt behaviour). In contrast, data collected within the framework of nomothetic measurement are viewed as samples from the total population of the respective characteristic in the total population of persons. Similar methodological distinctions have been suggested by Cattell (1944) who differentiates between norm-ative and ipsative personality measurement and, more recently, by authors like Bem (1983c) and Mischel (1983) who refer to the different foci of interest in terms of a variable-centred and a person-centred approach, respectively.

As noted above, the idiographic–nomothetic distinction originally referred to a difference in scientific *aims* rather than *objects*. Both Windelband and Allport made it very clear that one and the same issue can, in principle, be considered either from an idiographic or a nomothetic perspective, depending on the particular nature of the question to be addressed by the research. More recently, Epstein (1983b: 379) reiterated this point by emphasizing that 'idiographic and nomothetic procedures do not present different solutions to the same problem but solutions to different problems.' Nevertheless, it will become obvious in the course of this discussion that idiographic and nomothetic approaches have often been construed as essentially incompatible alternatives, particularly by nomothetically oriented personality researchers, and have been a constant object of controversy throughout the field's history (see, for example, Beck, 1953; Eysenck, 1954; Falk, 1956; and also see Pervin, 1984a, for a more recent review). In the course of the 1980s, however, this state of affairs has begun to change. Different approaches have been suggested which are designed to integrate the two research perspectives. The basic point made in this work is that much of the controversy surrounding the two terms has resulted from the failure to distinguish between the level of methodological strategies and the level of theoretical explanation (Marceil, 1977). There seems to be a growing consensus that it is perfectly possible to employ idiographic or individual-centred methods to test nomothetic, that is, general hypotheses (Bem and Allen, 1974; Lamiell, 1982; Pervin, 1984c). This reasoning and the empirical work derived from it will be presented in detail in Chapter 7.

Among the nomothetic contributions to personality measurement documented in several reviews (for example, Carson, 1989; Pervin 1985; Rorer and Widiger, 1983; West, 1986a), three approaches are particularly relevant to the debate on the cross-situational consistency of behaviour and its attempted resolution in the interactionist model. These approaches, which offer complementary not competing strategies to improve the reliability and validity of trait measures and their reflection in behaviour, will be introduced in the remainder of this chapter.

The first strategy aimed at increasing the accuracy of behaviour prediction consists in the search for *moderator variables* which influence the relation between trait measures and behaviour. This line of research is guided by the goal of identifying subgroups of persons, situations and traits that are characterized by typically high or low levels of behavioural consistency.

A second line of methodological development is based on the *principle of aggregation*, stressing the requirement to relate predictions of behaviour not to individual indicators but to aggregated samples of behavioural criteria across time or different situations. In this context reference will also be made to the latest round of controversy about whether the issue of consistency should be phrased in terms of the cross-situational generality – involving aggregation across different situations at any one time – or the temporal stability of behavioural patterns – involving aggregation across different points in time with regard to similar situations. Also to be included in this section is a review of the 'act frequency approach' (Buss and Craik, 1984 among others) briefly mentioned in Chapter 2 in the context of the summary view of traits. This approach has generated a prolific research output including a number of cross-cultural studies.

The third strategy, that of *peer-rating*, is also aimed at improving the measurement of behaviour. Here, however, the focus is on increasing the sample of raters rather than the sample of behavioural criteria. The peer-rating strategy involves reliance on informed raters, that is, people who are familiar with the persons under study and their characteristic ways of acting in various sections of their social environments. It enables the investigators to go beyond the level of self-reports and check their validity through comparisons with data obtained from knowledgeable informants. Moreover, peer ratings can be used to improve behavioural observations because it provides a strategy for sampling large and heterogeneous groups of raters.

The moderator variable strategy: beyond omnibus predictions

The moderator variable strategy is discussed here in the context of nomothetic approaches to personality despite the fact that some of its proponents (for example, Bem and Allen, 1974; Kenrick and Braver, 1982) have described it as an 'idiographic' approach to personality measurement. In the attempt to specify the conditions under which high levels of consistency may be found, the moderator variable strategy relies on generally applicable samples of traits, situations, and behaviours, and none of the studies to be reported below treats the individual as the unit of analysis. Therefore, the moderator variable strategy does not represent a genuinely idiographic approach and is classified more appropriately among the nomothetic attempts to specify the range of application of certain personality constructs.[1] In the development and increasing prominence of the *moderator variables strategy*, the investigation by Bem and Allen (1974) plays a central role. Their study was prompted by the authors' critique of the implicit assumption of nomothetically oriented research that traits are ubiquitous. According to this assumption of 'common traits', a given trait and its corresponding behavioural expressions apply, in principle, to all persons concerned, with individual difference referring only to the degree that a person 'possesses' the trait in question. In contrast, Bem and Allen argue that it may well be the case that certain traits are simply irrelevant to some persons, a claim made long before by Allport (1937; and see also Borkenau, in press, b). The issue of trait applicability thus becomes a qualitative question: whether or not a particular trait concept can be meaningfully applied to the description of the person. It is no longer just a quantitative question of the strength of the trait in the person as compared with others. One way of dealing with this issue has been presented by Baumeister and Tice (1988: 573) in their concept of 'metatrait'. A metatrait is defined as 'the trait of having versus not having a particular trait', whereby a 'metatrait is always associated with a particular trait'. As an illustration, consider once more the trait of dominance. In the traditional view, dominance is a trait that can be applied in very much the same way to all persons. Some people are characterized by high levels of dominance, while others are characterized by little or no dominance, but in each case, the strength of disposition towards dominant behaviour is regarded as being a stable characteristic of the person. According to the rationale put forward by Bem and Allen and elaborated by Baumeister and Tice, dominance as a stable characteristic may apply only to some people, while others fluctuate in their levels of dominant behaviour from one situation to the other. Consequently, it would be unreasonable to expect behavioural consistency across situations from the latter, 'untraited' group.

The question then becomes central of how to identify those people whose behaviour may be expected to be consistent across situations and over time due to their endowment with a corresponding internal disposition. Or, to put it differently: what are the crucial variables that act upon or *moderate* the relationship between internal characteristics and overt behaviour so as to produce systematic differences in the levels of consistency displayed by different groups of individuals? To address this question, Snyder and Ickes (1985: 896) favour a functional definition of moderator variables: 'Functionally, moderating variables in personality research are variables that shift the cause of behavior from a situational locus to a dispositional one and vice versa.' Baron and Kenny (1986) stress the importance of distinguishing between 'moderating' and 'mediating' variables, a distinction they claim many researchers have failed to observe. The crucial difference between the two concepts is described as follows: 'Whereas moderator variables specify when certain effects will hold, mediators speak to how or why such effects occur.' (Baron and Kenny, 1986: 1176). As will become clear in the course of this section, personality researchers have so far largely ignored the task of explaining the process whereby individual differences in consistency come about. Instead, they have concentrated on demonstrating the effect of moderator variables by showing that consistency between traits and behaviour as well as among behaviour in different situations is higher for some persons and/or situations than for others (see Borkenau (1985) for a critical review of the available methods for comparing 'consistent' and 'inconsistent' subjects).

In the now classic Bem and Allen (1974) study, a straightforward approach was adopted to address this issue. They proposed self-rated consistency as an important moderator variable referring to the extent that individuals describe themselves as generally consistent or inconsistent with respect to a given trait. Only those of their subjects who regarded themselves as consistent in this sense were expected to show high levels of consistency in their trait-relevant behaviour across situations.

The validity of this restricted consistency hypothesis was examined with respect to the two personality traits of friendliness and conscientiousness. Subjects were presented with a questionnaire measure of the two characteristics and also asked for a general evaluation of the extent to which they vary from one situation to another in how friendly or conscientious they are. On the basis of these ratings, they were classified as either consistent or variable. At the same time, observational measures of friendly and conscientious behaviour as well as ratings by parents and friends were collected in different situations. In support of their hypothesis, Bem and Allen found that correlations between the different measures of friendliness and conscientiousness (self-evaluations, observational data and evaluations by informed raters) were significantly higher for subjects classified as consistent than for those rated as variable. In the domain of friendliness, overall correlations among the different measures were $r = 0.57$ for the low variability as compared with $r = 0.27$ for the high variability group. For the trait of conscientiousness, findings were somewhat less clear-cut, with correlations of $r = 0.36$ obtained for the generally consistent and $r = 0.12$ for the generally variable subjects.[2] Since the two sets of data for friendliness and conscientiousness were collected from the same individuals, this suggests that self-rated consistency, instead of being a general moderator variable, may have a differential impact on different trait domains.

The main appeal of Bem and Allen's strategy of employing self-rated consistency as a moderator variable of the trait–behaviour relationship clearly lies in its simplicity. It is therefore not surprising that their study stimulated a series of replications which, however, have come up with generally less conclusive results. Underwood and Moore (1981) confirmed the patterns of findings obtained by Bem and Allen for the domain of sociability. Kenrick and Stringfield (1980) extended the hypothesis that self-rated consistency is a moderator of actually observed consistency by including the public observability of trait-related behaviour as an additional moderating variable and using a wider range of sixteen bipolar personality traits. A trait-by-trait analysis revealed, as in the Bem and Allen study, that the relationship between self-rated consistency and behavioural ratings by self, peers and parents varied substantially between different traits. The most pronounced differences between high and low self-rated consistency emerged for the traits of friendliness and conservatism, while almost no difference emerged for the traits of suspiciousness and group-orientedness. The observability of different traits generally enhanced the effects of self-rated consistency, with highest levels of observed consistency emerging for those traits which were rated by the subject as most consistent and highly observable at the same time. However, Rushton et al. (1981) identified a number of problems associated with Kenrick and Stringfield's interpretation of their data which referred, among other things, to the fact that ratings of consistency were methodologically confounded with the ratings of trait extremity, that is, the extent to which each trait was perceived as being characteristic of the person (see also Paunonen, 1988). While Kenrick and Braver (1982) attempt to clarify these points in their rejoinder to the Rushton et al. paper, not all of them are addressed convincingly.

The finding that self-rated consistency successfully predicts observed or peer-rated consistency only in certain personality domains but not generally was corroborated by Knapp and Sebes (1982). They found that behavioural responses to different situations in the domain of anxiety could be more accurately predicted for individuals who rated themselves as consistent in that domain but failed to show a similar relationship in the domain of extroversion (see also Campus, 1974; Vestewig, 1978).

Thus, there is some evidence to suggest that the extent to which individuals describe themselves as consistent on a particular trait predicts their actual level of cross-situational consistency as well as the level of agreement between different informed raters of their behaviour. Yet, the moderating effect of self-rated consistency appears to be limited only to certain personality domains. Unfortunately, none of the studies conducted in the Bem and Allen fashion offer an explanation for these differential findings which would allow the identification of those trait domains where the consistency of individual behaviour can be predicted on the basis of the person's self-rated level of consistency.

Further criticism of the reliance on consistency self-ratings as moderators of the trait–behaviour relationship has to do with the reliability and validity of such measures (Burke et al., 1984). Greaner and Penner (1982) examined the retest reliability of a global rating-scale measure of self-reported consistency after an interval of ten weeks and concluded that the resulting correlation of $r = 0.43$ between the ratings at the two data points casts serious doubts on the appropriateness of this strategy for classifying individuals as consistent or variable. As far as the convergent validity of different formats of consistency self-reports is concerned, Turner and Gilliam (1979) report at best moderate levels of correspondence between three select measures. Finally, the moderator variable approach has come under attack from studies that failed to find any relationship at all between various indices of self-rated consistency and actual consistency between trait measures and behaviour (see, for example, Chaplin and Goldberg, 1985; Paunonen and Jackson, 1985). To obtain a clearer picture of the support currently available for the moderating effect of self-rated consistency, Zuckerman et al. (1988) conducted a meta-analysis including eight pertinent studies. From this analysis, they concluded that there is at best weak support for the proposed link between a person's self-rating of consistency and his or her actual level of consistency as obtained through behavioural ratings, peer reports, or observation. Furthermore, they argued that self-reported trait-relevance, that is, the subjects' perceptions of the extent to which a certain trait is central to their self-concept, is a more adequate variable than self-rated consistency to test Bem and Allen's claim that not all traits are equally applicable to all persons. Nevertheless, their own study designed to test the relative importance of self-reported consistency and trait-relevance, respectively, showed that both variables, especially in combination, were significant moderators of consistency between self- and peer-ratings on different trait dimensions. These results were qualified, however, in a subsequent study by Zuckerman et al. (1989) which compared different strategies for measuring self-reported consistency and trait relevance. They found that moderator effects only emerged when a ranking procedure was used, as when subjects were required to assign a rank to each trait dimension in terms of its perceived relevance and level of consistency. In contrast, very little support for moderator effects was found using a rating procedure whereby judgements of consistency and relevance had to be made independently for each trait dimension. One conceptual implication of these findings could be that ranking procedures force people to discriminate between traits, yielding intra-individual or intra-trait differences. Rating procedures, on the other hand, are more closely related to inter-individual moderators, reflecting consistent differences in self-reported consistency and relevance across a range of trait dimensions (Koestner et al., 1989).

One reason for the conceptual and methodological inconclusiveness of the research reviewed so far is the essentially a-theoretical nature of the Bem and Allen procedure using a person's self-rated consistency as a moderator variable (see also Wallach and Leggett, 1972; Tellegen et al., 1982). This has been recognized and addressed by a number of authors who have argued in favour of selecting moderator variables that have a theoretical relevance to the issues of person–situation interaction and cross-situational consistency. In particular, the concepts of self-monitoring (Snyder, 1979, 1987), self-consciousness (Scheier, 1980) and social desirability (Crowne and Marlowe, 1964) have been proposed and examined as moderators of the link between traits and behaviour. Amelang and Borkenau (1984) support the prediction derived from the concept of social desirability that a person's situational variability of behaviour will depend on the extent to which he or she is characterized by the tendency to behave in a socially desirable way. Since the desirability of different behaviours is very much a function of the situation and/or the social agents present, the impact of stable personality traits on behaviour for people scoring high on social desirability must, by necessity, be limited.

From the concept of self-monitoring, the following prediction has been derived: 'low self-monitors', that is, people who rely on internal cues, attitudes, etc. as guidelines for their behaviour, will be less susceptible to situational influences and, accordingly, display higher levels of consistency across different situations than 'high self-monitors' who constantly adjust their behaviour to the demands and expectations of their environment. Support for this prediction has been found in various studies reported by Snyder and Ickes (1985: 902) which demonstrated substantially higher levels of cross-situational consistency as well as correspondence between self- and peer-ratings for low rather than for high self-monitors. Less conclusive findings, however, were obtained by Wymer and Penner (1985).

Similarly, the concept of self-consciousness (Scheier, 1980) suggests that individuals differ in the extent to which their attention is directed inwards or outwards, namely, to their social environment.

The more the individual's attention is typically directed towards him- or herself, the greater the self-consciousness. Different facets of self-consciousness have been distinguished by Fenigstein et al. (1975), whereby *private self-consciousness* is defined as a preoccupation with the self as an individual person and *public self-consciousness* refers to the person's awareness of the self as a social object. As far as the moderating effect of self-consciousness is concerned, the proposition is that the consistency and predictability of behaviour corresponds to the strength of the person's private self-consciousness: the higher a person's private self-consciousness, the higher his or her level of consistency and, hence, predictability. This hypothesis was confirmed in studies by Scheier et al. (1978), and Turner (1978). Underwood and Moore (1981) found higher correlations between trait measures of sociability and partner-ratings in an interaction situation for subjects scoring high as opposed to low on private self-consciousness. However, when they compared self-consciousness and self-rated consistency as different criteria of behavioural variability, they discovered little overlap or 'convergent validity' between the classifications resulting from each of the two measures. This means that many of the subjects in the high self-consciousness group had at the same time been classified as highly variable on the basis of their self-ratings. Similar findings are reported by Snyder and Ickes (1985) with respect to the relationship between self-monitoring and self-consciousness. This lack of congruence again points to the problem that little is known at present about how different moderator variables are interrelated and impinge on the link between traits and behaviour. It also casts doubts on the search for global moderators affecting the trait–behaviour relationship in diverse trait domains as opposed to moderators linked specifically with the trait in question, as in the concept of 'metatraits' discussed above.

The issue is complicated further by the fact that certain features of the situation may also function as moderator variables and affect the relationship between traits and behaviour (Snyder and Ickes, 1985: 904f.). In so-called 'strong' situations, such as situations in which the individual's behavioural choice is heavily constrained by norms and rules, systematic links between traits and behaviour are less likely to show up than in 'weak' situations containing less stringent behavioural prescriptions (see Chapter 2 for a similar point with respect to the 'strength' of experimental manipulations). Monson et al. (1982), for instance, found that individual differences on the trait dimension of introversion–extroversion were significantly better predictors of corresponding behavioural differences when situational pressures to show either introverted or extroverted behaviours were weak. Further evidence along these lines is reviewed by Ajzen (1988).

Altogether, the studies discussed in this section present a mixed picture of the moderator variable approach as a strategy for improving the prediction of behavioural consistency. Some success has undoubtedly been achieved in distinguishing subgroups of people, traits, and situations characterized by generally high levels of consistency (see Chaplin (1991) for a recent review). Yet, as Ajzen (1988: 90) has pointed out, the inevitable consequence of this strategy is that it also yields subgroups with low levels of consistency and, hence, poor predictability. In theory, the number and range of those subgroups could be narrowed by specifying an ever larger set of moderator variables. In practice, however, this makes the task of explaining why certain groups of people, traits, or situations are characterized by low levels of consistency even more pressing.

Furthermore, we are still a long way from understanding how different moderator variables on the person and the situation side interact with each other in their effects on the trait–behaviour relationship. In particular, it appears that the straightforward approach of employing a person's self-rating of consistency as a moderator variable is not only of limited success empirically but also fails to *explain* why some people are more consistent than others in certain trait domains. Thus, individual differences in consistency have to be observed and interpreted in relation to other psychological variables in order to furnish more precise conclusions on when and for whom consistency between personal qualities and overt behaviour is to be expected.

Aggregation and act trends: beyond single-act criteria

As the previous section has shown, the primary objective of the moderator variable strategy is to specify the conditions under which consistency over time and across situation can be expected. In effect, this means that the search for consistency should be limited to certain groups of persons, traits, and situations, defined on the basis of moderator variables serving to distinguish between high and low levels of consistency.

Another approach towards achieving progress in the search for consistency lies in the *aggregation* of behaviour across different occasions. Advocates of this approach argue that a major reason for previous failures to obtain evidence for consistency in individual behaviour lies in the lack of reliability of the behavioural measures employed. In the past, measures of personal dispositions were typically studied in relation to behavioural measures sampled on just one or, at best, very few occasions. Therefore, the resulting behavioural evidence was heavily fraught with problems of measurement error (see also Jaccard, 1979).

These problems can be remedied to a considerable extent by aggregating behavioural measures over multiple occasions and situations, thereby replacing traditional 'single act' criteria by more reliable 'multiple act' criteria. For example, to decide whether or not a person is consistently dominant, one would record the frequency and/or intensity of his or her dominant behaviours on a variety of occasions. The resulting average level of dominant behaviour would then be related to the person's score on a trait measure of dominance.

The most prominent and persistent advocate of the principle of aggregation is certainly Epstein (1979, 1980, 1983b, 1984). Epstein regards the sampling of behaviour on multiple occasions as an essential condition for predicting behaviour as well as detecting temporal and cross-situational consistency. His basic argument is as follows. As traits are defined in terms of broad response dispositions, they cannot be expected to predict single instances of behaviour. All they can do is predict average response tendencies observed over a sufficient range of time and situations (Epstein, 1984). His position is that single instances of behaviour are largely specific to the given situation, yet consistent, trait-related patterns may be discovered when behaviour is observed over multiple occasions.

Similarly, Rushton et al. (1983) attribute the lack of systematic relations between latent internal variables (cognitions, traits) and behaviour to the failure of most studies to include a sufficient number of measurements on the side of predictors and/or criteria variables. They quote evidence on different issues of personality development, such as the link between moral judgement and altruistic behaviour, which suggests the aggregation of data as a necessary strategy for reducing measurement error and increasing the reliability of the collected data (see also Rushton and Erdle, 1987).

The central propositions involved in the principle of aggregation are summarized in the following way by Epstein:

1 Stability can be demonstrated over a wide range of variables so long as the behavior in question is averaged over a sufficient number of occurrences.
2 Reliable relationships can be demonstrated between ratings by others and self-ratings, including standard personality inventories on the one hand and objective behavior on the other so long as the objective behavior is sampled over an appropriate level of generaliza-

tion and averaged over a sufficient number of occurrences. (1979: 1105)

The strategy of aggregation can be applied to different aspects or units of analysis over which data are averaged. Epstein (1980) distinguishes four types of aggregation.

Aggregation over subjects: This familiar principle involves the sampling of larger numbers of subjects for which empirical hypotheses are tested. Here, the aim is to counterbalance the influences of individual uniqueness on the obtained data by drawing random samples from the relevant subject populations (such as the population of adult females, the population of extroverts, etc.).

Aggregation over stimuli or stimulus situations: This strategy is aimed at reducing measurement error due to the specific features of single stimuli or experimental settings. In order to evaluate the replicability and generalizability of empirical findings, it is essential to check them across a range of different operationalizations. While this principle is generally observed in the construction of psychological tests where every theoretical construct is represented by multiple items (Paunonen, 1984), it is widely ignored in experimental research. Here, most of the findings rely on just one type of experimental manipulation (such as making subjects succeed or fail on an anagram task), taken as sufficiently representative of the theoretical construct in question (such as the experience of success and failure). This makes the findings of any single experiment highly vulnerable to error, resulting from factors such as the specific type of equipment used or the extent to which a cover story is transparent for the subjects. Thus, to cancel out such unique effects due to the nature of the studied stimuli, data should be aggregated across a sufficient range of stimuli and experimental situations (see, however, Monson et al. (1982) for a critical appraisal of this type of aggregation).

Aggregation over time: Here, the emphasis is not on collecting evidence from a diverse range of operationalizations but on repeating the same measures at different points in time. Running an experiment in several trials or sessions and subsequently averaging the obtained data would be an example of this strategy. The effect is to reduce error due to influences peculiar to a single data point, such as a noisy room or the experimenter's exceptionally bad mood.

Aggregation over modes of measurement: This last application of the strategy of aggregation aims at reducing method variance by cancelling out the unique effects of specific measurement devices. As Brody (1988: 23) points out, 'all available procedures for the measurement of personality are inadequate.' Therefore, aggregating personality measures across different methods so as to create a 'heteromethod measure' can serve to counteract the measurement error inherent in each single method. An example of this strategy would be to employ different instruments designed to measure extroversion and determine their convergent validity, that is, the extent to which they lead to similar extroversion scores for any one individual. By basing inferences about personality and behaviour on information derived from multiple measures of the same construct, method variance is reduced relative to 'true' variance that is psychologically informative about individual differences.

The theoretical arguments in favour of aggregation are substantiated by Epstein (1979) in a series of empirical studies pertaining to the third form of aggregation described above: aggregation over time. He employs a procedure analogous to traditional methods of establishing the reliability of a test. Every single behavioural act is treated as a single 'item' of a 'behaviour test'. In this way, it becomes posssible to determine the stability of behavioural data, for example, by correlating the data collected on odd days with those collected on even days (the familiar odd–even method for determining split-half reliability). According to the principle of aggregation, correlations between 'odd' and 'even' behavioural events are expected to increase in proportion to the number of days over which observations are aggregated.

Epstein (1979) presents four studies demonstrating that aggregation over multiple days does, indeed, lead to higher levels of behavioural stability in each of four different domains and data types. In Study 1, the stability of emotional experience was assessed over one month on the basis of subjects' self-reports. For a sample of six pleasant emotions (such as happy, calm), the average correlation between Day 1 and Day 2 was $r = 0.36$. When the correlation was computed for responses aggregated over the odd and even days of the one-month period, the coefficient rose to $r = 0.88$. Parallel findings were obtained in the second study. Here, subjects' behaviour pertaining to the domains of impulsivity and sociability was recorded by one of his or her peers over a period of fourteen days. Again, the observations revealed increasingly stable patterns of behaviour as a function of the number of days over which observations were aggregated. In Study 3, various responses from heart rate to borrowing a pencil from the tutor were recorded over twelve days as objective behavioural measures, substantiating the notion that higher levels of stability typically emerge from longer periods of observation. Finally, in the fourth study a wide range of self-reported and objective behavioural measures were aggregated over 14 days and subsequently related to subjects' profiles on a number of standard personality inventories. These data reveal that properly aggregated samples of behaviour correlate substantially with standard personality measures, supporting Epstein's claim that aggregation is a viable strategy for discovering consistency.

Considered in combination, the four studies reveal two additional important points. First, when only few data points are considered, there are marked differences between various behavioural measures in the extent to which correlations vary in magnitude. In Study 1, for example, measures of self-punishment recorded on Day 1 and Day 2 correlated $r = -0.04$, while two instances of subjects' tendencies to discharge tension correlated $r = 0.81$. When the data were aggregated, these differences disappeared and the resulting correlations presented a much more homogeneous picture in the range of $r = 0.70$ to $r = 0.90$.

Secondly, in Study 1, additional within-subjects correlations, that is, reliability indices established for each subject individually, were computed in addition to the averaged scores. These revealed significant individual differences. For example, in the category of pleasant emotions referred to above, a score of $r = 0.13$ was obtained for the least reliable subject in the sample, while the most reliable subject scored $r = 0.95$. This substantial range highlights the fact that aggregation is undoubtedly an essential requirement for discovering stable patterns of behaviour but is no guarantee for their emergence. Despite adequate measures, some individuals may simply not be stable in their behavioural profiles over time. This is not to say that they must necessarily be regarded as inconsistent in the traditional sense. Their behaviour may follow a changing, but systematic pattern, just as the concept of 'coherence' (see Chapter 2) would suggest. Thus, it must be said that aggregation *across subjects* is, in a sense, counterproductive to discovering consistency and variability in individual behaviour. However, to discover consistency in personality and social behaviour *at the level of the individual person*, aggregation over time, situations, and modes of measurement clearly represents an improvement over conventional single-act measures of behaviour.

Epstein has been concerned primarily with demonstrating the advantages of aggregating a single behavioural criterion over multiple occasions, operationalizations, or points in time. Other authors have shown that aggregating observations across *different* criteria (each observed on a limited number of occasions) also leads to improved behavioural predictions on the basis of latent dispositions. Gifford (1982), for instance, presented evidence that multiple-act criteria of 'affiliative behaviour' actually correlated higher with a trait measure of affiliativeness than multiple observations of just one criterion (repeated-measures single-act criterion). In the same vein, Moskowitz (1982) observed children's behaviour in the domains of dominance and dependency. Over an eight-week period, records were obtained of the frequency of five behavioural referents (for example, command, seek help) for each of the two constructs. The results were as follows: first, temporal stability of each behavioural referent increased substantially when aggregated over the total eight weeks as compared with just one week of observation; and secondly, behavioural referents were predicted more accurately by the aggregated scores of the remaining four referents than by each of the remaining referents individually. However, this latter finding, demonstrating the value of aggregated predictors as well as criteria, was limited to the domain of dominance. Dependency showed little coherence, even when aggregated scores were employed. Differences in predictability as a function of trait domain also emerged in a recent laboratory study by Moskowitz (1988) where predictions of single behaviours on the basis of aggregated predictors were found to be more successful in the domain of friendliness than in the domain of dominance.

Inconclusive findings such as these are responsible for the intense debate concerning the benefits and limitations of aggregation. This debate was first triggered by Mischel and Peake (1982a) and has produced a series of exchanges (Bem, 1983b; Conley, 1984b; Epstein, 1983a; Funder, 1983b; Mischel and Peake, 1982b, 1983b; Paunonen and Jackson, 1985; Peake and Mischel, 1984), the details of which will not be reiterated here. Essentially, the argument advanced by Mischel and Peake (1982a) was that while aggregation does increase the temporal stability of behavioural patterns, it does not increase their cross-situational generality in any comparable measure. Even worse, they argued, aggregation across situations has the effect of obliterating the discriminativeness of behaviour towards specific situations (see Campbell et al. (1987) for a similar point). To support this assertion, they present evidence from their Carleton Behavior Study, a longitudinal study observing students' behaviour in the domains of conscientiousness and friendliness. In this study, the sampling of conscientious and friendly behaviours led to a significant increase in stability (aggregation over occasions), but not in consistency (aggregation over referents). This led the authors to conclude that the value of aggregation, while undisputed as far as stability is concerned, does not extend to cross-situational consistency.

Reanalyses of the Mischel and Peake data by Conley (1984b) and Paunonen and Jackson (1985) produced substantially higher levels of consistency than those obtained by the original authors. They suggest that when appropriate procedures are applied, aggregation produces evidence for higher temporal stability as well as cross-situational consistency. Furthermore, Diener and Larsen (1984) conducted a study including a wide range of affective, cognitive, and behavioural responses and showed that stability and consistency strongly co-varied across responses. Those responses that were most stable over time were also most consistent across situations, although levels of stability generally tended to be somewhat higher than levels of consistency. Thus, as the debate stands at the moment, it appears that stability and consistency are more closely related than originally suggested by Mischel and Peake and that aggregation can, in fact, be used to improve empirical evidence for both notions (see also Brody, 1988: 17).

However, a different kind of criticisms has been levelled at the aggregation strategy by Monson et al. (1982). They argue that the reason why trait measures typically predict multiple-act criteria better than single-act criteria is that multiple-act criteria have a higher probability of including at least one predictable setting. In support of this assertion they demonstrate that if a set of behavioural criteria contains at least one criterion with good predictability, then an increase in the number of additional criteria does not lead to an increase in trait–behaviour correlations. Consequently, they argue, more efforts should be made to identify the conditions under which (single-act) behaviours may be accurately predicted rather than relying on the principle of aggregation as the strategy of choice for resolving the issue of consistency.

An alternative response to the Monson et al. (1982) criticism is to address explicitly the issue of the typicality of a given behavioural criterion with respect to the corresponding trait dimension. In their *act frequency approach*, Buss and Craik (1980, 1983a, b, c, 1984, 1986, 1989) have presented a research programme that deals constructively with this issue.

In line with the summary view of traits (see Chapter 2), Buss and Craik argue that the frequency with which an individual displays acts associated with a particular trait domain over a specified period of time provides the basis for applying the respective trait term to the person. Thus, to claim that someone is a hostile person is tantamount to saying that over a certain period of time the person has engaged in a number of hostile behaviours. In this sense, 'dispositional assertions are summary statements about behavior up to the present' (Buss and Craik, 1984: 244). Such summary statements capture regularities in individual behaviour and, moreover, facilitate actuarial predictions in the sense of projecting observed behavioural patterns into the future. If a person has shown a large number of hostile acts in the past, it is reasonable to infer from this observation an increased likelihood that he or she will continue to show hostile acts in the future.

In the act frequency model, acts are treated as basic units of analysis representing a particular trait domain. Trait domains, in turn, are regarded as 'natural cognitive categories', a concept adopted from social cognition research (see, for example, Rosch, 1975; Cantor and Mischel, 1979b). These trait categories are 'fuzzy sets' in that different category members, such as, behavioural acts, show varying degrees of typicality with respect to the category. Some acts may belong to more than one trait category, while others are indicative of only one trait (see also Borkenau, 1986). Thus, a trait category is composed of a set of single behavioural acts, some of which are better (highly typical) and others poorer (less typical) category members. To determine empirically how typical a given behavioural act is for the category in question, consensus among independent raters is generally used as a criterion. In their *internal structure*, categories differ in terms of the number of behavioural acts they contain as well as the range of typicality covered by the individual acts. As far as the *relationship between different categories* is concerned, the more two trait categories are regarded as being similar, or close to each other, the higher the proportion of behavioural acts that are common to both of them. In a similar reasoning, Broughton (1984) applied the prototype idea to the construction of personality scales.

By providing an absolute metric for establishing the strength of an act trend, the act frequency approach lends itself to three different modes of analysis. First, it may be applied to the study of 'modal human tendencies' where different groups of people are compared in terms of the absolute frequency with which they display trait-referent acts. In this way, it becomes feasible to answer questions such as: 'Is the act trend for introverted acts typically higher for Englishmen than it is for Italians?' Secondly, within groups of people, act trends provide information about individual differences in that they allow a person's act trend, as well as its stability over time, to be determined relative to that of other members of the sample. Thirdly, in an idiographic mode of analysis, the absolute frequencies of an individual's trait-referent behaviours at different times or in different situations can be interpreted as an idiographic index of temporal or cross-situational stability without having to resort to sample-based information about relative act frequencies (see Buss, 1985).

In the empirical study of act frequencies for a dispositional category, the first step consists in collecting a sufficient number of behavioural acts representing a category. This is usually achieved by an 'act nomination strategy' asking a sample of subjects to think of the most dominant, hostile, etc. persons they know and to list a specified number of acts observed in these people which express their dominance or hostility. To ensure that the acts sampled in this way are indeed representative of the respective category, individual acts are usually judged by independent raters in terms of their prototypicality for the category. These act nominations are then used as a basis for monitoring the behaviour of individuals over a set period of time to arrive at overall frequency tallies or 'act trends'. The task of determining individual act trends as well as base rates against which they can be judged is facilitated by the fact that frequency tallies of overt behaviours have an absolute zero point, namely when no trait-referent behaviours are shown within the period of observation.

The sequence of empirical steps involved in the application of the act frequency approach is illustrated in a study by Buss and Craik (1980) exploring the category of dominant acts. The aim was to demonstrate that act trends composed of multiple criteria for dominant behaviour can be successfully predicted by traditional trait measures of dominance, provided that the monitored acts represent typical examples of the category of dominant behaviours.

The procedure was as follows. First, a pilot study was conducted to generate a sample of 100 dominant acts through the 'act nominations' strategy briefly described above. In a second pilot study, a large sample of judges ($n = 79$) rated the dominant acts in terms of their prototypicality as well as social desirability. On the basis of these ratings, which displayed a high level of inter-rater agreement, the acts were ranked in terms of both their prototypicality and social desirability.

In the main part of the study, a new sample of subjects received the following instruments: the dominance scales from two standard personality inventories, the California Psychological Inventory (CPI) (Gough, 1957) and the Personality Research Form (PRF) (Jackson, 1967); the total list of 100 dominant acts whereby they were asked to indicate whether or not they had ever performed each of the behaviours, and, if so, how frequently they had performed it in the past; and a global self-rating scale of dominance. In order to explore the link between the trait measures of dominance and the corresponding act trends, correlations were first computed for each of the 100 acts between the reported act performance as well as frequency and the three traditional trait measures (CPI, PRF and global rating of dominance). These correlations were in the range of

$r = 0.10$ and $r = 0.20$, suggesting that trait measures of dominance are poor predictors of single dominant acts. In a subsequent analysis, the prototypicality ratings elicited in the second pilot study were used to divide the total set of dominant acts into four categories of typicality, whereby the first and last categories comprised the twenty-five most and least typical acts, respectively. Thus, each category provided a multiple-act criterion of dominant behaviour, with two categories containing highly typical and nontypical acts, respectively, and the two remaining categories containing acts of medium levels of typicality. By correlating the three traditional trait measures of dominance with the multiple-act trend for each category, the following results were obtained. Both the CPI and the PRF scores were significantly correlated with the multiple-act criterion yielded by the category of most typical acts, with correlations ranging from $r = 0.31$ to $r = 0.67$. A linear decrease in the magnitude of correlation coefficients was found as act categories became less typical. The global self-ratings of dominance generally turned out to be poorer predictors of dominant act trends across the four categories.

In conjunction with later studies exploring different personality domains (for example, Buss, 1984; Angleitner et al., 1990), these findings underline two central points. The first is that multiple-act trends can be more accurately explained by standard personality measures than single acts, a conclusion that is well in line with other recent research (see above). The second one is more peculiar to the act frequency approach, namely that the typicality of the acts chosen to represent the trait category determines the success of behavioural predictions. However, as Block (1989) points out in his critical analysis of the act frequency approach, the fact that most available studies have used retrospective act reports by the subjects rather than act trends recorded in ongoing situations and/or by independent observers must be seen as a limitation to be addressed by future research. It should also be noted that support for the act frequency approach was found to vary as a function of the specific trait domain under investigation (for example, Angleitner and Demtröder, 1988), but the reasons for such differences are yet to be explained.

An appealing feature associated with the use of multiple acts as trait referents is that the ascription of a trait to a person does not require the person to show one particular act frequently but only that a high frequency should be recorded across the full range of acts within the category. Thus, it would be conceptually equivalent, as far as the establishment of act trends is concerned, for an individual to report one particular dominant act repeatedly or to report a variety of dominant acts with lower frequencies for each. At the same time, the prototypicality ratings available for each behavioural criterion allow the investigator to identify both good and poor behavioural referents of a trait in question.

As far as the issue of consistency is concerned, the frequency tallies only speak to the issue of the temporal stability of act trends, but are mute with regard to the issue of cross-situational consistency. As Buss and Craik (1983a) acknowledge, neither the nature of the situations eliciting acts from a particular category nor the impact of behavioural constraints are explicitly taken into account in the original formulation of the act frequency approach. Subsequently, Buss (1985) presented an extension of the act frequency approach from 'dispositional act trends' to 'environmental act trends' as one way of addressing the impact of situations on trait-relevant behaviour. 'Environmental act trends' are defined as multiple indices comprising those behaviours to which the individual is exposed in his or her interactions with other people over a specified period of time. The frequency with which an individual is exposed to dominant acts from one or more of his or her interaction partners in a situation would be an example of an environmental act trend. In that sense, environmental act trends are direct counterparts of dispositional act trends, whereby the former represent situational and, in particular, interpersonal influences on the individual and the latter represent the individual's behaviour in relation to these influences. Thus, person–environment congruence can be determined by the extent to which the act trends of the person correspond to the environmental act trends representing the behaviour of his or her interaction partners. Buss (1985) quotes his earlier work (Buss, 1984), which examined the congruence of the behavioural profiles of married partners as tentative evidence for the validity of this approach. It remains to be seen, however, whether equally promising results will be obtained for other types of social interaction, including those involving more than one partner at the same time.

The act frequency approach can be regarded as a special case of applying the principle of aggregation to the aim of improving the ascription of traits to individuals. By using multiple acts and establishing the typicality of each act with respect to the trait category under consideration, they offer a refined procedure for describing the strength of trait-relevant behavioural manifestations under the summary view of traits. This purely descriptive use of the trait concept (in the sense of persons being more typically characterized by trait term X, the more X-referent acts they report to have shown in the past) involves stripping traits of any significance as explanatory constructs. Buss and Craik (1983a) intend to do just this, arguing that *demonstration* and *explanation* constitute two distinct tasks for personality research, and that the scope of the act frequency approach is explicitly limited to the first of the two tasks. Block (1989: 244), however, interprets this self-restriction as a position that 'ignores the explanatory endeavour of scientific personality psychology' (see also Moser, 1989).

Altogether, the work reviewed in this section clearly shows that aggregation of behavioural data across time, situations, and multiple acts is a viable strategy for improving the detection of trait-behaviour consistency and stability. In addition to the modes of aggregation discussed above, Epstein (1983b) referred to a further application of the aggregation principle: *aggregation over judges*. This idea, which involves ratings by multiple raters of a subject's behaviour, is more commonly known under the names of 'peer-ratings' or 'ratings by knowledgeable informants'. A number of authors have explored and demonstrated the utility of this strategy in personality measurement over the last years. Their work will be presented in the next section.

The peer-rating strategy: beyond self-reports

Critical voices on the use of self-reports as measures of individual behaviour have been cited repeatedly, last in connection with the reliance of Buss and Craik on retrospective self-reports of act frequencies. The criticism is directed first and foremost at the inaccuracy as well as unreliability of a person's own account of his or her behaviour (Pryor, 1980). Various sources of both deliberate and unintended biases in self-reports have been pointed out, such as memory distortions, the desire for positive self-presentation (Baumeister, 1982), and an overemphasis on the situational determinants of one's own behaviour (Watson, 1982).

To overcome these problems, two strategies suggest themselves. The first is to abandon the use of self-reports in favour of other sources of behavioural information, such as experimental responses, that are claimed to be more reliable and would be the strategy of choice for advocates of a situationist explanation of individual behaviour. An alternative response consists in complementing the use of self-reports by other data sources, such as direct observation and ratings by informed others and assessing the convergence of self-reports with those other measures. This latter strategy is at the focus of the present section. We will review a body of research analysing the extent to which ratings of somebody's personality and behaviour by informed others (friends, spouses, etc.) correspond with the person's self-reports as well as objective behavioural evidence gained mostly in laboratory settings.

A sample of fifty earlier studies on the relationship between self-perception and perception by others was summarized by Shrauger and Schoeneman (1979). In evaluating these studies, conducted between the late 1950s and early 1970s, they identified various conceptual and empirical shortcomings and concluded that approximately half the studies reviewed failed to show significant correlations between self-perceptions and others' actual evaluations. The majority of the remaining investigations yielded either significant but low correlations or ambiguous results (Shrauger and Schoeneman, 1979: 552).

However, subsequent studies on the convergence of self-reports with peer-ratings and observational data offer a more optimistic picture (Funder, 1989). The standard procedure employed by most of them involves the collection of parallel sets of behaviour ratings by self and others along with observations of overt behaviour. The number of informed raters varies considerably among studies. Some use only one or two raters, usually roommates (for example, Funder, 1980; Paunonen, 1984) or spouses (for example, Costa and McCrae, 1988a; Edwards and Klockars, 1981; McCrae, 1982; McCrae and Costa, 1982), while others obtain ratings from up to thirty informants (for example, Emmons, 1989a; Gormly, 1984). In each case, the persons participating as raters are 'significant others', well acquainted with the person they are asked to rate. Recently, however, Borkenau and Liebler (in press) reported that even in the case of no previous acquaintance between a rater and a target substantial levels of agreement are reached, provided the rater has some information (through videos, photographs, or sound recordings) of the target's behaviour (however, see Colvin and Funder (1991) and Paunonen (1991) for some limiting conditions).

Comparing self- and peer-ratings, most of these studies have found substantial correspondence between the two data sources. For a sample of married couples, Edwards and Klockars (1981) demonstrated that self-evaluations and mutual evaluations by both partners revealed significant agreements across a broad sample of personality characteristics. McCrae (1982) also obtained correlations of $r = 0.40$ to $r = 0.60$ between evaluations by self and partner for married couples on the trait dimensions of extroversion, neuroticism and openness. Correlations of similar magnitude were obtained for pairs of college roommates by Funder (1980), Gormly (1984) and Paunonen (1984).

However, differences in the level of self–peer agreement emerged in the McCrae study, depending on the observability of the trait in question. The more visibly a trait is manifested in overt behaviour – as, for instance, extroversion – the higher the agreement between self- and peer-reports of trait-relevant behaviour. This relationship, also found in other studies (for example, Cheek, 1982; Kenrick and Stringfield, 1980; Woodruffe, 1984), suggests that observability of traits should be taken into account as a moderator variable of the correspondence between self- and peer-ratings. However, Paunonen (1989) presents data showing that observability affects the agreement of self- and peer-ratings only under low and moderate levels of acquaintance between the person and the peer. Among well-acquainted pairs, high observability of a trait does not seem to be an essential prerequisite for self–peer agreement on ratings of the trait in question (see also Watson and Clark, 1991). In the same vein, Moskowitz (1990) demonstrated consistently high convergence between self- and other-ratings of subjects' dominance and friendliness when the other-ratings were provided by a friend as compared to ratings provided by previously unacquainted judges.

Cheek (1982) points out that peer-ratings can only be used as sources of information about personality and behaviour if they are ascertained to be sufficiently reliable. He carried out a study in which peer-ratings on four personality dimensions were aggregated across items as well as raters and subsequently correlated with the respective self-ratings. In this way, it was possible to determine the gradual increase in self–other agreement as a function of increasing the number of raters as well as items. As expected, it was found that with the number of raters and items rising from one to three, self–peer correlations also showed a linear increase.

However, the maximum number of three raters used by Cheek is certainly too low to fully appreciate the potential of the peer-rating strategy. Larger samples of raters are required to speak to the issue of the convergent validity of observer-ratings and self-reports. In an occupational context, Latham and Saari (1984) asked employees to describe their (hypothetical) responses to a number of critical incidents they might encounter at work. At the same time, four supervisors and between three and five peers were asked to give their description of the employee's response to the incident. Significant correlations were found between self-reports and both peer- and supervisor-ratings.

Broadening the range of informed raters still further, Woodruffe (1985) succeeded in obtaining peer-ratings from ten different persons for each of his sixty-six subjects. Each rater evaluated the person in question on the same personality scales (fourteen factors of Cattell's 16-PF) on which self-evaluations had previously been obtained. An average correlation of $r = 0.56$ was found between peer-ratings and self-evaluations across the fourteen personality dimensions. Closer inspection of the individual scales suggested, again, that the observability of the characteristic in question is a crucial factor in determining the level of agreement between self- and peer-ratings. High correlations between self-ratings and peers were typically found for the more publicly observable dimensions (such as 'reserved–outgoing' and 'likes to be in a group–happy to be alone'), while for less obvious personality characteristics (such as 'conservative–experimenting' and 'artless–shrewd') greater discrepancies were found between self- and peer-ratings. However, the level of acquaintance between subjects and their peer-raters was not systematically considered in this study.

The preceding discussion has shown that there is a substantial correspondence between self-reports and peer-ratings of individual behaviour, provided that a sufficiently large number of knowledgeable informants is employed. Two conclusions are suggested by this evidence. The first is that self-reports appear to be less prone to idiosyncratic biases than has been widely assumed in the personality literature, at least inasmuch as they do show substantial convergence with ratings by informed others. The second is that reliance on peers and other informed raters appears to be a valid method for tapping individual behaviour, either with the aim of checking the accuracy of self-reports or to substitute them in domains which are particularly susceptible to social desirability biases.

However, the question remains of how peer-ratings are related to other behavioural information, typically obtained through observation and recording of overt behaviour. A study that speaks directly to this issue was conducted by Moskowitz and Schwartz (1982). These authors investigated dominant and dependent behaviour in pre-school children across a time span of eight weeks, using frequency counts of various behavioural criteria as well as evaluations by teachers. They found that the convergent validity between behaviour counts and teacher evaluations increased significantly as a function of number of teachers and length of observation period. This result contradicts the notion that ratings by knowledgeable informants are generally inferior to objective behavioural information because of their susceptibility to systematic distortions. Indeed, Moskowitz (1986) sees a distinctive advantage of relying on informed raters in the fact that their evaluations are based on numerous and heterogeneous behavioural samples of the person they are asked to rate. Thus, raters are in a position to base their judgements on multiple observations of behaviour relevant to a particular personality dimension. On the other hand, it is this very feature of peer-ratings which makes them less suitable for examining situationally specific responses or interactions between personal and situational characteristics. In this case, a rater's previous knowledge of a person's behaviour could easily become a distorting influence on his or her behavioural ratings in a new situation.

Altogether, studies exploring the use of peer-ratings as a source of information in personality measurement complement the findings on the effect of aggregation across situations and data points. They suggest that personality ratings by raters who are familiar with the person under study can constitute valid sources of information on an individual's personality. The evidence clearly suggests that it is feasible to draw upon a substantial number of judges to provide independent evidence that shows good convergence not only with the ratings of other judges but also with the individual's self-reports on the respective personality variables. In terms of practical applicability, an essential prerequisite for the success of the peer-rating strategy is the selection of suitable raters. Specific samples of informed raters have to be selected for each individual, which makes the peer-rating strategy rather time-consuming and cost-intensive. This point is illustrated by Woodruffe's (1985) study where ten raters were employed for each subject. As a result, 660 raters were needed to participate in the study on top of the sixty-six original subjects. On the other hand, the increasing number of studies using the peer-rating strategy with good results is a clear demonstration that peer-ratings provide a feasible, ecologically valid source of information in personality measurement.

Summary

Starting from a brief review of the nomothetic–idiographic controversy in personality measurement, the present chapter introduced three approaches developed within the nomothetic mainstream aiming to yield more conclusive empirical evidence of consistency.

The first strategy consists of the search for *moderator variables* which are supposed to influence the relationship between trait measures and behaviour. Initiated by the well-known study of Bem and Allen (1974), this line of research is guided by the aim to identify subgroups of persons, situations and traits that are characterized by typically high or low levels of behavioural consistency. Furthermore, other authors have recently begun to examine the role of certain cognitive principles, such as the cognitive accessibility of attitudes and self-descriptive contents as moderators of consistency. Thus, the identification of moderator variables serves an essential purpose in the attempt to overcome the shortcomings of traditional omnibus models of behaviour prediction by delineating specific types of individuals, traits and situations for which cross-situational consistencies may be expected (Ajzen, 1987).

A second nomothetic approach for providing more convincing evidence of consistency is based on the *principle of aggregation*. Proponents of this approach, most notably Epstein, stress that the task of predicting behaviour on the basis of dispositional constructs can only be successful if multiple indices of behaviour are considered, that is, if trait measures are related not to single instances of behaviour but to aggregated samples of behavioural criteria across time or different situations. Evidence of cross-situational consistencies between trait measures and aggregated behavioural patterns was found in a number of recent studies. These findings suggest that while single instances of behaviour may be determined to a large extent by the specific features of the situation, stable behavioural patterns can be shown to exist as a function of personality dispositions if behavioural acts are aggregated across a representative number of situations and occasions (see also Brody, 1988). Moreover, the act frequency approach introduced by Buss and Craik offers a procedure for establishing multiple-act trends as manifestations of a given trait, whereby the prototypicality of each act with respect to the trait dimension in question is treated as a central issue.

Finally, a third strategy aimed to improve the methodological prerequisites for demonstrating consistency relies on *peer-ratings* as a source of information about a person's behavioural performance in different situations. The peer-rating strategy is also committed to the principle of aggregation, but the focus is on increasing the sample of raters rather than the sample of behavioural criteria. Relying on informed raters, that is, people who are familiar with the persons under study and their characteristic ways of acting in various sections of their social environments, enables the investigators to go beyond self-report data and also to check their validity by comparing them to the data obtained from knowledgeable informants. In this way, evidence of consistency has been obtained by relating subjects' self-reports to information collected from spouses or roommates.

The three approaches presented in this chapter have explored different avenues for discovering and measuring the stability and consistency of personal qualities. Peer-rating, aggregation, and the moderator variable strategy share in common the basic feature of searching for nomothetic, or general principles of personality functioning that would hold, in much the same way, for large numbers of people or groups of people. Inevitably, the search for general explanations can only be successful at the expense of disregarding any information peculiar to the individual member of the sample. Indeed, it requires that all those features of personality and behaviour that are idiosyncratic to an individual be treated as measurement error. According to the predominant view of personality psychology as 'differential psychology', the focus is on investigating *differences between individuals* rather than the individual per se. Thus, none of the three strategies facilitates a better understanding of the stability and consistency *of individual behaviour* and of the exact nature of the interaction between the individual and the situation. In contrast, the work examined in the next chapter is committed to an idiographic perspective on the study of personality, guided by the aim to explore and explain as comprehensively as possible the personality and behaviour of the individual person.

Notes

1 The terminological problem surrounding the two concepts becomes apparent in statements like the following: 'we have retained the use of the term idiographic to describe analyses that might better be described as nomothetic analyses of selected subgroups based on moderator criterion splits, or more simply [sic!], individualized nomothetic analyses.' (Kenrick and Braver, 1982: note 1; see also Mischel and Peake, 1983a: note 6).

2 For details of their analysis, in particular their 'ipsatized variance index', see Bem and Allen (1974) and see also Tellegen (1988) for a critical analysis.

7

Personality Psychology is about Individuals: Rediscovering the Idiographic Legacy

The introduction to the previous chapter briefly reviewed the definition and history of the nomothetic and idiographic research traditions in personality psychology. What was said then, and needs to be reiterated at the outset of the present chapter, is that the development of a distinctly idiographic research tradition has never had a high priority for personality psychologists. From Allport (1937) up to the present day, nomothetically oriented approaches have clearly dominated the field, both in terms of quantity and impact. Therefore, the present review of progress achieved in the idiographic study of personality is bound to be somewhat fragmented and preliminary. One reason for the imbalance between idiographic and nomothetic research efforts to the disadvantage of the former lies in the fact that a number of influential representatives of the nomothetic mainstream have repeatedly raised doubts about the relevance and even scientific acceptability of an idiographic approach to the study of personality (see for example, Eysenck, 1954; Holt, 1962; Paunonen and Jackson, 1985). Jaccard and Dittus poignantly describe the crux of this challenge and argue against it:

> Strictly idiographic approaches frequently are characterized as antithetical to the identification and development of universal laws that govern human behavior. This assertion is untrue. The idiographic researcher is interested in explaining the behavior of a given individual and, to do so, seeks a general theoretical framework that specifies the constructs that he or she should focus upon and the types of relationships expected among these concepts. This search for guiding framework is no different from that of the scientist who adopts nomothetic perspectives. The major difference is that the idiographic theorist desires to apply the framework to a single person in order to understand the factors guiding that person's behavior. (1990: 315)

Jaccard and Dittus's defence of an idiographic orientation to the study of personality marks the end of a decade during which the long-standing disregard for the study of individual uniqueness has slowly begun to falter. Pervin (1984c: 268f.) has noted a resurgence of interest in the study of individuals as opposed to individual differences, which he regards as a 'healthy development for personality psychology'. A diverse collection of papers devoted to *The Individual Subject and Scientific Psychology* (Valsiner, 1986a) bears witness to this trend. Its stated aim is to counteract the 'gradual disappearance over the past decades of the treatment of individual subjects as viable sources of scientific generalizations in our discipline' (Valsiner, 1986a: vii). The same zeitgeist is also reflected in a survey by Rosenberg and Gara who asked Fellows of the 'Society of Personality and Social Psychology' (APA, Division 8) to comment on past and present interest patterns in both fields. They conclude:

> Within such forecasts of theoretical and substantive integration, there are still perhaps matters of emphasis that certain Fellows saw as necessary to redress past neglects. In this regard, the view expressed most frequently is that the field needs to place an increased (renewed?) emphasis on idiography. (Rosenberg and Gara, 1983: 70)

Yet at the same time, this renewed emphasis has also mobilized once again the opponents of idiographic research, and the old controversy between the two positions has been rekindled.

One factor responsible for the issue being as contentious as it has been long-lived is the terminological confusion that surrounds the term 'idiographic'. In part, this confusion stems from the failure to observe the crucial distinction between the level of theoretical concepts and the level of methodological strategies. Depending on whether idiographic is used in a theoretical or a methodological argument, different meanings have been associated with the term (Pervin, 1984a):

1   In a methodological context, idiographic denotes such strategies of data collection and analysis which aim at gaining complex information about single individuals. Examples of genuinely idiographic research methods are case studies, content analyses of qualitative data and more specific data collection methods, such as the Q-Sort Technique (Butler and Haigh, 1954; Ozer and Gjerde, 1989) and the Repertory Grid Test (Kelly, 1955; Krahé, 1990).

2   With respect to the problem of predicting behaviour, idiographic means to focus on those sources of information which facilitate reliable predictions about the behaviour of individual persons.

3   At a more general theoretical level, the term idiographic is associated with a view of personality which emphasizes the uniqueness of the individual person and is directed at the holistic measurement and description of single individuals (Runyan, 1983).

These characteristics illustrate that the idiographic approach to personality is rooted in a fundamentally different understanding of the aims and goals of scientific research than other empirical disciplines, most notably the natural sciences. Generally speaking, the idiographic approach is concerned with the individual person as the central unit of analysis. More specifically, this concern embraces several related issues, as Runyan (1983: 405) points out:

1 The study of individualized traits or dispositions.
2 The identification of central themes within an individual's biography.
3 The analysis of the (ipsative) ordering of responses within the individual.
4 The discovery of patterns of variables within the single case.
5 The examination of correlations of variables within the single case.
6 The selection of particular traits on which to assess individuals.
7 The exploration of causal relationships between variables within the single case.
8 Descriptive generalizations about the single case.
9 The analysis of the particular subjective meaning of events and circumstances to the individual.
10 Idiographic predictions based on trends or patterns in the data of a single case.

None of these objectives can be reached conclusively on the basis of a traditionally nomothetic orientation in which information about the individual person is inevitably qualified by the data obtained for other members of the sample. Thus, Runyan concludes:

> There is, in short, an important place within psychology for both *idiographic goals* – of generalizing about, describing, explaining, predicting, and intentionally changing the behavior of particular individuals, and *idiographic methods* – or research methods capable of contributing to the attainment of each of these goals. (Runyan, 1983: 419)

Strategies for capturing individual uniqueness

To illustrate possible avenues for translating this plea into specific research strategies, three examples will be discussed in more detail in the present section. The first is Harris's (1980, 1984) strategy of *idiovalidation* aimed at discovering individual personality profiles. His approach is based essentially on the same logic as Allport's method of *matching* (Allport, 1961: 387). In a sense, it can be regarded as an 'individualized' version of the principle of *aggregation over modes of measurement* (see Chapter 6) advocated by

Epstein. In the context of an idiographic approach, the question to be resolved is stated as follows:

> Is it possible to infer from different methods of measurement a true underlying personality profile for an individual that is both stable over time and stable in different daily life situations? (Harris, 1980: 734).

The general idea is that 'true' personality profiles can never be established unambiguously. They can only be approximated through appropriate measurement. Appropriate measurement, according to Harris, involves the combination of personality scores related to any one trait (or, more generally, construct) into a composite score, that is, aggregating information across different measures of the same construct. Consequently, the resulting *composite profile* is defined as 'the summation for each personality construct of the scores or ratings obtained by separate methods of measurement, each adjusted to a common metric (Harris, 1984: 588). Three types of measure have been particularly prominent in traditional personality research and thus suggest themselves as building blocks for the idiovalidation strategy. These are personality inventories, observer-ratings and self-reports.

Harris (1980) presents a study which illustrates the type of conclusions furnished by such a combined data set. Four groups of undergraduates who had been previously acquainted for different lengths of time (between five hours and eight months) participated in the study. Data were collected at two data points with intervals ranging between three and nine months for the four groups, and subjects had close daily contacts in between. On each measurement occasion, they were asked to do the following:

1   To complete the 'Personality Research Form' (PRF) (Jackson, 1967).
2   To rate every other group member on the variables measured by the PRF so as to provide a 'mean rating by others' score for each participant.
3   To rate themselves on the PRF variables as they typically perceived themselves.
4   To rate themselves once more on the PRF variables from a specific perspective, namely as they perceived themselves in their familiar home environment.

The obtained data were first analysed individually for each subject and then combined into an average score for the twenty-nine members of the sample. The focus of the analyses was on the following issues:

The temporal stability of each of the four measures: Correlations between scores obtained at the two data points were fairly high, ranging from $r = 0.50$ to $r = 0.85$ when averaged across members of the different groups.[1] More significant, however, is the range of individual correlations obtained for each of the four measures. These reflect huge individual differences which are psychologically very informative from an idiographic point of view but would have been averaged out in a nomothetic analysis.

The temporal stability of the composite profile: As predicted by the idiovalidation approach, aggregating individual methods into composite scores results in an increase in the obtained stability scores. More importantly, however, combining information from multiple methods into a composite score substantially reduces the range of individual coefficients, with the lowest individual score being $r = 0.24$. Thus, a more homogeneous pattern of findings emerges from the composite scores.

The correspondence between pairs of methods: These analyses are based on the familiar validation strategy of correlating measures which are assumed to tap the same construct. The correlations between all possible combinations of single methods were examined for each subject individually and subsequently averaged into a median score for the entire sample. The scores thus yielded by the idiovalidation strategy range from $r = 0.36$ to $r = 0.56$. As Harris (1980: 737) concludes, they are of a magnitude that 'one might hope to achieve in the more successful conventional validity studies involving diverse methods of measurement of a single personality attribute.'

The relative contribution of each measure to the composite profile: Arguing that composite personality profiles are superior to single measurements requires evidence that each individual measure contributes significantly to the composite profile. Otherwise, it could be argued that increasing the number of measures simply enhances the likelihood of including at least one valid method. Each of the methods used by Harris showed substantial correlations with the composite profile, a finding which lends convincing support to the rationale of the idiovalidation strategy.

In conclusion, Harris (1980, 1984) presents a strategy for identifying reliable (that is, stable) and valid personality profiles for the individual person. By adapting a procedure commonly accepted in nomothetic research, namely the 'multimethod technique', to the aims of idiographic inquiry, he illustrates a feasible way of utilizing information about individual persons in its own right, unconfounded with information pertaining to other members of a sample.

A second example of an empirical strategy for exploring individual uniqueness is provided by Pervin (1976). The focus of his study is on examining the interaction of the person with his or her specific environment, relying on in-depth information from four subjects. As he describes it: 'The effort is to understand personality as the individual's pattern of stability and change in relation to defined situational properties' (Pervin, 1976: 466). His four participants first provided a list of situations they typically encountered in their current lives. Subsequently, they were asked to describe each situation in terms of: its characteristic properties or 'situation traits'; the feelings typically elicited from the person; and the behaviour typically shown in the situation. Finally, quantitative ratings were obtained indicating the extent to which each situation trait, feeling and behaviour applied to each situation. In this way, four sets of data were obtained for each of the four participants: situations, situation traits, feelings, and behaviours. They were subjected to a series of factor analyses, including an analysis based on all four data sets. The information resulting from this latter analysis will be briefly illustrated for one subject, called Jennifer (see Pervin, 1976: 467). The life space of Jennifer at the time of the study is represented by four major factors: home, accounting for 35 per cent of the variance, school and work (18 per cent), friends, alone (6 per cent) and uncertain (5 per cent). On the 'home factor', *situations* such as 'being honest with parents about leaving' or 'someone else coming home upset' have high factor loadings, as have the *situation traits* 'emotional' and 'volatile', the *feelings* 'angry' and 'involved' and the *behaviours* 'caring' and 'confused'. In contrast, the 'home–family' factor obtained for another subject, Harry, includes only positive, pleasurable situations as well as attributes, while a separate factor, 'tension', combines such situations as 'arguing with my wife' with feelings of frustration and anxiety. Altogether, a comparison of the four subjects reveals considerable differences in the number, content and interrelationships of factors, situations and descriptive attributes, highlighting the necessity to look into individual experiences in order to understand individual personalities.

A final example of the scope of an idiographic analysis of personality is provided by McAdams's (1988, 1989) work on *life narratives*. Adopting Murray's (1938: 39) dictum that 'the history of the organism *is* the organism', McAdams argues that personality can and should be defined in terms of the person's construction of the history of his or her life. As he describes the main tenet of his approach: '*Identity is a life story* – an internalized narrative integration of past, present, and anticipated future which provides lives with a sense of unity and purpose' (McAdams, 1989: 161). It is clear from this definition that the psychological understanding of life stories requires an in-depth analysis of individuals' autobiographical accounts of their lives. However, this does neither preclude nor replace the search for general structural principles that form the theoretical frame of reference for the identification of specific narratives. To arrive at such a theoretical framework, McAdams integrates ideas and concepts from the work of three key figures in psychology: Murray's (1938) theory of motivation, Piaget's (1952) work on cognitive development, and Erikson's (1963) theory of identity formation.

The construction of identity as a life story is seen as beginning in early adolescence when the individual has reached, in Piaget's terms, the cognitive developmental stage of 'formal operational thought' needed for a coherent life story embracing the person's past as well as future. Nevertheless, the precursors of the emerging life story reach back as far as the first year of life. In line with Erikson's theory of psychosocial development, the dominant aspect of the child's first year of life is the development of an emotional bond between the infant and the caregiver. The nature of this bond determines the *tone* of the individual's subsequent life story in the sense of a global optimistic versus pessimistic outlook on life. Against this general affective quality of a child's early experiences, the next facets of the life story to develop, in the stage of pre-operational thought, are *images* conceptualized as ingredients of fantasy-based stories which become 'the raw stuff, later transformed and refined, of narratives of the self' (McAdams, 1989: 164). In the subsequent stage of concrete thoughts, these images are placed into a narrative context of temporal and causal sequences referring to different *themes* or goals pursued by the individual.

Tone, image, and theme can thus be regarded as building blocks for the development of the life story. This begins in early adolescence with the formation of a coherent 'ideology' reflecting the individual's efforts to define a valid system of values for him- or herself. In this system of values, two dimensions are considered of central importance: *agency*, referring to themes of power, control and mastery; and *communion*, referring to intimacy, cooperation and love. Once a personal ideology has been tentatively established, first versions or 'drafts' of the identity story are worked out as the person attempts to delineate the *setting* and the *scenes* of his or her life course. The subsequent years of early and middle adulthood are seen as being devoted largely to the refinement and elaboration of this first identity draft, whereby identity is differentiated into a number of *imagoes*, that is, idealized and personified images of the self. The last stage in the development of the life story, beginning in middle adulthood, is devoted to the construction of a *generativity script* outlining what the person hopes to do to leave a legacy of the self for the next generation. Thus, the generativity script is very much oriented towards the future, extending the perspective of the life story beyond the individual's own lifetime (McAdams et al., 1986).

This model of the emergence of a life story containing the gist of an individual's personality provides a kind of 'grid' for discovering the meaning and structure of particular life stories. Two methods for eliciting autobiographical life stories have been employed by McAdams (1988). One method asks persons to keep an 'identity journal' over an extended period of time. The journal is prestructured along the defining aspects and central questions identified in the theoretical framework outlined above, including questions about the person's earliest memories, critical life experiences, moral beliefs, and hopes and dreams for the future. In the second method, these questions or prompts are submitted in individual interviews. Detailed coding systems are subsequently applied to the data for identifying the tone, imagoes and central themes, such as power and intimacy, in individual life stories. McAdams (1988) presents a wide range of examples from this rich case material. These examples illustrate that the analysis of narrative identities is directed at the holistic understanding of individual personalities as they are reflected in people's constructions of their lives.

Throughout the preceding discussion, we have referred repeatedly to the criticisms raised against the idiographic approach by proponents of a strictly nomothetic perspective in personality research. Now it is time to review their arguments in more detail. In addition to warnings against an overemphasis on the idiosyncratic organization of personality (Kenrick and Dantchik, 1983), the following major criticisms have been levelled against the idiographic approach in the course of its history (see Runyan (1983) and Pervin (1984a) for a more detailed analysis):

Results from idiographic studies have no potential for generalizability: This criticism, raised for instance by Bandura (1986: 11), is based on a misunderstanding concerning the level at which generalizability is sought. It is certainly fair to say that idiographic studies provide no immediate clues for generalizing to other individuals. However, they do offer the potential for generalizing to other attributes or behaviours characteristic of the individual thus studied. For example, conducting an idiographic study about Person A's level of aggressive behaviour towards her or his subordinates does not furnish generalizations to the corresponding levels typically characteristic of Persons B or C. Yet, it does form the basis, in principle, for deriving generalizing inferences about Person A's behaviour in other domains and/or situations, such as dominance towards his or her spouse. Thus, idiographic research is aimed at generalizing within the individual, whereas nomothetic research seeks to generalize across individuals. There is no inherent conflict between these aims, and they can both be accommodated within the boundaries of personality research (Jaccard and Dittus, 1990: 317). Triandis et al. (1984) demonstrated the feasibility of comparing idiographically obtained data, reflecting the person's subjective model of social behaviour, across different individuals. They conclude that 'studies combining idiographic analyses with foci that reflect sociocultural variables will eventually lead to a more fruitful personality/social psychology' (Triandis et al., 1984: 1401). Epstein also highlights the complementary rather than mutually exclusive nature of idiographic and nomothetic research strategies:

> Nomothetic procedures are important for investigating individual differences and differences in performance among groups of subjects, but provide no information on processes within individuals. Idiographic approaches, on the other hand, provide information about processes within individuals, but provide no information on individual differences or on the generality of findings across individuals. Thus, each procedure has its advantages and limitations, and neither is a substitute for the other. (Epstein, 1983b: 379)

As far as the issue of interindividual generalizations is concerned, Thorngate (1986) has presented a persuasive argument against the claim that idiographic research strategies fail to provide information about general principles of psychological functioning. He points out that the study of averages (for example, behavioural decisions aggregated across judges) is often ill-suited to provide information about what people do 'in general', as it typically cancels out systematic patterns in individual persons. Rather than searching for nomothetic laws on the basis of averaged data, their discovery requires a strategy in which individual uniqueness is preserved: 'To find out what people do in general, we must first discover what each person does in particular, then determine what, if anything, these particulars have in common' (Thorngate, 1986: 75). In the same way, Rosenzweig (1986: 241) claims that 'it is quintessential to regard the individual person as an idioverse – a universe of events – through which both general scientific principles and statistical generalizations find implicit expression' (see also Lerner and Tubman (1989: 366) for a similar argument).

There are no unique traits that would apply to only one individual: Taken literally, this criticism is undoubtedly true, as traits are by definition differential constructs referring to the person's standing on a trait dimension relative to that of other people. At the other extreme, the traditional position of invoking traits as explanatory constructs which are applicable to everyone has been shown to be equally misguided. Indeed, it was the very assumption of the general applicability of trait terms as well as its poor empirical support which gave rise, for instance, to the moderator variable strategy discussed in the previous chapter. It must be said that the trait concept has proven problematic for personality psychology independent of the idiographic–nomothetic controversy (see Chapter 2). Its significance becomes even more questionable in the context of idiographic research.

The study of individual cases is useful for generating hypotheses, but not for testing them: In response to this criticism, we can refer to the two examples by Harris and Pervin discussed above. These authors have shown that it is perfectly possible to employ quantitative methods to the study of individual data, and there is nothing which precludes the application of these methods to the testing of hypotheses within an idiographic frame of analysis. Further examples of how the same statistical procedures can be applied to both idiographic and nomothetic analyses are presented later in this chapter.

It is virtually impossible to conduct an idiographic study of every individual: This point cannot possibly be rejected, but what are its implications? The implications are serious if one endorses the view that the study of individual persons cannot yield any information that is relevant to a more general understanding of psychological principles. If, on the other hand, one joins the increasing number of authors who accept that information derived from idiographic investigations can be combined, in a meaningful way, into conclusions about groups or samples, then the inevitable selectivity of idiographic research efforts ceases to be a genuine problem. It should be noted in passing that the comprehensive study of all potentially relevant groups of individuals represents an equally illusory goal.

There is nothing wrong with the idiographic study of individuals, but it is not science: This argument appears to be based on an implicit, somewhat elusive understanding of science, apparently committed closely to the conception underlying the natural sciences. In the light of this ambiguity, Runyan argues that 'if the thrust or intent of this criticism is that it is impossible to apply systematic, reliable, quantitative, or experimental methods to the study of individual cases, this criticism has been refuted by the proliferation of quantitative and experimental studies of the single case' (Runyan, 1983: 422).

In the same vein, Harris, like Pervin, has demonstrated that the same methodological tools and principles advanced for nomothetic research can be applied, with slight modifications, to the aims of idiographic research. It is difficult to see why an accepted analytical strategy like factor analysis should suddenly become less 'scientific' only because it is applied to individual rather than group data (for further examples see Jaccard et al., 1988; Schulenberg et al. 1988; Zevon and Tellegen, 1982). In fact, there is a growing number of studies where the data are subjected to both idiographic and nomothetic modes of analysis to facilitate a direct comparison between the two strategies (for example, Chaplin and Buckner, 1988; Dolan and White, 1988; Klirs and Revelle, 1986; Lord, 1982).

The abstract argument for an idiographic approach is appealing, but there are no adequate methods available for its realization: Recent reviewers of the idiographic approach generally agree on the fact that the methodological spectrum available for studying the single case is substantially broader than commonly assumed by those working in the mainstream of personality research. Nevertheless, one cannot fail to note a relative scarcity of procedures designed explicitly to meet the objectives of idiographic research. This is true with respect to both general measurement strategies and specific research instruments. As Ross (1987: 170) points out for one form of personality assessment: 'What is needed are personality tests for use in application that assess the individual as individual and not in comparison to some more or less relevant group. Of such tests there are all too few.'

There is no progress to be achieved through the idiographic approach which goes beyond the potential of nomothetic inquiry: This final criticism is raised by Paunonen and Jackson (1985, 1986a, b), who are among the most rigorous current critics of the idiographic approach and, indeed, its reconciliation with the nomothetic approach proposed recently. After reviewing various proposals for idiographic strategies, including the work of Bem and Allen (1974) as well as Kenrick and Stringfield (1980) mentioned in the previous chapter, Paunonen and Jackson conclude: 'Whereas many limitations thought to be inherent to nomothetic measurement can be surmounted by adherence to modern assessment standards, the promise of idiographic measurement for the study of personality has yet to be realized' (1985: 509). Essentially, their argument is that nomothetic measures provide explanations and predictions of behaviour which are just as good and often show strong agreement with corresponding idiographic indices. The reason why they should be preferred, according to these authors, lies in the fact that nomothetic research strategies are more generally applicable and allow wider generalizations than idiographic analyses.

However, this argument suffers from two problems. First, it is based on the assumption that nomothetic and idiographic approaches are by their very nature in opposition to each other. This view bars the way to a constructive combination of both perspectives (see also Pervin, 1984a). Secondly, it is based on comparisons between the two strategies which rely on identical types of data and differ only with respect to the statistical analyses to which these data are subjected. However, it is an essential requirement for idiographic research that the information entered into the analysis is valid for the individual subject. For example, administering a standard personality questionnaire in a typical nomothetic study assumes that its items tap contents that are equally meaningful to all respondents. Otherwise, interindividual comparisons would be precluded. But this assumption is questionable from an idiographic point of view arguing that research instruments must refer to contents (traits, behaviours, etc.) that are subjectively meaningful for the individual person. Thus, a comparative evaluation of idiographic and nomothetic research strategies can only lead to valid conclusions if both sets of methods are appropriate translations of their respective methodological rationales. As far as the issue of cross-situational consistency is concerned, a nomothetic analysis would typically examine subjects' behaviour across a range of situations preselected by the investigator and identical for all subjects. In contrast, an idiographic analysis of the same problem requires the relevance of the situations across which consistency is sought to be established individually for each participant. As Bem (1983a) and Lamiell (1981) emphasize, it is only by observing this basic rationale of the idiographic approach that its full potential for understanding and explaining the behavioural patterns of individual persons can be realized. Referring to the contentious issue of generalizing from the findings obtained through idiographic analysis, Lamiell points out: 'There is no logical a priori reason to reject a paradigm for the scientific study of personality in which generality is sought with reference to the *process* of personality development but in which comparability in the *substance* of individuals' personalities is neither presumed nor precluded' (1981: 285). Similarly, Pervin (1984a: 279) pleads for a revision of the traditional antagonism between the nomothetic and the idiographic approach: 'The utility of the idiographic approach lies not in contradistinction to the nomothetic approach, but in its compatibility with it, and not in contradistinction to science, but in its commitment to it.'

Thus, there seems to be growing consensus that it is possible, in principle, for idiographic and nomothetic approaches to join forces so as to contribute to a more comprehensive analysis of the issues of personality psychology (see also Brody, 1988: 121; Laux and Weber, 1987; Silverstein, 1988; Thomae, 1987). In the next sections, different approaches will be reviewed which are committed to this view and offer research strategies combining both nomothetic and idiographic objectives in personality research. The next section begins by looking at Lamiell's *idiothetic approach* which is one of the most radical departures from the traditional individual difference paradigm dominating the study of personality.

The idiothetic approach to consistency

As the label suggests, Lamiell's (1981, 1982, 1987) 'idiothetic' approach is designed to offer a perspective on personality measurement in which the aims of *idio*-graphic and nomo-*thetic* inquiry are integrally combined. His line of thinking can be regarded as one of the most prominent, albeit deliberately controversial, contributions recently made to the field of personality. At the outset of his most comprehensive account of the idiothetic model so far, Lamiell warns his readers that 'much of what I have to say is wholly antithetical to what are, at least to those who answer to the appellation of "personality psychologist", deeply entrenched beliefs' (1987: xvi; see also Ross, 1987). The present discussion will be limited to the general rationale and procedure of the idiothetic model in the context of personality psychology. For more information on details of measurement and empirical results, the interested reader is referred to Lamiell (1987). It should also be noted that the name and overall objective of the idiothetic approach have recently been introduced into applied social psychology by Jaccard and his co-workers who have developed an idiothetic perspective on the study of behavioural decision making and consumer choice (Jaccard and Wood, 1986; Jaccard et al., 1988).

To highlight the epistemological foundations of his approach, Lamiell goes back to the fundamental distinction between *differential psychology* aimed at exploring individual difference with respect to specific personality constructs (that is, traits), and *personality psychology*, which concentrates on investigating issues of personality structure and development at the level of the individual. In his view, the failure to observe this distinction is responsible for the profound crisis in which the field of personality has found itself over much of its recent history. In particular, he argues that the perennial issue of consistency in individual behaviour, while phrased essentially as a problem of personality psychology, has traditionally been approached through the methods of the individual difference paradigm. 'Knowledge of the sort contained in the empirical findings generated by individual difference research is therefore ill-suited to the task of advancing a theory of personality, however useful the same knowledge may be for other purposes' (Lamiell, 1986: 4).

To underscore this claim, Lamiell (1982: 8f.) uses the example of the correlation coefficient to illustrate that group statistics do not furnish conclusions about individuals except in the rare case of perfect association. For any correlation of less than $r = \pm 1$, the only permissible interpretation is that the members of the sample differ in the extent to which the variables in question are associated. This interpretation, however, is of limited relevance to the researcher who wants to explore the relationship between two or more variables. In stressing this point, Lamiell is in full agreement with Epstein, who is equally critical of the use of correlations as idiographic indices: 'Too often, the highly questionable assumption is made that correlations derived from nomothetic studies of groups of individuals are applicable to processes within individuals' (Epstein, 1980: 803). Valsiner (1986b) presents additional evidence that psychologists, like laypersons, show a strong tendency towards inappropriately translating group-based correlational findings into statements about the psychological functioning of an individual person. Even the most ardent critics of idiographic research, and the idiothetic model in particular, such as Paunonen and Jackson (1986b: 473) have to concede that probabilistic inferences about individuals based on normative data are at best justified if the individuals belong to different samples showing different levels of consistency.

On the basis of this critique, Lamiell's main argument is directed at highlighting the need for an alternative paradigm to investigate temporal as well as cross-situational regularities in individual behaviour. Such a paradigm should combine idiographic methods of analysis with the development of general principles of personality: 'The key to any such reconciliation lies in the fact that there is nothing in the search for general principles of personality which logically requires that the status of an individual on a given attribute be defined relative to the measured status of others on the same attribute' (Lamiell, 1981: 285).

By rejecting individual rank orders as a source of information about single members of a sample, a primary task for the idiothetic approach consists in defining an alternative frame of reference for interpreting any pattern of individual behaviour as a weak, average or strong manifestation of an underlying personality characteristic. This problem is addressed by assigning crucial significance to the total range of behaviours indicative of the respective characteristic that the person could, in principle, have chosen to perform. Thus, individual behaviour is interpreted against the standard of what the person could have done, not against the standard of what other people did in the same situation. To be translated into an empirical research strategy, this rationale requires the following steps.

First, for each domain to be studied, a comprehensive list of possible behavioural options has to be collected. The total number of options contained in this list determines the maximum strength or extremity of the underlying attribute that an individual may display in his or her behaviour. Consider, for example, the domain of friendliness. If it were decided that this domain was comprehensively characterized by a set of twenty different behaviours, each potentially feasible for the person, then he or she could be said to be the more friendly the higher the number of friendly acts performed over a specified period. It should be noted, though, that the maximum score that can possibly be assigned to an individual is defined by the constraints of the sampling procedure. Secondly, not all behaviours sampled in this way will be equally central or pertinent to the domain in question. Therefore, an index of relevance is needed which can be used as a weighting factor for each behavioural item. For instance, all behavioural items could be judged in terms of their similarity and subsequently be subjected to multidimensional scaling. In this way, the coordinates of each behaviour on the underlying dimension(s) could serve to indicate its relevance for the domain.

Thirdly, behavioural reports need to be obtained from the subject for each of the items representing the domain. In their most straightforward form, these reports are operationally defined as 'yes/no' responses to the question of whether the person has shown that behaviour in a certain period of time. In addition, more detailed information could be collected about the frequency with which each activity is performed over a specified period. Fourthly, on the basis of these behaviour reports, the strength of the behavioural performance, and by implication the strength of the underlying attribute, can be expressed as the ratio between the actual number and frequency of behaviours performed and the maximum number and frequency of behaviours the person could possibly have reported on the respective instrument. In this analysis, the relevance weights attached to each behavioural criterion are taken into account on each side of the ratio (for computational details see Lamiell, 1982).

Using this procedure, both cross-situational consistency and temporal stability can be conceptualized and measured directly through comparing the relative strengths of behavioural tendencies shown in two or more situations. As Lamiell, Trierweiler and Foss (1983) showed, such a strategy facilitates the empirical assessment of individual patterns of behaviour which are at the same time informative about the individual person and – through aggregation across persons – about the validity of general hypotheses on consistency and stability in personality.

The relevance of the idiothetic approach to the study of dynamic person–situation interactions is briefly outlined by Lamiell (1982). He claims that idiothetic analysis provides a framework in which both the person and the situation are embraced simultaneously. At a theoretical level, it is the concept of the 'psychological situation' which corresponds most closely to this objective. From the viewpoint of the idiothetic model, 'a *psychological situation* is defined as an *interval of time* (not necessarily a physical location) during which certain concepts dominate the perception and construal of one's alternative possibilities for action' (Lamiell, 1982: 56). This perspective suggests that personality variables should be conceived not as stable traits but rather as 'mediating cognitive processes' in the sense postulated by modern interactionism.

In their empirical applications of the idiothetic model, Lamiell and his co-workers have so far concentrated on the question of whether impression formation by naive or 'intuitive' observers actually follows the principles of the idiothetic model. In forming impressions about others, can persons be shown to proceed along the lines of a 'personal qualities' approach as opposed to an 'individual difference' strategy? In answering this question, Lamiell et al. argue that the reasoning strategy proposed by the idiothetic model is *dialectical* in nature. This means that observers contrast their observations of others' behaviour with mental negations of those observations (for example, 'what would the conclusion be if the person had not shown this behaviour?'). In a series of studies, Lamiell and his colleagues (for example, Lamiell, 1982; Lamiell, Foss, Larsen and Hempel, 1983; Lamiell, Foss, Trierweiler and Leffel, 1983) have shown that personality judgements made by naive observers can, in fact, be attributed to their reliance on dialectical reasoning. In contrast, traditional personality research is accused of inappropriately adopting a *demonstrative* reasoning strategy whereby observations of one person are compared with and interpreted in relation to observations of other persons' behaviour. This discrepancy in the reasoning strategies underlying intuitive and scientific models of personality is held responsible for the persistence of the consistency paradox. According to Lamiell et al., therefore, the paradox could be resolved if scientific researchers of personality finally recognized the need to adopt dialectical reasoning as their general methodological rationale.

Not surprisingly, such a provocative attack on the traditional foundations of personality measurement has been quick to elicit critical responses from members of the nomothetic mainstream. These criticisms have concentrated primarily on the empirical procedures and findings in support of the idiothetic model (for example, Conger, 1983; Paunonen and Jackson, 1986a, b; Woody, 1983). Among other points, Paunonen and Jackson (1986a) object that idiothetically defined behavioural tendencies fail to take into account differences in the base rates of behavioural criteria. To illustrate their point, they choose the example of a person scoring 0.50 on an idiothetic measure of aggressive behaviour which suggests that the person has performed about half of the aggressive acts covered by the measure. Assuming that the measure comprises an equal number of verbal and physical acts of aggression, it could be the case that the person has shown all the verbally aggressive acts and none of the physically aggressive acts, or vice versa. Since instances of physical aggression are typically less frequent, that is, have lower base rates, than verbal aggression, at least among adults, a score of 0.50 based on the performance of physical aggression suggests a much higher level of aggressiveness than an identical score based on verbal aggressive acts. Thus, for behavioural categories comprising a wide range of behaviours with different base rates, a person's identical scores in two or more situations do not provide conclusive evidence of high levels of consistency. In defence of the idiothetic model, however, it has to be said that this problem is made somewhat less serious by the inclusion of relevance weights for each behavioural alternative which should reflect, at least to some extent, differences in behavioural base rates.

Another, more general objection is that idiographic indices of consistency and stability are not needed, since corresponding nomothetic indices produce almost identical results while avoiding the problems associated with the former. To substantiate this point, Paunonen and Jackson ran a simulation study showing that the correlation between the two types of indices is $r = 0.94$. However, a recent study by Rogers and Widiger (1989) identifies a number of limitations which question the impact of this simulation as a challenge to the idiothetic assessment of consistency.

In responding to these criticisms, Lamiell and Trierweiler (1986) accept some of the points pertaining to their empirical procedure. Yet, they emphasize that the overall objective of the idiothetic approach is neither properly appreciated by Paunonen and Jackson nor seriously compromised by their criticisms.[2]

In conclusion, the idiothetic approach represents an ambitious programme for a thorough revision of the traditional foundations of (nomothetic) personality measurement. It questions the appropriateness of the individual difference paradigm for contributing in any way to our understanding of individual behaviour as well as its underlying causes. A new frame of reference for defining and assessing the strength of individual behavioural tendencies is introduced, namely the potential minimum and maximum levels of behavioural performance, which does not rely on comparisons between persons. This frame of reference is closely linked with a particular strategy of forming impressions about personality through dialectical reasoning, which is shown to be followed by the intuitive psychologist and is advocated as the strategy of choice for the professional personality psychologist as well. Compared to its innovative force at a conceptual and general methodological level, the empirical procedures that have so far been offered as part of the idiothetic approach seem much less convincing. As the critique by Paunonen and Jackson has illustrated, the present ways of defining and computing indices of stability and consistency suffer from shortcomings which need to be addressed. Thus, as matters stand, the relevance of the idiothetic approach clearly lies in its general rationale whereas the specific empirical procedures are still in need of refinement.

Integrating idiographic and nomothetic measures of personality

As stressed throughout this chapter, the view that idiographic and nomothetic aims not only can but should coexist and cross-fertilize each other is gaining acceptance in personality research. The conviction has grown 'that a combined idiographic–nomothetic approach provides important advantages. One of the most important of these is that it allows relations within individuals to be compared among individuals' (Epstein, 1983b: 380; see also Walschburger, 1986: 339). This section presents different contributions sharing the goal of providing empirical strategies that can be used simultaneously for the purposes of both idiographic and nomothetic inquiry.

When the *act frequency approach* (Buss and Craik, 1984) was discussed in Chapter 6, its potential applicability to the idiographic analysis of consistency was briefly mentioned. To reiterate, this approach is based on the general idea that traits should be defined operationally in terms of their prototypical manifestations in overt behaviour. These acts as well as the frequency with which they occur can be established either as samples from the behavioural repertoire of defined groups (nomothetic application) or as samples from the behavioural repertoire of individual persons (idiographic application).

While the previous chapter illustrated how the act frequency approach may be used in the (nomothetic) study of individual differences, there is no empirical evidence so far showing its applicability to the (idiographic) study of intra-individual regularities. Therefore, rather than presenting an exemplary piece of research, it is necessary to rely on the general strategies outlined by Buss and Craik (1984, 280ff.) for 'individualizing dispositional assessment' by means of the act frequency approach.

The most straightforward application in the service of idiographic inquiry consists of the recording of act trends for individual persons over time as well as situations. In this way, it becomes possible to establish individual base rates against which act trends observed in particular 'critical' situations or periods of time may be assessed.

For example, observing a person's act trend of dominant behaviours across a range of different situations provides a basis for identifying deviations, that is, substantially higher or lower frequencies of dominant acts, in particular classes of situations. Such deviations hold important clues to the understanding of the interaction of dispositions and situations at an individual level. Apart from exploring the strength of an act trend, this strategy illuminates, at a descriptive level, the specific nature of the acts typically characteristic of the person under study. It may thus be discovered, for instance, that two individuals who show the same overall act trend, differ vastly with regard to the specific acts of which this trend is composed.

For a committed idiographer, however, the previous strategy is fraught with the problem that the behaviours on which the act frequency tallies are based are nomothetically determined, that is, selected on the basis of an inter-individual consensus about their meaning as well as typicality. In principle, this problem could be overcome by leaving both act nominations and typicality ratings to the individual under study. The person could thus be asked to sort his or her behavioural performance in a specified period or situation into subjectively appropriate categories as well as rate the different acts for prototypicality according to his or her own, possibly idiosyncratic, definitions. According to Buss and Craik, 'an ultimate step would be to enlist the individual in segmenting his or her monitored stream of behavior . . . as well as generating categories of acts from it' (1984: 282). However, these suggestions are only programmatic at this stage. Whether they will eventually prove fruitful for the idiographic study of act frequencies has yet to be seen.

The template matching approach

Another attempt to develop a methodological approach suitable for both nomothetic and idiographic assessment of personality is the *template matching technique* (Bem, 1983b). According to this approach, the problem of behaviour prediction can be phrased as a problem of matching individual personality profiles measured at any one time against the typical profile or 'template' associated with the situation in question. Again, the frame of reference for establishing these 'templates' can either be provided by relevant others (nomothetic version) or the individual's own profile averaged across different occasions (idiographic version).

The development of the template matching technique by Bem and his co-workers (Bem, 1983b; Bem and Funder, 1978; Bem and Lord, 1979) is to be understood against the background of the authors' commitment to an interactionist view of personality. It reflects their claim that both person and situation variables have to be integrated into a common methodological framework, that is, studied in relation to each other, in order to understand and predict individual behaviour. The aim is to explain behaviour by exploring the match between the characteristics of the person and those of the situation, an aim which is similar in a sense to Buss's (1985) extension of the act frequency approach relating dispositional act trends to environmental act trends (see Chapter 6). Accordingly, the template matching approach envisages a methodological strategy for describing persons which lends itself at the same time to the description of situations, and vice versa. As Bem and Funder put it when they first introduced template matching: 'We believe that the development of such a common descriptive system would be an important step toward a coherent theory of person–situation interaction' (1978: 486).

The general problem addressed by the template matching technique is the following: a given situation typically provides various behavioural alternatives, and the crucial task is to predict which of these alternatives an individual will actually choose to perform. In order to solve this task, a two-step procedure is adopted. First, each behavioural alternative is linked to a *template* containing personality descriptions of the hypothetical ideal person most likely to show that behaviour in the situation. As an example, consider the situation of a road traffic accident in which a person is seriously injured. For a motorist arriving at the scene there are broadly speaking two behavioural options, namely, to withdraw from the situation or to take action. By generating hypothetical personality profiles for both the typical 'withdrawer' and the typical 'action taker' in an emergency situation of this kind, it is possible to grasp the 'personality' of that situation. Secondly, in order to predict the behaviour of individual persons, personality descriptions of these individuals are obtained and compared with each of the different templates. The idea is that a person will show the behaviour associated with the template that corresponds most closely to his or her personality profile. In this example confined to the case of just two templates, an individual whose personality description shows high similarity to the template construed for the typical 'action taker' should be more likely to respond to the situation by taking action than by withdrawing.

For the match between individual personalities and templates to be determined and expressed in quantitative terms in a diverse range of situations, a descriptive instrument is required which can be applied in the same way to hypothetical as well as real persons in relation to a variety of situations. To serve this purpose: the descriptive language itself must not be situation-specific; the instrument must be person-centred rather than variable-centred, that is, provide information about the relative importance of personality characteristics within the person rather than about the relative standing of the person on that characteristic;[3] and the instrument must facilitate direct comparisons between two persons, two templates, or a person and a template.

One well-established instrument in personality research which meets these requirements is the Q-sort technique introduced by Butler and Haigh (1954), and it is this instrument that has been used extensively for the purposes of the template matching approach. Bem and his colleagues have chosen Block's (1961) California Q-sort version which consists of 100 descriptive personality statements. In the standard application of a Q-sort, the subject is asked to sort these statements into nine categories representing the extent to which they are characteristic of his or her real self as well as ideal self. By yielding formally equivalent distributions, such Q-sorts can be used, for instance, to assess the quality as well as magnitude of discrepancies between the person's real and ideal self.

In template matching, the Q-sort technique is used to elicit both the templates and the personality descriptions of the actual subjects. The latter may be obtained either through self-reports or through peer-ratings. To arrive at the templates pertaining to a given situation, three strategies have been explored so far.

The first of these strategies involves constructing templates on the basis of existing data on the relationship between personality and behaviour in the area under investigation. This was illustrated by Bem and Funder (1978) who studied children's behaviour in a situation involving delay of gratification. Apart from recording delay times, Q-sorts for each child were obtained from his or her parents. The templates were constructed by dividing the total sample into long- and short-delaying boys and girls and collapsing the individual Q-sorts across the members of each group (see Bem and Funder (1978: 491) for procedural details). The extent to which each child's individual Q-sort is correlated with the template pertaining to his or her group represents the criterion for evaluating the validity of the template matching strategy.[4]

A second possibility for arriving at the templates characterizing different responses to a situation is to ask observers to provide Q-sorts for the typical person showing the behaviour in question. The feasibility of this strategy was demonstrated by Bem and Lord (1979). They presented five observers with a description of the familiar 'Prisoner's Dilemma Game' and asked them to provide Q-sorts of the typical subject pursuing each of three strategies: maximizing the joint gain of both players; maximizing his or her own absolute gain; and maximizing his or her own relative gain. The resulting three templates were then correlated with the Q-sorts obtained from the roommates of participants in an actual Prisoner's Dilemma Game who had followed one of the different strategies. It was found that the individual Q-sorts correlated significantly higher with the templates pertaining to the strategy actually chosen by the person than with the templates pertaining to the two remaining strategies. Adopting a similar reasoning, Niedenthal et al. (1985) suggested that university students' choices between different housing options can be predicted by the extent to which the person's self-concept matches that of the prototypical resident in the respective option.

A final strategy for defining templates characteristic of a particular situation is to draw upon formal psychological theories. Bem and Funder (1978) provide an example of this strategy applied to forced-compliance situations. They asked a dissonance theorist, a self-perception theorist, and a self-presentation theorist to construct, from their theoretical points of view, templates (Q-sorts) of the hypothetical persons most likely to show attitude change under forced-compliance conditions. These templates were compared with the Q-sorts as well as attitude change scores obtained for participants in a forced-compliance experiment. The extent to which the similarity of individual Q-sorts with the different theory-specific templates is correlated with the actual attitude change scores indicates the success of each theory in predicting behaviour. The results show that dissonance theory did worst and self-presentation did best in this comparison (see Funder (1982) for a conceptual extension of this study).

From what has been said so far, it is clear that the template matching technique facilitates behavioural predictions both at an individual and a group level. Just as it is possible to interpret individual self–template correlations, individual Q-sorts may be aggregated to furnish predictions about defined groups. In a direct comparison of a nomothetic and an idiographic version of the template matching technique, Lord (1982) has demonstrated that predictions of conscientious behaviour in different situations can be made more accurately on the basis of idiographically derived templates than on the basis of templates derived from Q-sorts averaged across the entire sample.

Personality information in the form of Q-sorts is elicited in global, context-free terms and only subsequently related to the situation-specific templates. In contrast, Bem's (1983b) development of an extended version, the 'contextual template matching' technique, is designed to create a direct link between the description of the person and the situation. At the core of this version is a set of descriptive attributes referring to situations (S-set) which is formally equivalent to the attributes of the Q-set. Just as the typical Q-sort consists of describing a person through the attributes of the Q-set, the S-sort consists of describing a situation in terms of the attributes of the S-set. Once the characteristic features of a situation have been established in this way (usually through multiple raters), individual Q-sorts may be obtained *with direct reference* to the situational properties. In a first test, the contextual template matching technique was applied to a reanalysis of the Bem and Funder study of forced-compliance situations (see above). It could be shown that significantly better behavioural predictions were achieved on the basis of a contextual matching of individual characteristics and templates, leading Bem to conclude: 'Contextual template matching, then, implements a stronger version of inter-actionist thinking. It does not simply add together person information and situation information independently, but rather treats the person-in-context as the fundamental unit of analysis' (1983b: 211). Apart from the obviously very time-consuming nature of this strategy, a potentially serious conceptual problem remains. This is that in contextual template matching, a situation is first split up into single features and then 're-synthethized' into a global situation profile after the situation-specific Q-sorts have been obtained. Such a procedure is based on the problematic assumption that there is a simple additive relationship between the characteristic features of a situation and disregards possible interactions between situations. In conclusion, the template matching technique has the advantage of providing a flexible language for describing both the person and the situation which facilitates – as Lord (1982) has demonstrated – behavioural predictions at an intra-individual as well as an inter-individual level of analysis. However, as it presently stands, template matching provides no more than a methodological strategy with no or little theoretical underpinning, and it is this feature that has earned its authors the accusation of 'blunt empiricism' by Mischel and Peake (1982a). Yet, this does not preclude the possibility that the template matching strategy, like the act frequency approach, will eventually be linked to a particular model or theory within the broad spectrum of an interactionist understanding of personality (see Hyland, 1985).

Both the act frequency approach and template matching represent attempts to integrate idiographic and nomothetic research strategies within a unified methodological framework. In addition, a small range of individual studies is available offering direct comparisons of the advantages and drawbacks of idiographic as opposed to nomothetic measures of personality.

Combined idiographic–nomothetic analyses
A strong case for the simultaneous pursuance of idiographic and nomothetic goals is stated by Zevon and Tellegen (1982) who investigated the individual structure of mood ratings over time. They asked subjects to complete daily mood protocols over a period of ninety days and subsequently factor-analysed the protocols individually for each participant to explore the structural organization of mood. These analyses revealed that the two a priori postulated factors, positive and negative mood, were confirmed for the large majority of subjects (see also Larsen, 1987; Watson, 1988). Moreover, the individual factor solutions showed a high degree of congruence with a composite, nomothetic factor solution based on the aggregation of factor loadings across subjects. To illustrate the information gained by an idiographic complement to the nomothetic analysis of mood states, one should take a closer look at those three subjects for whom the expected two-factor solution could not be confirmed. First, it is only due to the idiographic approach adopted by Zevon and Tellegen that these individuals were explicitly identified instead of simply being absorbed into error variance in the group data. Secondly, exploring why the data patterns of these subjects fail to go along with the

majority of respondents may yield a clue to the psychological principles underlying the structure of mood change. In the Zevon and Tellegen study, the authors were prompted by the three 'deviant' subjects to examine whether the members of their sample had shared a semantic consensus on the interpretation of the mood adjectives used in the protocols. In fact, an adjective-sorting task checking whether subjects' categorizations of the mood adjectives corresponded to the a priori classification underlying the mood protocols confirmed that two of the deviants had interpreted the mood adjectives in an idiosyncratic way. Thus, the idiographic analysis of mood protocols not only facilitated the identification of exceptions to the general pattern of a two-factor solution; it also suggested a more thorough analysis of the causes of these exceptions which proved fruitful for interpreting the obtained data as a whole. This study, the authors claim, thus illustrates that 'scientific idiography can be a crucial way station to nomothetic description' (Zevon and Tellegen, 1982: 121).

The benefits of combining idiographic and nomothetic measures of personality variables are further illustrated by Hermans (1988). He introduces the concept of 'valuation' referring to the personal meaning assigned by the individual to the experiences encountered in his or her life. Valuation is an idiographic concept inasmuch as it refers to the unique life situation of the person. In contrast, Hermans argues, affective responses associated with those valuations may be described in a nomothetic fashion since there is a common range of affective states with which people respond to events in their lives. In his 'self-confrontation' technique, subjects are requested to generate a list of valuations from their previous experience and subsequently rate each valuation in terms of a number of affective responses. On the basis of these data, it is possible to carry out idiographic comparisons of the affect profiles pertaining to different valuations named by the person or to the same valuation rated at different data points. At the same time, individual patterns may be assessed against standard patterns (for example, the typical 'winner' or 'loser' experience) to arrive at information about whether a person's valuation system contains experiences that are associated with similar affective profiles as those associated with the standard. Thus, Hermans found, for example, that the majority of subjects had named valuations that were associated with the affective responses characteristic of the winning and the losing pattern, yet the contents of those valuations were essentially idiosyncratic. In conclusion, Hermans points out that 'each valuation can be studied within three frames of reference: other people, the person at the present moment, and the person at a preceding moment in time. These three frames of reference are seen as mutually complementary in the biographical study of the individual' (1988: 807).

Chaplin and Buckner (1988) approached the issue of the relationship between nomothetic and idiographic personality measurement from a different angle. They conducted a series of studies aimed to reveal the standards of comparison invoked by persons when they provide self-ratings of their personal characteristics. Subjects were instructed to rate themselves on a variety of personality attributes, successively adopting three different standards of comparison: a *normative* standard, requiring them to rate themselves compared to other people of their age and sex; an *ipsative* standard, whereby they were asked to rate their standing on a particular attribute relative to their standing on other personality attributes; and finally, an *idiothetic* standard, instructing them to rate their average standing on a given trait relative to the possible minimum and maximum of trait-referent behaviours.

Each of these standards was related to subjects' *implicit* self-ratings on the same attributes, namely, ratings for which no explicit standard was prescribed and which could thus be assumed to reflect subjects' intuitive standards in evaluating their personality characteristics. The analysis revealed, across three independent studies, that there was a small but consistent tendency for ratings based on normative standards to be less similar to implicit self-ratings than ratings based on the ipsative and idiothetic standards. At the same time, the authors report that each of the three standards was most closely related to implicit self-ratings for a certain number of subjects. These findings illustrate that individuals differ in terms of the standards which they employ when asked to make personality ratings of themselves and, possibly, others. Thus, they challenge the (mostly tacit) assumption that laypersons rely on the nomothetic standard underlying traditional psychometrics in their ratings of personality.

Still another possibility of studying personality in an idiographic frame of reference without relinquishing the formal interindividual comparability of the data is illustrated by Lippa and Donaldson (1990). The aim of their study was to examine the correspondence between two different ways of measuring consistency in interpersonal encounters across different situations. The first method involved a computer-guided description of each person's most important interaction partners, the situations in which these interactions typically take place and his or her behaviour typically shown towards each partner. The second operationalization of consistency was based on the subjects' completion of a diary, at hourly intervals over a ten-day period, recording the specific setting, interaction partner(s) and behaviours at each point in time. Indices of consistency were derived individually for each participant from these two data sources. Intra-individual correlations revealed substantial levels of correspondence between the two measures of consistency. Both measures, in turn, were significantly related to an individual difference measure of self-monitoring (Snyder, 1974), indicating higher levels of consistency for low self-monitors than for high self-monitors (see Chapter 6 for the moderating effect of self-monitoring on cross-situational consistency). Thus, Lippa and Donaldson (1990) illustrate another possibility of combining idiographic measurement strategies with traditional nomothetic constructs of personality research.

A more pessimistic note is struck by Asendorpf (1988) about the feasibility of enriching nomothetic procedures by taking idiographic information into account. He studied the relationship between different behavioural indicators of shyness and dispositional ratings of shyness by self and peers. Stable individual differences were found in subjects' typical behavioural manifestations of shyness. Some subjects, for instance, consistently showed gaze aversion when interacting with strangers and persons in authority, while others responded to these situations with pauses in speech. This finding suggested the creation of an index of consistency based on these idiosyncratic response patterns by selecting each person's most typical response as a predictor of the dispositional shyness ratings. Yet, when trait–behaviour consistency was examined by relating behavioural profiles to trait ratings of the subjects' shyness by themselves and observers, no support was found for the empirical superiority of this 'salient response' index over nomothetically defined criteria (either by aggregating across response modes or by selecting the single most valid response for the sample as a whole). Thus, Asendorpf (1988: 165) concludes: 'As convincing as the call for more respect for the individual case may be from a theoretical stance, it is difficult to realize with real behavioural data for real people in real situations.'

Altogether, the research presented in this section illustrates that the integration of idiographic and nomothetic research perspectives is a possible, if not easy, task. Apart from developing new methodological frameworks, specific procedures and analytical tools need to be devised that cannot normally build upon the existing stock of traditional research strategies. However, as the examples quoted above have shown, something is definitely to be gained from this endeavour in terms of creating a closer link between central constructs in personality psychology, such as the concept of consistency, and their appropriate empirical assessment.

Understanding personal life plans

The work presented in the previous sections has concentrated mostly on short-term predictions and explanations of individual behaviour within the framework of idiographic analysis. The need for such a person-centred approach to enhance the predominantly nomothetic analysis of personality becomes even more compelling if one tries to understand an individual's unique biography as it unfolds in the course of development. Building upon the work of seminal figures in personality psychology some fifty years ago (for example, Allport, 1937; Murray, 1938), the study of individual lives has recently been rediscovered as a central task for personality psychologists committed to the personological tradition (for example, Klinger, 1977; Rabin et al., 1990; Runyan, 1982, 1990). The history of the study of individual lives in the social sciences is reviewed in the introductory chapter of Runyan's (1982) important volume *Life Histories and Psychobiography* which also presents a thorough discussion of the theoretical and methodological issues involved in the analysis of individual biographies.

The present section will review several new concepts and units of analysis designed to capture an individual's characteristic way of dealing with the manifold tasks, themes and events of his or her life. A cursory look at these concepts – such as personal projects (Little, 1989), personal strivings (Emmons, 1989b), and life tasks (Cantor and Langston, 1989) – reveals that special emphasis is placed by recent work on two aspects of this process: the *motivational* basis of individual life plans and their *cognitive* organization. In addition, the need to combine the advantages of an idiographic and a nomothetic outlook on personality is stressed throughout the different contributions. This aspect, shared with the work discussed in the earlier parts of this chapter, distinguishes them from other, more radically idiographic approaches, such as *psychobiography*, which focus first and foremost on the life history of single individuals without the aim of inter-individual generalization (see Howe, 1982; Runyan, 1982: ch. 10).

Personal projects
Little's (1983, 1989) work on *personal projects* is well suited to illustrate the feasibility of applying evidence from idiographic analysis to general aims not only in psychological explanation and

intervention but also in social policy decisions. Personal projects are defined as 'extended sets of personally relevant action' (Little, 1987: 230) comprising an individual's plans and activities at varying levels of complexity and temporal extension. Thus, 'calling my mother tonight', 'working harder for the rest of the term' and 'showing greater concern for the needs of others' would all be examples of the overall category of personal projects. Since the formulation and pursuance of personal projects are shaped jointly by the specialized competencies and orientations of the individual and the requirements and resources of his or her environment, the analysis of personal projects is proffered as 'an inherently interactional perspective on personality' (Little, 1989: 16).

For the empirical analysis of personal projects, Little (1983) has developed a four-step procedure. The initial step consists of obtaining an idiographic sample of a participant's projects through a 'Personal Project Elicitation List'. The free-response format of this instrument allows persons to list as many and diverse projects as they consider relevant for portraying a full picture of their current concerns and activities. Alternatively, the range of projects to be elicited can be restricted a priori to certain domains of interest or problem areas, such as family relationships or achievement-related contexts. These data in themselves provide a basis for idiographic descriptions of an individual's current goals and aspirations as well as for nomothetic taxonomies of salient projects in different populations or life domains.

Going beyond this content-oriented classification of personal projects, the second stage of analysis requires respondents to describe their projects on a set of standard rating dimensions (such as enjoyment, visibility for others, difficulty). The dimensions are selected so as to represent five theoretical factors considered central to the understanding of the psychological significance of a project for the person. These five factors refer to the *meaning* of a project (whether it is seen as worthwhile or worthless), its *structure* (whether it is well organized or blurred), *community* (whether or not the project is visible to and accepted by others), *stress* (whether or not the person's skills are sufficient to cope with the project satisfactorily), and, finally, *efficacy* (whether the project is progressing well or running into difficulty jeopardizing its successful completion). The resulting 'Project Rating Matrix' provides a comprehensive description of each project as well as facilitating comparisons across projects in terms of the different dimensions.

To assess the hierarchical organization of a person's project system, two complementary procedures, called left and right laddering, are applied to the Project Rating Matrix as a third step. For each project, subjects are required to indicate, on the left of the project description, *why* they pursue this project and, on the right, *how* they are trying to accomplish it. These why- and how-questions are then laddered by further questions until a terminal point is reached.

While the first three steps are concerned with single projects as units of analysis, the final step addresses the relationship between different projects in a person's system as well as between the project systems of different individuals. Different projects can be in harmony or in conflict, both at an intra-individual and an inter-individual level. To assess these relationships, a 'Cross-Impact Matrix' is used, asking respondents to rate the impact of each project on all remaining projects in their system. In contrast, the 'Joint Cross-Impact Matrix' requires relevant others to rate the impact of the person's projects on their own project system. Both strategies lead to inferences about the degree of cohesion or conflict characteristic of a particular project system.

The tension, or harmony, within a person's project system can be regarded as a major determinant of the successful handling of his or her projects. Not surprisingly, the perceived efficacy in pursuing one's projects, defined by the two components of 'progress' and 'outcome', has emerged as a central aspect of psychological well-being. Little (1989: 25) presents evidence that high life satisfaction is systematically related to the ease and efficacy with which the person pursues his or her personal projects, while dissatisfaction with life and depressive affect are associated with project difficulty and lack of efficacy. To remedy such negative effects, an intervention programme has been developed in which the person and the counsellor use the five central factors of project analysis (meaning, structure, community, stress, and efficacy) to identify and tackle sources of inadequate project handling. At the same time, environmental changes facilitating successful project completion may be initiated on the basis of a consensual compilation of projects and problem areas. Little (1989) reports the development of a data bank containing information on the predominant projects of a total community as well as special groups within the community. Such a data bank can serve as a starting point for policy decisions aimed at promoting the successful pursuance of those projects.

In sum, Little's work outlines a continuous path from the purely idiographic sampling of personal projects over the assessment of interindividual conflict in the handling of projects to the relevance of personal project information at the community or societal level. He offers a methodological strategy that may enable personality psychologists to develop a better understanding of 'the serious business of how people muddle through complex lives' (Little, 1989: 15).

Life tasks

According to Cantor and Kihlstrom (1987), success in 'muddling through' the changing demands and opportunities encountered in the course of one's life is determined to a large extent by the person's *social intelligence.* The concept of social intelligence captures an individual's knowledge repertoire of the concepts and rules that allow him or her to respond adequately to socially defined expectations and life tasks. Through their social intelligence, individuals are able to interpret situations and plan their behaviour in a way that translates a common problem, such as becoming a parent, into a personalized task with idiosyncratic solutions (Cantor and Kihlstrom, 1987: 1; see also Cantor, 1990).

By placing their analysis of *life tasks* into the theoretical context of goal-directed thought and action, Cantor and her colleagues emphasize the motivational aspects underlying an individual's efforts to shape his or her life in a characteristic way. Cantor and Langston (1989: 130) define life tasks as 'those tasks that individuals find highly salient and attention consuming and that are seen as organizing daily life activity around self-goals'. This broad definition embraces a diverse range of tasks varying, both from one person to another and from one period in an individual's life to the next, in terms of their *scope, persistence,* and *source* (that is, whether they are self-initiated versus externally encouraged). While life tasks represent continuous challenges to the individual, their psychological significance becomes most obvious at points of transition in a person's life which alter the relative importance and salience of different tasks. There are both similarities and differences between the concept of life tasks and Little's work on personal projects. The two approaches are similar, for example, in that they both use a person's idiographically defined sample of current life projects as starting points for their analyses. One important difference, however, is that personal project analysis, in its current form, is concerned mainly with the meaning, that is, the cognitive representation of an individual's project. In contrast, Cantor and colleagues focus on the *process* of handling life tasks, namely, the chain of problem-solving strategies involving the entire sequence of 'appraisal, planning, retrospection and effort' (Cantor and Langston, 1989: 131).

This process-oriented perspective calls for longitudinal research following a person's handling of life tasks through the different phases of strategic action. In what can be regarded as a paradigmatic example of the study of life tasks, Cantor et al. (1987) examined the spectrum of life tasks facing young people in their transition from home to college life. Spanning a period of over two years, this study looks at students' characteristic ways of approaching the tasks of college life from their first to their senior year. To begin with, all participants in their study were asked to provide a list of their current life tasks and then code each task into one of six consensually defined categories. Three of these categories referred to achievement tasks ('getting good grades', 'setting goals', and 'managing time'), while the other three referred to interpersonal tasks ('being on one's own away from family', 'developing an identity', and 'making friends'). It turned out that a high percentage of idiographically defined tasks could be assigned, by the persons themselves, into this set of predefined categories. Yet, similar tasks were grouped into different categories by different people, underlining the significance of relying on idiosyncratic perceptions of life tasks as a first step. This finding was confirmed in a later stage of the study when subjects were asked to code on-line protocols of their daily experiences into the six categories.

Parallel to the analysis of the nature and meaning of life tasks, characteristic strategies of approaching these tasks were studied. Cantor et al. argue that it is possible to distinguish different 'strategy packages' referring to a person's distinct patterns of approaching, carrying out and evaluating his or her solving of life tasks. Two strategy packages in particular have been studied so far. The first is termed *defensive pessimism* (Norem, 1989) and refers to the strategic anticipation of the worst possible outcome of a task, the setting of low expectations, and the extensive preparation for the demands of the task, all despite a previous history of successful performance. This set of cognitive strategies has been shown to be used by individuals feeling habitually anxious and out of control as a means of keeping their anxiety at bay and thus preventing it from exerting a debilitating effect on their task performance. Its counterpart, referred to as *'illusory glow' optimism*, involves the anticipation of positive outcomes and the setting of realistically high outcomes based on previous successful performance. It is important to note that both strategies are adaptive in that they enable their respective followers to achieve positive outcomes against the background of their specific personality characteristics. Thus, while optimists and pessimists do not differ in terms of their overall success in handling life tasks, they do show substantial differences in personality background and strategic action. For example, the magnitude of a person's discrepancy between actual self and ideal self is negatively related to academic performance among optimists, while it shows a positive relationship with performance for defensive pessimists. While the perceived personal insufficiency reflected in self-concept discrepancies thus seems to be a debilitating factor for optimistic persons, it appears to have a performance-enhancing, motivating effect on defensive pessimists. In a similar vein, strategic differences in the handling of life tasks have recently been studied with regard to the social domain under the heading of *social constraint versus other-directedness* (Cantor and Langston, 1989: 141ff.).

Altogether, the analysis of life tasks offers a perspective on personality development that stresses the person's flexible response to the recurrent and changing demands in his or her life. 'Social intelligence' provides the overarching concept for understanding these efforts to select, from the diversity of socially defined life tasks, those to be transformed into self-defined goals that are then pursued in the way best suited to and reflective of an individual's characteristic dispositions, styles and strategies.

Personal strivings

As Cantor and Zirkel (1990) point out, the study of life tasks focuses on the person's dynamic and flexible approach to the changing nature and quality of tasks encountered in the course of development. Emmons (1989b) argues that this feature limits the usefulness of life tasks, and also personal projects, as units of analysis for the study of personality designed to uncover stability over time and consistency across situations. In contrast, his analysis of *personal strivings* is directed at capturing relatively stable and enduring motives which impose meaning and order on seemingly diverse patterns of individual behaviour (Emmons, 1989a, 1991; Emmons and King, 1989). Personal strivings are defined as 'idiographically coherent patterns of goal strivings and represent what an individual is typically trying to do. . . . Each individual can be characterized by a unique set of these "trying to do" tendencies' (Emmons, 1989b: 92). In this sense, personal strivings can be understood as idiographic versions of one of the most prominent nomothetic concepts in personality psychology, the concept of 'motive dispositions' (see, for example, McClelland, 1985). Unlike personal projects and life tasks, which can be expressed at varying levels of abstraction, personal strivings are located at a fixed level of abstraction between dispositional motives as superordinate concepts and specific concerns and actions at subordinate levels. They express an individual's self-defined specification of a general motive. At the same time, they need to be further specified in terms of concrete tasks and, finally, actions designed to meet the intended goal. The relatively stable and enduring nature of personal strivings implies that they do not come to an end once a specific task pertinent to a striving has been accomplished. Instead, strivings are persistent motivational tendencies requiring sustained efforts to meet a desired goal (or avoid an undesired one). It is clear, though, that these efforts need to take different shapes in different life domains and at different points in the person's development.

For example, a striving such as 'becoming a more independent person' may lead to different tasks for a person in late adolescence (for example, becoming more independent from parents; being less dependent on the approval of friends), which, in turn, suggest different actions (such as leaving home; acting against the advice of a friend). In adult life, the same striving may be expressed in the attempt to stand up against one's boss, at the task level, by disregarding orders or voicing open criticism, at the specific action level.

For the empirical analysis of personal strivings, a 'Personal Strivings Assessment Packet' has been developed which is very similar to the strategies used by both personal project and life task analysis. Following the open-ended generation of striving lists, respondents are asked to indicate the specific activities they typically adopt to accomplish each striving. The self-generated striving lists can be complemented by and checked against strivings provided by informed peers. Emmons (1989a) reports evidence showing a far-reaching correspondence between self-generated and peer-generated strivings in a sample of narcissistic individuals.

Beyond this purely idiographic analysis, people then rate their strivings on a set of eighteen nomothetically defined dimensions to arrive at basic factors underlying the consensual representation of strivings. Emmons (1986) identifies three central meaning dimensions along which personal strivings can be described. They are interpreted as referring to the degree or *intensity* of pursuing a striving, the *success* in living up to a striving, and the *ease* with which success on a striving may be achieved. These three basic dimensions bear striking resemblance to the meaning, stress, and efficacy dimensions identified by Little (see above) as defining characteristics of personal projects.

In a subsequent study, Emmons and King (1989) showed that emotionally reactive individuals (namely, those responding with high affective intensity and extreme mood variability to events in their lives) are characterized by more independent striving systems than less emotionally reactive persons. At the same time, they display lower levels of differentiation within their strivings (such as generating fewer plans for trying to achieve a striving) than their less emotionally reactive counterparts. In interpreting these findings, Emmons and King argue that high emotional reactivity predisposes the individual to seek out congruent situations and settings, that is, those which facilitate the experience of extreme affective responses (see Chapter 5 for a discussion of Emmons and Diener's congruence model). Both high independence between strivings and low differentiation within strivings, in the sense of few specific action plans, can be regarded as cognitive mechanisms minimizing the potentially moderating influence of other strivings or plans which would weaken the person's emotional reactivity to a particular success or disappointment encountered in the process of pursuing his or her strivings.

Altogether, personal strivings are suggested as units of analysis that convey an optimal amount of information about an individual. As Emmons (1989b: 121) concludes: 'More discriminating than global motives yet more stable than specific plans, personal strivings occupy a desirable yet unexplored position in the hierarchy of personality functioning.' However, it has become clear that there is a significant degree of both conceptual and methodological overlap between personal strivings, life tasks, and personal projects that raises the question of the distinctive qualities of each approach. Whether there is a place for three such similar models in a science of personality guided by the search for parsimonious explanation or whether they will eventually be merged into one general conceptualization of personality based on the goal concept remains to be seen.

Summary

This chapter has brought together a diverse body of research emphasizing the need for a more thorough analysis of the individual person in personality psychology. Following a brief review of the different meanings associated with the term 'idiographic', a general agenda was presented of the issues covered by the idiographic analysis of personality. We then looked at three empirical examples to illustrate the range of concepts, questions, methods and conclusions which can be, and have been, addressed within the framework of the idiographic approach. The first example was Harris's strategy of idiovalidation which demonstrated how familiar strategies in nomothetic research, such as the multitrait–multimethod approach, can be adapted to the aims of idiographic analysis. From a different perspective, the potential of free-response data for describing the current life spaces of individual persons was illustrated in a study by

Pervin. Finally, McAdams's analysis of autobiographical accounts of life narratives was quoted as an example of how to implement the claim for a holistic analysis of the person. Against the background of these examples, the concluding part of the first section examined the validity of seven recurrent criticisms levelled at idiographic strategies of personality measurement. In the course of this discussion, it became increasingly clear that the long-standing view of the basic incompatibility of nomothetic and idiographic objectives is no longer tenable. Instead, there is a growing consensus emphasizing both the possibility and the need to combine the assets of both perspectives to promote progress in personality psychology.

The second section, therefore, introduced a set of methodological approaches designed to transcend the antagonism of idiographic versus nomothetic research traditions. They are linked together by the aim to explore different avenues for testing general propositions about personality on the basis of idiographically defined data. Following a look at Buss and Craik's outline of an idiographic version of the *act frequency approach*, Bem's *template matching strategy* was discussed in some detail. This approach emphasizes the need to go beyond the trait concept and define as well as predict behaviour with direct reference to the situation in which it takes place. Accordingly, the aim is to provide a methodological tool offering a 'commensurate' language for describing both persons and situations. Lamiell's proposal of an *idiothetic model* of personality represents a more radical departure from the conventional paradigms of personality psychology. He pleads for abandoning the traditional individual difference paradigm as altogether unsuitable for the study of individual persons and, instead, calls for a person-centred perspective on personality. At the core of his approach lies the conviction that reliance on techniques of data collection and analysis that yield information about individual persons is by no means incompatible with the search for general principles of personality. This conviction also received support from a number of studies comparing idiographic and nomothetic measures of personality within a single design.

The final part of the chapter was devoted to recent research efforts extending the study of personality over longer periods of time and more complex units of analysis. Adopting the concept of goal-directed activity as their basic principle, these approaches concentrate on exploring the process by which individuals define and pursue the tasks of their lives. Personal projects, life tasks, and personal strivings are examples of concepts located at a 'middle level' of analysis between overarching motives on the one hand and specific plans and activities on the other. Such middle-level units are advocated as holding the greatest potential for progress in the study of personality (Buss and Cantor, 1989: 11). Moreover, these frameworks for understanding personal life plans cogently demonstrate that it is not just feasible but imperative to use a person's idiosyncratic definition and selection of life tasks, projects or strivings as points of departure for any subsequent attempt at deriving normative patterns of personality.

In conclusion, the spectrum of methodological strategies reviewed in the last two chapters demonstrates that new and promising avenues for progress in personality measurement have been explored in recent years. The most notable achievement in these developments is the growing recognition that nomothetic and idiographic approaches each have an important place in personality research and can be fruitfully combined in order to advance our understanding of individual uniqueness *and* individual differences in personality.

Notes

1   It is important to note that these average correlations differ from nomothetically established correlations in one essential respect: in the present analyses, individual correlations were established first on the basis of each subject's original responses. These individual correlations were then combined into average scores. In a traditional nomothetic analysis, subjects' original responses are first averaged into mean scores, and it is these means which form the basis for computing a group correlation.

2   Since much of this exchange refers to the details of the empirical strategies adopted by Lamiell and his co-workers, a comprehensive review of the dispute is beyond the scope of this chapter.

3   This means, for instance, that one would want to know whether 'trying to be in control of things' is more characteristic of the person than 'the wish to be liked by others' (rather than knowing whether 'trying to be in control' is more characteristic of Person A than of Person B).

4   The results and implications of this study, which have been highly controversial, will not be discussed here because the study is referred to only to illustrate one possible strategy for deriving templates (compare, however, Bem, 1983c; Funder, 1983b; Mischel and Peake, 1982a).

8

The Role of the Situation in Personality Research

As long as much of the energy expended by personality researchers was dissipated in the conflict between trait theorists and situationists, there was little chance for a constructive treatment of the situation as a concept in personality psychology. It was only when the consistency controversy eventually gave way to an interactionist understanding of personality that the analysis of situations gained a place on the agenda of personality research. As Cantor and Kihlstrom (1987: 84) have noted: 'The study of *situations* is back in fashion and for good reasons.'

Chapter 4 briefly sketched the role of the situation in the modern interactionist view of personality. The present chapter extends this perspective by looking in greater detail at recent contributions towards a 'psychology of situations'. The growing recognition of the need for social and personality psychologists to devote more attention to the systematic analysis of situations has led to a diverse range of theoretical suggestions and empirical research. This work is documented, for instance, in three volumes by Argyle et al. (1981), Furnham and Argyle (1981), and Magnusson (1981a). It is also covered extensively in Snyder and Ickes's (1985) chapter in the *Handbook of Social Psychology*.

This chapter will select examples from the variety of research devoted to the analysis of situations that are especially relevant to the study of personality and social behaviour. In particular, two lines of thinking and research into the role of the situation in personality psychology will be presented which address the following general questions:

1 How do situational factors interact with specific characteristics of the person in producing a particular kind or pattern of behaviour?
2 How does an individual's personality influence his or her choice of situations?

The first line of research is based on a conceptualization of situations that focuses on their *subjective presentations* in an individual's perceptions and cognitions. Central to this work is the idea that in order to have an impact on individual behaviour, the information contained in an objectively definable situation has to be processed like any other kind of information, and that it is the outcome of this processing that impinges on the person's subsequent behaviour. As Geis (1978: 126) puts it: 'Persons respond to situations *as perceived.*' To the extent that persons have not only different perceptual and cognitive abilities but also different experiential backgrounds, it is assumed that they will transform an identical set of objective situational features into different subjective representations. Accordingly, the impact of situations on behaviour is regarded as being shaped and mediated to a significant degree by the subjective meaning attached to them. This meaning, in turn, is very much a function of personal variables, including dispositions and cognitive skills. Therefore, Cantor and Kihlstrom (1987: 86) assign a central role to the analysis of subjective representations of situations: 'For social cognition theorists, it is becoming clear that part of the richness of the social knowledge repertoire derives from intuitive concepts of situations and the typical persons, behavioral episodes and affective impressions associated with them.'

The second part of the chapter will discuss a body of research aiming to explore the processes whereby *individuals select and influence the situations* in which they act. While researchers studying the subjective representation of situations treat the situation primarily as an independent variable influencing the behavioural performance of the individual, the reverse perspective is adopted by this line of research. As the idea of a multidirectional interaction between person and environment suggests (see Figure 4.2 above), the person is an active and intentional participant in the interaction process. Very often, people are in a position to choose certain situational settings in preference over others and aim to manipulate existing situations in such a way that they become more amenable to their goals (Showers and Cantor, 1985). In Chapter 5 it was demonstrated that people generally experience more positive emotions when they are in situations which are congruent with their personal dispositions. Similarly, the idea of conceptualizing personal adjustment in terms of a person–environment match has come up repeatedly in the preceding chapters, and it is clear that the individual is actively involved in bringing about this match.

Irrespective of whether situations are analysed in terms of their subjective meaning or as products of the individual's action, that is, treated as either independent or dependent variables, several layers of situational analysis have to be distinguished, each providing information at a different level of complexity. The following categorization of the units of situational analysis has been suggested by Magnusson (1978), but various other authors have made highly similar distinctions (for example, Furnham and Argyle, 1981; Pervin, 1978; and see Edwards, 1984, for a review). The categories are ordered along a continuum of increasing complexity, with each successive unit containing a combination of elements specified at the preceding levels.

The most fundamental level at which situations may be studied is that of *situational stimuli*. These consist of single objects or acts inherent in a situation which are meaningful in their own right, that is, they do not necessarily have to be linked to other information in order to be understood. Consider the example of taking a written examination at the end of term. In this context, a specific array of tables and chairs, blank sheets and writing material and the presence of fellow students would each be examples of distinct situational stimuli.

At the next higher level, *situational events* or episodes comprising specific parts of a total situation may be studied. In our example, 'receiving the exam papers', 'being allowed to start' and 'being told to stop' would be examples of such episodes. Situational events have a dynamic quality about them in that they are composed of a set of interrelated actions by one or more persons.

When situational stimuli and events are observed comprehensively and combined into an overall picture, we are talking about the level of the *total, actual situation*. What is characteristic of the total situation is a unique occurrence in time and space, such as taking a social psychology exam after the first year.

In contrast, at the level of *situational settings* situations are defined in generalized terms independent of specific occurrences. From this perspective, one would be interested in identifying the characteristic features of exam situations in general. Accordingly, the study of situational settings is designed to discover typical events and sequences of events that would recur in much the same way in any situation of that type.

Finally, the broadest level at which situations can be studied is the level of *life situations* or environments. They comprise the totality of social and physical factors which affect the person and are affected by his or her actions at a certain stage of development. The life situation pertaining to our example of the exam situation could be defined in this way as 'being an undergraduate in his or her first year at university', involving all the particular circumstances associated with this point in life.

Thus, the first task facing researchers who aim to study the role of situations is to make a decision about the level of analysis at which their specific research question can be most adequately addressed. Subsequently, they have to decide on their general methodological strategy which will depend, to a significant degree, on the particular type of theoretical framework within which the analysis is located. Furnham and Argyle (1981) have provided a comparative overview of the different strategies for analysing social situations which is presented in Table 8.1. It should be noted in passing that among the academic traditions named in the table as being associated with the different methods, the field of personality does not feature at all, a fact that reflects what was said at the beginning of this chapter about the long-time neglect of situational factors in personality research.

Looking at it from the last column, Table 8.1 illustrates how the levels of situational definition described above are associated with different research traditions. These associations result in a variety of differences in empirical analysis, from the selection of appropriate samples over choosing a particular method of data collection to the final analysis of the data.

There is a further crucial respect in which psychological disciplines differ in their characteristic forms of situational analysis. This has to do with the decision to study situations either in terms of their *objective* properties, which may be established independently of any individual observer, or in terms of their *subjective* meaning, reflecting the way it is perceived by the individual (see Magnusson, 1978: 3; Pervin, 1978: 81). For example, a group encounter can be described objectively in terms of the number of participants and whether it is a single-sex or mixed-sex group, or it can be described in terms of its subjective, psychological significance, for example, a mixed-sex group being perceived as more threatening than a single-sex group.

Treating situations as objective entities has been the predominant form of situational analysis throughout the consistency debate and, indeed, still continues to be so in most experimental work in the fields of social psychology and environmental psychology. However, from the point of view of personality research, and modern interactionism in particular, defining and studying situations solely in terms of their objective features is regarded as too limited. The analysis of situations in objective terms is based on the assumption that the features of any given situation, such as working in an extremely noisy environment, has similar effects on all the individuals present. In contrast, personality researchers have emphasized that individuals differ in their responses to a given situation because their specific personality characteristics as well as biographical background lead them to perceive and interpret an identical set of

Table 8.1 *Methods for analysing social situations*

	Academic tradition	Descriptive vs. hypothesis testing	Subjects	Within/between situation analysis	Methods of data collection	Type of data	Treatment of data	Level of definition
Dimensional (Perceptual)	Psychophysics, Social psychology	Descriptive	Observers usually grouped according to some criterion	Between	Questionnaire, Sorting task	Rating scales, Similarity rating	MDS, Factor analysis	Situational episode
Componential (Structural)	Linguistics, Ethology	Hypothesis testing and descriptive	Observers who have experienced these situations	Within (and between)	Questionnaire, Sorting/rating tasks	Rating scales, Similarity ratings, 'Parsing' data	Cluster analysis, ANOVA, Appropriate statistics	Situational stimuli (objects, acts)
Process (Applied)	Applied psychology	Hypothesis testing and descriptive	All participants in a setting	Within and between	Observation, Behavioural measures, Interview	Rating scales, Behavioural counts, Self-reports	Varied	Total actual situations
Environmental	Evaluation assessment research, Architecture	Hypothesis testing and descriptive	Users, planners, assessors of an environment	Within and between	Questionnaire, Observation, Behavioural measures	Varied	Varied	Situational events and total situation
Ecological	Anthropology, Microsociology	Descriptive	Whole population of a setting	Between	Observation	Detailed notes	Development of taxonomy	Situational settings
Ethogenic (Roles–Rules)	Microsociology, Philosophy	Descriptive	Selected participants in a natural episode	Within	Interview, Observation	Accounts	Selection of 'representative' accounts	Situational episode

Source: reprinted with permission from Furnham and Argyle (1981: xxxvii)

objective properties in different ways (see, for example, Edwards, 1984; Forgas, 1979a; Geis, 1978; Magnusson, 1981a: Part III).

Nevertheless, even the most determined interactionist would have to acknowledge that the subjective representation of situations results from characteristic modes of perception and cognitive representation *as they are applied to* situational features which often have an objective reality independent of the particular individual perceiving them. Thus, in order to understand the process whereby situations acquire subjective meaning for the individual, it is necessary to consider briefly some of the issues associated with the conceptualization of situations as objective entities.

Situations as objective entities

Looking at situations in terms of their objective properties, the idea is that a situation may be defined and described in terms of its temporal and spatial boundaries, including the people who are present and act in the situation. A classroom situation would thus be characterized by the presence of several, usually younger, people plus a further, typically somewhat older person, who come together for a specified period of time at a particular location. Also included in this perspective are those features of a situation that cannot be determined objectively by observation but are consensually regarded as being part of the situation, such as different roles and normative rules. What makes these features 'quasi-objective' in a sense is the fact that they belong to the situation irrespective of whether or not the individual person recognizes them as such. In the example of the classroom situation, a difference in status as well as power between students and instructor which endows the latter with certain rights and duties is an integral part of the situation, even though single individuals may fail to recognize this.

Attempts at describing situations in terms of their objective properties are typically guided by the aim of reducing the almost infinite complexity of situations to a limited number of situation categories. For example, van Heck (1989) presents a taxonomy of everyday situations based on the situation terms provided by natural language. After extracting a total of 248 non-overlapping situation concepts from a dictionary analysis and having them described in terms of an empirically derived range of characteristics, a factor analysis yielded the following ten broad factors:

1 Interpersonal conflict.
2 Joint working and exchange of thoughts, ideals, and know-ledge.

3   Intimacy and interpersonal relations.
4   Recreation.
5   Travelling.
6   Rituals.
7   Sports.
8   Excesses.
9   Serving.
10   Trading.

By classifying situations into systematic taxonomies, the task of explaining and predicting behaviour can be approached with respect to defined classes of situations rather than individual situations or heterogeneous sets. Accordingly, the search for taxonomic descriptions of situations which would facilitate the analysis of the interplay of person and situation variables is an important part of the emerging 'psychology of situations' (Pervin, 1978).

Depending on the particular purposes underlying the search for a descriptive classification of situations, different approaches have been suggested towards distinguishing situations by their objective properties (see Jaspers, 1985). Frederiksen (1972) suggests classifying situations according to their tendency to elicit similar behaviours. Price (1974) has demonstrated that a classification of situations based on consensual ratings of which behaviours are appropriate in them allows one to identify classes of behaviour that are uniquely appropriate in certain classes of situations (see also Schutte et al., 1985). Yet another strategy involves the systematic ordering of situations on the basis of the behavioural rules that are prevalent in them (Argyle et al., 1979). In each case, what these criteria allow is to partition a heterogeneous range of situations into more or less coherent groups which can then be matched against corresponding groups of behaviours and/or personality characteristics. Argyle et al. (1981: 6ff.) have proposed a comprehensive set of features by which situations – defined as a type of social encounter with which members of a culture or subculture are familiar – may be characterized:

1   The potential offered by situations for attaining certain goals.
2   Rules containing consensual positions as to the range of behaviours permitted, not permitted or required in the situation.
3   Roles which define and link into a common network the actions, privileges, responsibilities, etc., of individual participants.
4   Behavioural repertoires specifying the range of meaningful actions in a situation.
5   Characteristic sequences, as opposed to single instances, of behaviour.

6 Concepts for handling the situation shared by the participants.
7 Distinctive features of the physical environment in which the situation is embedded.
8 Specific forms of language and communication prevalent in the situation.
9 Difficulties presented by the situation requiring specific skills to be dealt with satisfactorily.

Additional attributes for distinguishing situations have been proposed by other authors (see van Heck, 1989; Magnusson, 1981b), including the persons typically found in a situation, the complexity and clarity of situations as well as their strength, that is, the extent to which they override individual differences and elicit uniform patterns of behaviour from the persons involved.

In their search for an empirically derived taxonomy of situational attributes, Baumeister and Tice (1985) developed an interesting rationale. They argued that since social psychological experiments typically seek to explore the impact of situational influences on behaviour, the independent variables used in a sufficient number of experiments can be regarded as a comprehensive sample of situational attributes. Accordingly, they used the total pool of independent variables of studies published in the odd-numbered volumes of the *Journal of Personality and Social Psychology* as input data for their taxonomy. These single situational attributes were then classified into fifty-one non-overlapping categories representing the following five dimensions of situational structure:

1 *Stimulus environment*, comprising the enduring physical and social structure of the situation and including attributes such as 'publicness' and 'type of task'.
2 *Characteristics of the subject*, such as 'dispositions' and 'prior experience'. (The authors are aware of the fact that this is not strictly speaking a situational category and suggest that for a clear-cut differentiation between person and situation this category should be dropped.)
3 *Cognitive and affective dynamics of the situation*, including 'situational demand intensity' and 'subject's goal'.
4 *Relationship background*, referring to the different aspects of the relationship between the persons involved in the situation, such as 'subject's amount of knowledge about other person' and 'attempt to influence subject'.
5 *Matrix of possibilities*, denoting those aspects of the situation that relate to the subject's choice of behavioural responses. This category includes attributes such as 'range of options' and 'expectation of future interaction'.

The advantage of this taxonomy lies in the fact that a systematic strategy was adopted to derive the initial sample of situational attributes. On the other hand, it is based on a rather restricted understanding of situational attributes in terms of variables that lend themselves to and are typically encountered in social psychological analysis. This limitation is explicitly recognized by the authors who point out that 'we would be remiss if we failed to state the plausibility that such an effort [that is, to derive a second theory of situations from organizational or sociological publications] would furnish a view of situational structure that differs from the one we obtained using social psychology' (Baumeister and Tice, 1985: 171).

While the previous taxonomies concentrated exclusively on the classification of situations, Kenrick et al. (1990) were interested in exploring the intersection of certain trait dimensions with certain situational settings. Using six central trait dimensions including the 'Big Five' (see Chapter 3) and twelve situation categories (six 'domicile' and six 'non-domicile' settings), they tested the proposition that situation categories differ in the extent to which they invite the behavioural manifestation of different traits. Their findings show, for example, that a greater variety and frequency of trait manifestations in behaviour were reported for the non-domicile settings, such as academic situations and play and entertainment situations, than for the domicile settings, such as eating room or dormitory.

As valuable as such detailed taxonomic descriptions of situations undoubtedly are, they can only be a first step towards developing a theory for explaining *why* and, more importantly, *how* different categories of situations are linked to different patterns of behaviour for different groups of people. In the taxonomy of Argyle et al. (1981), for example, the concept of goal attainment is the focal point to which all subsequent elements of situational analysis are subordinate. They argue that 'situations emerge within a culture because they have the function of enabling people to attain goals, which in turn are linked to needs and other drives . . . All other features of situations can be explained in terms of facilitating the attainment of these drive-related goals' (Argyle et al., 1981: 10). What Argyle et al. regard as a major advantage of focusing on the objective situation is that it provides a kind of yardstick against which the individual's perception of the situation can be checked, and possibly identified as being mistaken. They argue that any social-skills training requires such a yardstick, since it is geared primarily towards helping the individual to adjust his or her definition of a situation to the consensually accepted meaning.

In a similar vein, Price's (1981) approach to the prevention of psychological distress and disorder is directed at identifying those life situations that make individuals particularly susceptible to the development of such problems. As he points out: 'Even for disorders that have a specific etiology of genetic origin, situational factors may still determine to a very large extent whether the disorder in question will actually occur or not' (Price, 1981: 107). As a tentative taxonomy of the defining features of high-risk situations, Price suggests that a combination of low social support, high competition, low participant involvement and high task orientation are among the features likely to be conducive to the precipitation of psychological disorder.

These examples illustrate that the description and analysis of situations in terms of objective and quasi-objective features can provide informative answers to a number of research questions and clinical objectives, such as the training of social skills and the prevention of emotional disorders. At the same time, it has become quite clear that even in these contexts the study of the subjective interpretation of situations cannot be ignored. For example, the question of why and how an individual who seeks professional help has developed an idiosyncratic, dysfunctional definition of a certain type of situation needs to be addressed for any intervention to have a lasting effect. Underlining this point, Jessor (1981) demonstrated that different types of problem behaviour in adolescents can be explained far better on the basis of the environmental factors *as perceived* by the adolescents (for instance, the perceived approval of friends and parents) than on the basis of environmental factors defined *in demographic terms* (for example, socioeconomic status).

Thus, there can be no doubt that the influence of situations (as defined in objective or consensual terms) on the behaviour of the individual person is mediated to a large extent by the subjective meaning assigned to them. This is also stressed by Block and Block in their analysis of how an objectively or consensually defined situation (that is, the 'canonical situation') is transformed into a subjectively meaningful cognitive representation (that is, the 'functional situation'):

> The difference between the canonical situation and the individual's functional situation is, logically, attributable to the operation of the individual's personality structure (the individual's developmentally achieved perceptualizing schemata) as further influenced by the immediately present motivational state of the individual. (1981: 87)

The relationship between the objective features and the subjective perception of situations is conceptualized in a similar way by Dworkin and Goldfinger (1985) who refer to Gibson's (1979) concept of situational 'affordances' for a taxonomic description of situations. They argue that each situation contains different 'affordances', that is, positive or negative potentials for action, and that individuals differ with regard to the particular affordances towards which they direct their attention. On a steep cliff walk, for instance, an inexperienced walker might direct all his or her attention to the cliff's 'affording' his plunging 100 feet down, while a dedicated mountaineer would attend primarily to the affordance of a magnificent view. Similar differences between the two persons might be expected in their anticipation as well as their memory of the event. Applying this reasoning to the analysis of the social affordances of different situations, Dworkin and Goldfinger (1985) addressed the question whether persons differing on the trait of sociability would also differ in their processing of the social versus non-social affordances of situations. They demonstrated that both highly sociable and anti-sociable subjects showed a stronger tendency to direct attention to social (as opposed to non-social) situational stimuli than moderately sociable subjects, whereby this difference was found to hold for the anticipation and memory of social versus non-social stimuli as well.

Baron and Boudreau (1987) view the concept of affordance as a key notion in understanding the interaction of personal and environmental factors. They argue that affordances are simultaneously objective and subjective because their physical properties can exert an influence on the person only if he or she possesses the complementary characteristic to make use of or 'tune into' a certain affordance. For example, for a situation affording favourable self-presentation to be used towards this goal, the person must be capable of both detecting this affordance and taking appropriate behavioural steps. At the same time, people have to communicate their own 'social affordances' (for example, being a compassionate friend or helpful neighbour) as part of their social competence, and the authors quote evidence that highly socially competent persons are indeed more successful in both detecting and sending affordance information.

In summary, then, studying situations as defined in objective or quasi-objective, that is, consensual terms only partially illuminates the influence of situational features on behaviour. From the perspective of personality psychology, the study of the psychological meaning of situations for the individual should take priority over the study of situations and settings in objective or physical terms. Similarly, Zavalloni and Louis-Guerin see the study of 'internal environments' as a central task conjoining environmental and social psychology:

The psychological context, the knowledge and skills of the individual, including his particular interpretation of the situation, interact with the experimental stimuli or with real-life events. Interactive particularism (idiographic orientation) is thus replacing the search for regularities in an aggregate (sample) of individuals as a research goal. (1979: 310)

Thus, any theoretical framework that is concerned with *individual patterns* of behaviour in response to a given situation is bound to assign crucial importance to the analysis of situations in terms of their perceived significance.

Situations as subjective realities

Descriptions of situations in objective terms are, by definition, largely independent of the perspective of an individual observer. In contrast, understanding the subjective meaning that a person assigns to a situation places critical importance on the individual's information processing and impression formation. While some features of these processes are likely to be shared, others are most certainly idiosyncratic and can be properly understood only against a person's unique experiential background. The basic approach underlying this type of inquiry is epitomized in the well-known *Thomas theorem*: 'If men define situations as real, they are real in their consequences' (Thomas, 1928: 572). This means, as Ball (1972) elaborates, that the 'definition of the situation may be conceived of as the *sum of all recognized information, from the point of view of the actor, which is relevant to his locating himself and others, so that he can engage in self-determined lines of action and interaction*' (1972: 63, emphasis in the original). Although the concept of the definition of the situation has acquired a specific meaning in the context of symbolic interactionism and ethnomethodology, it also captures in a broader sense the modern interactionist notion of the 'psychological meaning of situations' (see Stebbins (1985) for a recent review). From a similar sociological perspective, Turner (1988: 2) points out that the effect of situations on the individual 'is determined in part by meanings that the individual attributes to the situation *which could not be predicted perfectly from knowledge of the social structure that generated the situation or from an objective characterization of the situation*' (emphasis in the original).

As with the study of 'objective' situations, an essential task for the analysis of situations as subjective realities consists of classifying situations so as to reduce them into more manageable units. Three basic approaches for categorizing situations on the basis of their subjective meaning have been distinguished by Magnusson and

Stattin (1982): the *perceptual approach*, whereby situations are grouped together on the basis of how they are perceived and interpreted; the *reaction approach*, classifying situations in terms of the immediate physical and affective responses they produce; and the *action approach* looking at the more complex patterns of behaviour that different situations typically elicit from the person.

This part of the chapter will examine some of the research strategies associated with these basic approaches. The 'perceptual approach' is best represented by a group of studies designed to discover the central dimensions underlying the subjective interpretation of situations. This approach is linked to both the action and reaction approaches by another group of studies exploring the relationship between situation perception and behavioural responses to those situations. To the extent that there is a systematic relationship between situation perception and behaviour over different situations, this can be interpreted as evidence for cross-situational consistency as proposed in the interactionist concept of 'coherence' (see Chapter 2).

The cognitive representation of situations

Clarifying the central dimensions of people's perception and interpretation of situations is an essential step towards the systematic investigation of the psychological meaning of situations. Nevertheless, only a few studies are available to date which have addressed the dimensional structure of situations. These studies provide descriptive information about how everyday situations are perceived by different social groups and individuals (Edwards, 1984). Other cognitive approaches, to be discussed later in this section, have concentrated less on identifying the central *dimensions* of situation perception than on the issue of how the *sequence of events* that make up a situation is organized in memory (the script concept) and on how situations are consensually perceived and categorized in terms of their characteristic features (the prototype approach).

The empirical paradigm for investigating the *dimensional structure* of situation perception is best illustrated by the work of Forgas (1979a, b, 1982) on social episodes. *Social episodes* are defined as 'cognitive representations of stereotypical interaction sequences which are representative of a given cultural environment' (Forgas, 1979a: 15). The process of episode cognition reflects the individual's knowledge of the socially accepted rules and norms of appropriate behaviour in different interaction situations and its application to specific interpersonal encounters. The cognitive structure of this implicit situational knowledge is represented in the *episode space*. Therefore, the major empirical objective of the social episode approach lies in the modelling of consensual episode spaces to reveal the perceived patterns of relationship between different kinds of social encounters within a cultural milieu (Forgas, 1979a: 172).

In order to address this task, Forgas (1979a: 116) introduced a 'perceptual' strategy for the study of social episodes. This strategy, which has been used in the majority of studies based on the social episode concept, involves five successive steps:

1 The sampling of episodes representing the subjects' daily inter-action routines (for example, by obtaining diary records over a certain period of time).

2 The selection of appropriate measures for tapping the subjects' perception and evaluation of the sampled episodes (for example, by presenting bipolar adjective scales on which each episode is rated and from which psychological distance measures between episodes can be derived).

3 The analysis of episode (dis-)similarities by statistical methods. The methods preferred by Forgas and most other researchers in this area are multidimensional scaling procedures. These methods facilitate the identification of central dimensions under-lying the cognitive representation of different episodes and also provide the basis for developing descriptive taxonomies.

4 The interpretation of the obtained statistical solutions, which involves the labelling of the dimensions constituting the episode space. Typically, no more than four or at most five dimensions are found to be sufficient to represent the total range of situations for a given sample.

5 The formulation and testing of hypotheses about differences in episode cognition between individuals and groups, as well as about potential determinants of the perception of social epi-sodes.

With the exception of the last step, which has so far remained largely programmatic, this procedure underlies most of the studies exploring the dimensions of situation perception. Differences between studies, therefore, mainly refer to the range of situations to which their analysis is addressed. While Magnusson (1971) and Battistich and Thompson (1980) study broad samples of situations from their subjects' everyday lives, other authors have concentrated on specific situational domains, such as 'interpersonal relations' (Wish, et al., 1976), 'aggressive episodes' (Forgas et al., 1980), or 'helping episodes' (Amato and Pearce, 1983). Not surprisingly, the situational dimensions that emerge from these analyses differ as a function of the specific type of situation investigated. At the same time, however, there appears to be a common dimension underlying the perception of apparently very different kinds of situations. This universal dimension refers to the intensity or involvement with which the person participates in the situation. In order to facilitate a comparative appraisal of the different studies of situational dimensions, their main features are summarized in Table 8.2.

What becomes clear from Table 8.2 is that only a minority of dimensions, such as 'group versus individual activity', refer to the objective or physical features of situations (for further examples see Amato and Saunders, 1985; Magnusson, 1974; Russell and Pratt, 1980; Taylor, 1981). Almost all the dimensions uncovered by multidimensional scaling refer to the *psychological properties* of situational events as opposed to *physical aspects*. This finding, however, is partly due to the fact that the scales on which the situations are rated by the respondents (see Step 2 above), and which to some extent predetermine the subsequent interpretation of the dimensions, address the subjective meaning rather than the objective properties of situations. On the other hand, these scales are typically selected on the basis of pilot data from independent subjects who are asked to list the characteristic features of the situations in question (see, for example, Battistich and Thompson, 1980; Forgas et al., 1980). Therefore, it seems fair to conclude that people do, indeed, tend to interpret situations in subjective/ psychological rather than objective/physical terms.

While the studies reviewed so far have been concerned primarily with analysing the consensual interpretation of situations, a few studies have compared the characteristic perceptual dimensions of different groups or looked at individual differences in situation perception. Forgas (1976) compared the episode spaces for members of two cultural milieux, housewives and students. He found that while the episode space of the housewives was best represented by a two-dimensional solution, a three-dimensional solution was most adequate for the student sample. The first two dimensions were highly similar for both groups and were interpreted as 'perceived intimacy and involvement' and 'subjective competence', respectively. The additional dimension obtained for the student sample was interpreted as a general evaluative, 'pleasant–unpleasant', dimension. A comparison of the dimensional location of select episodes revealed a further interesting result: activities involving socializing and entertainment outside the home (such as 'having a drink with some friends in a pub') were strongly associated with feelings of incompetence for the housewives, while the same situations were closely linked to feelings of competence and self-confidence for the students. Using a similar procedure,

Table 8.2 *Studies exploring the perceptual dimensions of situations*

	Magnusson (1971)	Wish et al. (1976)	Forgas (1978)	Battistich and Thompson (1980)	Forgas et al. (1980)	Amato and Pearce (1983)	King and Sorrentino (1983)
Type of situation	Heterogeneous	Interpersonal relations	Interaction episodes	Heterogeneous	Aggressive episodes	Helping episodes	Interpersonal goal-oriented situations
N of subjects/ raters	3	87	15	216	137	45	200
N of situations	36	45	17	30	22	62	20
Dimensions	1 positive/ rewarding 2 negative 3 passiveness 4 social interaction 5 activity	1 cooperative/ friendly vs. competitive/ hostile 2 equal vs. unequal 3 intense vs. superficial 4 socioemotional/ informal vs. task-oriented/ formal	1 anxiety 2 involvement 3 evaluative 4 socioemotional vs. task-oriented	1 emotional involvement 2 group vs. individual activity 3 social isolation 4 behavioural conformity	1 probability of occurrence 2 justifiability 3 provocation 4 control	1 spontaneous/ informal vs. planned/formal help 2 serious vs. non-serious 3 direct vs. indirect help	1 pleasant vs. unpleasant 2 accidentally vs. intentionally caused 3 physically vs. socially oriented 4 sensitive vs. insensitive 5 intimate vs. non-intimate 6 non-intimate/ uninvolved vs. intimate/ involved 7 work- vs. relaxation-oriented

Forgas (1983a, b) found systematic differences in the cognitive representation of episode spaces due to individual differences on certain personality and social skills measures. For example, subjects scoring high on personality measures of introversion and/or low on measures of assertiveness and social competence were shown in the Forgas (1983a) study to organize situational information predominantly in terms of the 'self-confidence' dimension. A different perceptual style emerged for subjects characterized as extroverted and 'high self-monitors' (Snyder, 1974) who tended to interpret situations mainly in terms of the 'pleasantness' and 'involvement' dimensions.

In summary, then, the studies discussed so far convey two important messages. First, they highlight the necessity to explore the subjective representation of situations, not just their objective properties, in order to understand the impact of situations on behaviour. In interpreting situational information, individuals rely much more on the psychological characteristics of the situations than on their physical features. Secondly, the last set of studies in particular suggests that there are significant differences in the cognitive representation of situations as a function of social group membership or specific personality characteristics. These findings strongly imply that the study of person–situation interactions can only be expected to yield meaningful results if these characteristic differences are taken into account both conceptually and empirically.

While the studies exploring the dimensional structure of situation cognition have yielded mainly descriptive results, other recent approaches have been interested in exploring the *functional* significance of the way in which situational information is cognitively organized. With this objective in mind, the concept of *cognitive prototypes* has been applied to the analysis of situation cognition (Cantor, 1981; Cantor et al., 1982; Eckes, 1986). Central to the prototype concept is the idea that the cognitive representation of social stimuli (persons, events, settings) is organized in clearly discernible, yet partly overlapping categories. The meaning of each category is best captured in the 'category prototype', that is, an idealized member of the category that incorporates the consensual features typically assigned to the category in question. To the extent that individual members of a category are similar to the prototype, they can be described as better (more central) or poorer (more marginal) members of the category.

Cantor et al. (1982) presented subjects with a taxonomy of four broad situation categories (social, cultural, stressful, and ideological) specified on the three levels of superordinate, middle level and subordinate categories distinguished by the prototype model (for example 'being in a social situation' – 'being at a party' – 'being at a birthday party'). For each situation category, subjects generated lists of characteristic attributes from which the category prototypes – defined as consensual feature lists – were derived. Comparing the feature lists of different situations, the similarity between situation prototypes can be expressed by the ratio of shared to non-shared attributes in the respective feature lists. This procedure not only provides information on which situations are perceived as being similar to each other but also reveals the criteria, namely, the features, on which judgements of situational similarity are based.

In support of the prototype model, Cantor et al. (1982) demonstrated that situations in each of the four broad classes of the taxonomy were regarded as significantly more similar to other situations within their class than to situations belonging to one of the remaining three general categories. In a number of earlier studies, the cognitive organization of social stimuli in the form of prototypes was shown to facilitate the processing of information about objects and persons (for reviews see Mervis and Rosch, 1981; Taylor and Crocker, 1981). Prototypical objects were found to be associated more frequently with a given category label and recognized more rapidly than less prototypical stimuli. Furthermore, prototype-consistent information about persons was recalled more accurately than prototype-inconsistent information and led to more differentiated as well as more confident impressions about the persons described.

It remains to be seen, however, whether the same facilitating functions of cognitive prototypes will also be demonstrated for the processing of information about situations. Evidence suggesting a positive answer to this question comes from a study by Schutte et al. (1985). They constructed a prototypical and a non-prototypical description of three situations: 'in a park', 'in a bar', and 'in a job interview'. Following the presentation of either set of descriptions, two dependent measures were obtained from the participants: the accuracy with which they recollected the elements of the descriptions in a recognition task; and their predictions of the likelihood that they would show each of a list of fifteen behaviours in each of the three situations described. The hypotheses were that compared to the non-prototypical group, subjects given the prototypical descriptions would tend to recognize falsely the highly typical elements *not* given in the original description and show less variability in the range of behaviours which they predicted they would show in these situations. Both hypotheses received clear support from the data, suggesting that the cognitive organization of situational stimuli as conceptualized in the prototype approach is, indeed, functionally linked to subsequent cognitive operations as well as predicted behavioural responses.

A second line of research exploring how situational information is cognitively organized is based on the *script concept* (Abelson, 1981; Schank and Abelson, 1977). Cognitive scripts are defined as 'conceptual representations of stereotyped event sequences' (Abelson, 1981: 715). Thus, the emphasis is on the dynamic flow of interpretations and inferences in the course of an interaction. The script model postulates that individuals acquire a specific knowledge of event sequences as a result of their experiences with different situations. This scripted knowledge consists of structures that describe 'appropriate sequences of events in a particular context' (Schank and Abelson, 1977: 41). It enables people to respond adequately to a situation and to make sense of the behaviour of their interaction partners. The basic elements of a script are single interactions, whereby strong (as opposed to weak) scripts specify a causal ordering of the different elements. It is important to note that a situation is translated into different scripts according to the role perspectives of the participants: the restaurant script, for example, consists of different elements for the waitress than for the customer. The interpretation of social situations on the basis of scripts entails two basic mechanisms of information processing: the person has to identify the appropriate script applicable to the specific situation and he or she must be able to infer lacking information by retrieving stored situational experience. To facilitate the decision which script to retrieve from memory, scripts are identified by 'headers' as part of the cognitive representation of events, and the most essential or 'normative' elements are marked as 'pointers'.

According to the script model, social situations are cognitively represented in terms of characteristic (inter-)actions rather than characteristic attributes. Due to its dynamic nature, scripted knowledge specifies action rules for appropriate behaviour which can be used directly as guidelines for individual behaviour. Cross-situational coherence may thus be conceptualized as a function of the correspondence between 'scripts in understanding' and 'scripts in behaviour' across different situations (Abelson, 1981: 719). Such a systematic relationship between script cognition and behaviour can only be detected, however, if both the conditions that evoke a given script and the defining elements of the script have been established.

Empirical studies on the cognitive representation of scripted knowledge typically present subjects with sequences of events which they are later asked to reproduce from memory. In this way, it has been demonstrated that people not only show a strong tendency towards false recognition of non-mentioned, but highly central events (Graesser et al., 1980), but also tend to rearrange a distorted causal ordering of events when reproducing script-based stories (Bower et al., 1979). These results support the basic tenet of the script model, namely that individuals do not store the entire host of information characterizing a situation, but confine themselves to only the most characteristic elements (including explicit memory of unusual events) from which the complete sequence of interaction may be reconstructed when required.

Both the script concept and the application of the prototype approach to the study of social situations contribute to our understanding of the principles whereby objective or quasi-objective situational stimuli are transformed into cognitive representations that have a particular meaning for the individual. The work discussed in the next section further extends this perspective by looking into the link betweeen the cognitive representation of situations and subsequent behaviour.

Situation perception and behaviour: the issue of
coherence
In general terms, the basic question underlying this issue is the following: is there a systematic relationship between the way people perceive and interpret certain situations and the way they behave in those situations? More specifically, the hypothesis has been put forward and tested that persons tend to show similar *behaviours* across situations to the extent that they *perceive* the respective situations as being similar (see, for example, Klirs and Revelle, 1986; Krahé, 1986, 1990; Magnusson and Ekehammar, 1975, 1978; Pervin, 1981). If there is such a correspondence between situation perception and behaviour, then this may be interpreted as evidence of 'coherence', namely as a lawful pattern of behavioural stability and change across time and situations.

Before reviewing the empirical evidence, it is important to bear in mind that from a traditional situationist perspective the issue of consistency has been approached in a fundamentally different way. Persons are expectd to show similar behaviours across situations – typically represented by experimental treatments – which are regarded (and selected) *by the investigator* as similar with respect to an underlying trait. Accordingly, failure to observe similarity in behaviour across situations thus defined has been interpreted as evidence against the concept of consistency in personality. Adopting the interactionist concept of 'coherence' rather than that of consistency in the situationist sense (see Chapter 2), several studies have explored the link between perceived situational similarity and behavioural similarity. Based on the distinction of a stimulus-analytical versus response-analytical approach to the study of situations, Ekehammar et al. (1975) have examined the correspondence of data generated by each of the two approaches. In the response-analytical method, their subjects were presented with a sample of twenty-four stressful situations which they rated in terms of the affective response, that is, the degree of unpleasantness, each situation would typically evoke in them. In the stimulus-analytical method, a new sample rated the same set of situations in terms of how similar they perceived each pair of situations to be. Each set of ratings was subjected to factor analysis, and the resulting factorial structures were compared for their degree of correspondence. This analysis revealed a significant similarity between the two sets of data, supporting the idea that perceptions of and responses to situations are, indeed, linked in a systematic fashion.

To provide a more immediate examination of the proposed co-variation between situation perception and behaviour, however, both perceptual and response data should be obtained from the same subjects. In Magnusson and Ekehammar's (1975) study, subjects were asked to rate a set of twelve stressful situations both in terms of their perceived similarity and in terms of the responses each situation would typically evoke in them. Using the same analyses as the above study by Ekehammar et al. (1975), they, too, found that both types of ratings yield highly similar factor structures. This means, for instance, that the majority of situations with high loadings on the first factor extracted from the perceptual similarity ratings also showed high loadings on the first factor extracted from the response similarity ratings.

While these results support the idea that perceived situational similarity and behavioural similarity are closely related both conceptually and empirically, they do not tell us anything about the co-variation of situation perception and behaviour *at the level of the individual person* (Klirs and Revelle, 1986: 35). However, since it is precisely this intra-individual correspondence which is at the core of the concept of coherence, evidence on this point is critically important. As a first step, Magnusson and Ekehammar (1978) examined the congruence between how individuals perceive situations and how they actually react in the same situations. To this end, their subjects were presented with descriptions of twelve anxiety-provoking situations covering four types of stressful situations: 'threat of punishment', 'ego threat', 'threat of pain', and 'inanimate threat'. The subjects had to complete two tasks: to provide ratings of perceived similarity between each pair of situations; and to rate each situation in terms of the experienced intensity of twelve reactions, whereby these reaction ratings were subsequently converted into similarity matrices using four different indices of profile similarity (for details see Magnusson and Ekehammar, 1978: 44). Unlike the two studies discussed before, the correspondence between perceived and behavioural similarity was assessed by computing individual correlations between the two data sets for each of the thirty-nine participants. Magnusson and Ekehammar found that, depending on the index of profile similarity applied to the reaction data, between 67 per cent and 85 per cent of the intrasubject correlations were in the expected direction, 33 per cent to 44 per cent respectively were statistically significant. The average correlations between situation perception and reaction ranged from $r = 0.11$ to $r = 0.17$. Magnusson and Ekehammar (1978) conclude that their findings corroborate the interactionist emphasis on the subjective meaning of situations as determinants of behavioural regularities. Using a wider range of situations as well as a different method of data analysis, namely multidimensional scaling, Klirs and Revelle (1986) present further evidence in support of the postulated correspondence between perceived similarity and response consistency across situations. Yet they only provide partial support for the idea that an idiographic mode of analysis is superior to a nomothetic or combined idiographic/nomothetic approach in predicting behavioural variability from perceived situational similarity.

It may be argued, however, that both Magnusson and Ekehammar (1978) and Klirs and Revelle (1986) have overlooked an important point in their so-called idiographic analyses. By presenting an identical, that is, nomothetically defined, set of situations to each of their subjects, they fell short of the idiographic requirement that the situations investigated need to be ascertained as representative examples from the individual's realm of experience.

Measuring perceived similarity and behavioural similarity with respect to situations from each subject's personal experience, Krahé (1986) found an average intra-individual correlation between perceptual and behavioural similarity of $r = 0.37$, which represents a substantial increase over the Magnusson and Ekehammar (1978) findings. A highly similar result is reported by Champagne and Pervin (1987). They also examined cross-situational coherence with respect to an idiographically sampled range of situations and found a mean correlation of $r = 0.36$. The importance of studying consistency with respect to individually selected situations is corroborated by Dolan and White (1988). In two related studies, they explored coping strategies in response to daily hassles encountered by their participants over several weeks. They found that the consistency of coping responses was substantially higher when examined at the level of the individual subject as opposed to the sample as a whole. Furthermore, their findings support the interactionist model in that consistency was found to be higher for hassles associated with particular contexts, such as work, health or finances, than for the total range of hassles across different contexts.

In addition to adopting a stringent idiographic approach to the study of coherence, the studies by Krahé (1986) and Champagne and Pervin (1987) share a further objective. They both seek to identify those features of situation perception underlying a person's subjective ratings of situational similarity which are related, in turn, to similarity in behaviour. Previous studies demonstrating a link between perceived situational similarity and behavioural similarity have relied on global judgements of perceived similarity between situations. Such global rating scale measures of perceived situational similarity, while easy to administer, have the drawback of being uninformative in terms of the structural principles underlying the cognitive organization of situational experience. What are the properties that people have in mind when they rate two situations as being similar or different? To what extent are different cognitive representations of situations related to behavioural profiles in these situations?

Rather than relying on global, a-theoretical measures of perceived situational similarity, theoretical conceptualizations of situation cognition are required which specify principles of the cognitive organization of situational experience. As a first step towards this task, concept-based measures were derived in the Krahé (1986) study from the three models of situation cognition discussed in the previous section: the *prototype approach*, the *social episodes model*, and the *script approach*. In the first part of this study, the twenty-three participants were asked to list twelve anxiety-provoking situations they had experienced in the past. Three situations were elicited from each of the following categories specified in the interaction model of anxiety (see Endler 1983; and Chapter 4): physical danger, social evaluation, interpersonal situations, and ambiguous situations. Subsequently, each subject made pairwise ratings for his or her sample of situations of the extent to which their behaviour had been similar in the two situations along with providing the global ratings of perceived similarity mentioned above. In addition, participants described each situation from their list either in terms of its characteristic features (*prototype* group), its precise course of events (*script* group), or by judging it on a number of evaluative attribute scales (*social episode* group). For each individual, these concept-based measures of situation cognition were transformed into similarity matrices which could be correlated with the ratings of behavioural similarity. The intra-individual correlations between similarity in behaviour and similarity in situation cognition as conceptualized by the three models were significant for the majority of subjects, suggesting that empirical evidence for cross-situational consistency can well be obtained, provided that appropriate strategies are employed for sampling both situations and their perceptual representations.

Champagne and Pervin (1987) relied on the theoretical framework of social learning theory in deriving their concept-based measures of situation cognition (Bandura, 1977; Rotter, 1954, 1981). They argued that a central criterion for perceiving situations as similar is the extent to which they provide similar reinforcement contingencies. Thus, situations for which the individual expects similar outcomes as a result of his or her behaviour should produce more similar patterns of actual behaviour than situations associated with more diverse reinforcement contingencies. When this hypothesis was examined with respect to idiographically sampled lists of situations, average correlations between reinforcement contingencies and behavioural similarity were found to be $r = 0.30$ for the simple 'outcome probability' ratings and $r = 0.32$ for the 'outcome probability × outcome value' ratings. These coefficients were only slightly lower than the average correlation of $r = 0.36$ between global ratings of perceived situational similarity and behavioural similarity.

Considered in combination, the last two studies illustrate, at least tentatively, how the link between situation perception and behaviour can be conceptualized from different theoretical viewpoints. Although their findings do not warrant the conclusion that more complex, theory-guided measures of situation cognition produce higher levels of cognition–behaviour co-variations than global ratings, these measures were shown to be equally well-suited to reflect cross-situational coherence. Their main advantage over global rating measures is that they illuminate the principles and criteria by which situations are cognitively construed as similar or different. There can be no doubt that a better understanding of these principles is an essential prerequisite for predicting individual behaviour as a function of the dynamic interaction between person and situation.

The studies discussed in this section are among the few attempts to put the interactionist concept of 'coherence' into practice as an alternative to the traditional notion of 'consistency'. The major difference between the two strategies is that the search for consistency has been directed at discovering stable individual differences in behaviour due to some underlying trait, an endeavour that has produced at best mixed results (see Chapter 2). In contrast, the search for coherence aims to reveal lawful, idiographically predictable patterns of behaviour (Magnusson, 1976). This means, as Mischel (1983) has pointed out, that one needs to explain both the stability and discriminativeness in individual behaviour, a task that has two important requirements. The first is that both the situations and the behaviours studied need to be representative of the individual's personal experience (see also Edwards and Endler, 1989). This requirement can best be met by adopting an idiographic or person-centred mode of analysis. The second requirement involves going beyond the *demonstration* of a systematic relationship between similarities in situation perception and similarities to support the concept of coherence. In order to *understand* the lawfulness of individual behaviour patterns, the development of theoretical explanations of the process as well as properties of situation cognition and their relationship to subsequent behaviour remains a serious challenge for personality psychology.

Situations as chosen by the individual

In everyday life, we often find ourselves confronted with situations we would not choose to be in but nevertheless have little chance of avoiding or escaping. A dangerous traffic situation, an unpleasant encounter at work or the necessity to defend one's opinion against alternative viewpoints are examples of not unusual situations that are more or less forced upon the individual regardless of his or her wishes. On the other hand, there is also a considerable degree of freedom for the individual person not only in choosing certain situations in preference over others but also in influencing and shaping a particular situation according to his or her ideas. Frequently, people are in a position to affect the unfolding and subsequent course of a situation by their own actions and also their cognitive activities. They can actively manipulate the way they are seen by others, influence the physical and psychological properties of the situation, and decide to leave the situation once they feel it is no longer satisfactory to them. Therefore, if the study of the psychological situation is to become an integral part of personality research, then the issue of how persons create and choose between different situations must also be addressed. In this vein, Buss (1987) has argued that the study of naturally occurring links between personal dispositions and features of situations should replace the widely criticized ANOVA strategy (that is, the apportioning of the variance accounted for by person factors, situation factors and their interaction term; see Chapter 4) as the research paradigm of modern interactionism. He suggests three basic mechanisms by which such person–situation links are created:

1 Selection – the preference for entering certain situations at the expense of others.
2 Evocation – the process of unintentionally eliciting certain responses from the environment, especially from other persons.
3 Manipulation – the active and intentional attempt to alter and control the features of the situation, most notably the behaviour of interaction partners.

So far, few research efforts have been devoted to these issues compared with the amount of work on how people *respond* to situations in which they find themselves. Nevertheless, some promising developments towards examining the role of situations *as being chosen, shaped and influenced* by the individual participants have emerged in recent years. They will be reviewed in the following sections.

Situated identities
Starting from a distinctly sociological orientation, Alexander and his co-workers (see for example, Alexander and Rudd, 1981; Alexander and Wiley, 1981) have proposed a theoretical model pertaining to the issue of how people decide between different courses of action in a given situation. Their *situated identity theory* is based on the postulate, derived from symbolic interactionism (Goffman, 1959), that people must mutually negotiate their respective identities before any social interaction is possible. In this process of identity negotiation (and continuous re-negotiation as the interaction carries on), the definition of situational meaning by the participants is of central importance. It is stipulated that in any social encounter, people are concerned with creating a particular social identity, that is, a particular way of portraying themselves to others. The exact nature of the intended social identity is determined in large part by the characteristics of the respective situation, and it is this feature that is stressed in the concept of situated identities. As Alexander and Rudd (1981: 83) point out, the actor faces 'a limited set of feasible behavioral alternatives, and each alternative carries its own consensually defined identity'.

Thus, in a situation where the person has a choice between different behavioural options, each option is assumed to be associated with a particular situated identity. Operationally, this identity may be defined in terms of the dispositional inferences an observer would make about a person choosing the particular option. From this operational definition, it becomes clear that situated identity theory applies to those types of situations where others are 'psychologically present', that is to say, are imagined as potential interaction partners by the actor without necessarily being physically present. For example, in a typical everyday helping situation, such as witnessing somebody accidentally dropping a banknote, different responses are possible. The observer may pick up the note and return it, pick it up and put it in his or her own pocket, tell the other person that he or she has dropped something, or simply ignore the incident. Each of these options is associated with a different situated identity, that is, suggests different inferences about the person behaving in that way (see Kaplan (1986) for a similar argument with regard to the self-referent aspects of social identity).

Situated identity theory has been developed as a model for predicting which behavioural option is most likely to be chosen by the person. In general terms, the process of identity formation is conceived of as consisting of two stages (see Alexander and Lauderdale, 1977). In the first stage, the person confronting a situation where a choice between different behavioural options is required has to *anticipate* the situated identities that would result from his or her choice of each of the different alternatives. On this basis, the person decides in favour of one course of action, whereby the prediction is that he or she will typically choose the option that is associated with the *most socially desirable* identity. Thus, the basic tenet of the theory is that:

> the achievement of a favorable identity is the leading consideration in interactive social situations . . . In effect, situated identity theory argues that the relevant cues in the behavioral settings are *first* translated into identity potentials, and that these identity potentials provide the basis for specific behavioral choices. (Alexander and Lauderdale, 1977: 226 and 232)

This conceptualization of the process of situated identity formation has several important implications. The first is that in order to anticipate different situated identities, the person must arrive at a subjective interpretation of the given situation, that is, establish situational meaning. Secondly, since it is assumed that the person will be motivated to identify (and subsequently perform) the most socially desirable option, the normative expectations inherent in the situation are crucial determinants of the ascription of situational meaning. That is, individuals can only make a decision on what they consider to be the most socially desirable behaviour if they are aware of the normative standards applying to the respective situation. Thirdly, social desirability has to be defined more precisely with respect to the evaluative dimensions that are relevant to the situation. Depending on the nature of the situation, different identity dimensions (such as competence, spontaneity, friendliness) will be salient and have to be explicitly identified to define the exact meaning of a 'favourable' identity. Finally, in order to make clear-cut predictions of behavioural choices, situated identity theory requires that the different behavioural options differ noticeably in terms of their social desirability and that they do not differ substantially in other important respects that might account for the person's deciding in favour of a less desirable option.

Returning to the example of the dropped banknote, the above analysis suggests the following sequence. First, the observer would have to form an impression of what the different options (returning the note, keeping it, informing the other person, or ignoring the incident) would 'tell' about him- or herself. In so doing, consideration of the normative evaluations associated with each option play a crucial role. To the extent that he or she shares the consensually accepted norms for appropriate behaviour in this type of situation, the person would probably conclude that ignoring the incident would create an unfavourable situated identity in the sense of being seen as uncooperative, while picking up the note and keeping it would create an even less desirable identity. The remaining two options (returning the note versus informing the loser) are both linked with a positive public identity and are therefore likely to be chosen. However, from the point of view of situated identity theory they are probably too similar in terms of social desirability to allow a clear-cut prediction of what the person will eventually decide to do.

Empirical evidence in support of the predictions of situated identity theory is reviewed by Alexander and Rudd (1981) and Alexander and Wiley (1981). So far, most of the studies have been concerned with demonstrating that observers can accurately predict the behaviour of actors on the basis of their perceptions of the situated identities associated with different behavioural choices. In particular, the theory has been applied to the behavioural choices faced by participants in a variety of classical social psychological studies, such as cognitive dissonance or conformity experiments. Employing a role-playing or simulation paradigm (Alexander and Scriven, 1977), observer subjects are typically presented with descriptions of one of the experimental conditions and asked to make a response *as if* they were subjects in the original experiment. Furthermore, they are asked to define the situated identities associated with the different response options in each condition by rating a person performing a given option on a number of evaluative scales. The overall favourability of these ratings is interpreted as the situated identity score pertaining to the respective choice.

A typical example of this research strategy as well as the answers it is designed to provide is the study by Alexander and Lauderdale (1977). The authors simulated the procedure of a conformity experiment which examined the extent to which high versus low ability subjects switched over to their partner's judgement in a visual judgement task. In the original study, it had been found that subjects who were first led to believe they lacked the ability required to solve the task and then interacted with a high ability partner revised their initial choices significantly more frequently to conform with their partner's choice than did high ability subjects interacting with a low ability partner. In the Alexander and Lauderdale simulation of this experiment, subjects received a detailed description of either the high or low ability condition of the original experiment, following which they completed two tasks. First, they were asked to make a choice (either stay with the initial judgement or switch over to the partner's choice in each of twenty trials) from the point of view of the original subject. These simulated scores were compared with the original responses and revealed a high degree of correspondence. From the point of view of situated identity theory, this correspondence is taken as evidence that both the original subjects and the observers in the simulation study responded to similar normative expectations inherent in the situation. The question remains, however, whether the choices shown by the experimental subjects (and accurately simulated by the observers) are actually those associated with more positive situated identities. To address this issue, subjects were informed, in the second part of the study, about the alleged 'actual' choices of a subject in the original experiment. The fictitious choices were manipulated such that the original participant was portrayed as sticking to his initial choice for twenty, sixteen, twelve, eight, four, or zero times in either the low or high ability condition. They were then asked to rate that subject on thirty-five evaluative dimensions as well as indicate the ten most relevant dimensions in forming their impression. While subjects did agree in their evaluations of persons sticking to their original choices, there was marked disagreement on how to evaluate a high shift rate to the partner's choices on the part of the 'low ability subjects'. An inspection of the mean situated identity scores revealed a parallel pattern. In the high ability condition, subjects were evaluated less favourably the more often they switched over to their partner's choices. This is a clear indication that for high ability subjects staying with their initial judgement is perceived by observers as being linked with the most positive situated identity. In the low ability condition, a different picture emerged. Showing both high stay rates *and* high change rates was perceived more favourably than showing an equal proportion of change and stay. This suggests that for some subjects staying with one's initial choice despite low ability is perceived as the socially desirable option, while for others conforming to the high ability partner is seen as the appropriate response under the circumstances.

Thus, Alexander and Lauderdale (1977), along with subsequent research (Alexander and Beggs, 1986; Alexander and Rudd, 1984) succeeded in showing that subjects' choices between different behavioural alternatives are indeed a function of the situated identities associated with each behavioural option in a given situation. The fact that highly similar patterns of results were shown by the experimental subjects and the observers simulating their responses indicates that the normative structure of the situation rather than internal psychological processes of the individual experimental subjects is the major determinant of behavioural decisions. Further support is lent to this reasoning by Bem and Funder (1978) who referred to the situated identity approach to illustrate their template matching technique (see Chapter 7). They used a template of the typical 'attitude changer' in a forced-compliance experiment, defined from the point of view of situated identity theory as a 'person likely to conform to norms', and showed that the amount of attitude change by subjects in an actual forced-compliance experiment correlated significantly with that template.

So far, research based on situated identity theory has concentrated on predictions in cases where little is known about the actor. In these cases, the consensually defined social desirability of different behavioural choices is regarded as the main source of information on which predictions about the person's behavioural decision can be based. If information about the actor's personality or previous behaviour is available, then the theory stipulates that rather than choosing the most socially desirable option the actor will decide in favour of the option that is most consistent with his or her previously construed social identity in similar situations (Alexander and Rudd, 1981). This prediction highlights the need for situated identity theory to define explicitly the terms under which situations are regarded as similar or even equivalent. The theory holds that two situations are equivalent if the choice alternatives in each of them are characterized by the same identity dimensions and receive the same ratings on those dimensions (Alexander and Wiley, 1981: 286). Let us consider the example of a person who is known to be concerned with adjusting his or her behaviour to the expectations of the social environment (such as the typical 'high self monitor'; Snyder, 1987). This person should show a consistent preference for norm-conforming behavioural choices across situations to the extent that the respective situations provide behavioural options that are similar in terms of their salient identity dimensions. However, empirical studies exploring the impact of specific knowledge about the actor on predicting his or her choices between subsequent behavioural options in similar situations are as yet lacking.[1]

In conclusion, situated identity theory offers a general framework for conceptualizing the meaning of situations which can broadly be characterized as a 'self-presentational' approach. At the core of this approach is the idea that people anticipate and are concerned about the social identity or image of themselves that a particular choice of action is likely to convey. As Alexander and Wiley summarize:

> The definition of the situation for a given actor is the configuration of situated identities that is created by each of the perspectives that are salient for him or her. We view this social reality as a continual flow of sequential choice possibilities, at each point of which the actor confronts an array of actionable alternatives. Each alternative is defined by the situated identity it can actualize. Thus, the actor chooses the personage he or she will become at each choice-point in an activity sequence. (1981: 288)

Situated identity theory thus acknowledges the actor's active role in interacting with his or her environment, whereby the communication of a favourable identity is regarded as a central concern involved in the subjective construction of situational meaning. This concern is salient not only in the diversity of social interactions encountered by the individual in his or her everyday activities. It is also actualized in a particular type of encounter that has special relevance for social as well as personality psychologists, namely responses to experimental settings and even to the items of personality inventories designed to elicit a particular personality profile from the individual (Alexander and Beggs, 1986). Thus, situated identity theory can also be taken as a starting point for reconsidering the relationship between subject and investigator as a central element of those contexts where information about the interaction of person and situation is typically obtained.

The influence of individuals on situations

In our discussion of situated identity theory, we have looked at a conceptualization of situational meaning that concentrates on individuals' choices of different behavioural alternatives available *within* a particular situation. In the present section, the emphasis will be on the principles underlying individuals' choices *between* different situations as well as their attempts to modify situations according to their personal preferences. It is this approach towards exploring how people actively shape their social environments as a function of their characteristic personal dispositions that Snyder and Ickes (1985) have designated as the 'situational strategy' for the study of personality and social behaviour. In general terms, the rationale of this strategy is described as follows:

> The underlying theme of the situational strategy for understanding individuals and their behavior in social contexts is the proposition that, as a consequence of their transactions with their social worlds, individuals construct for themselves social worlds that are suited to expressing, maintaining, and acting upon their conceptions of self, their social attitudes, and their characteristic dispositions. (Snyder and Ickes, 1985: 932)

Reversing the traditional question of how situations affect individuals, this perspective seeks to explain how individuals choose between as well as act upon situations so as to create settings for themselves in which they can best express and satisfy their personal goals (Snyder, 1981, 1983). This means that the clue to understanding the behaviour and personality of the individual is seen as lying in the particular situations the person chooses to seek or to avoid (Argyle, 1977; Endler, 1983; Mischel, 1977). Thus, the aim of the situational strategy is to define and explain an individual's personality in terms of the social environments the individual creates for himself or herself.

To choose the situations of their lives in the way stipulated by the situational strategy, individuals must have a relatively specific situational knowledge, that is, they must be able to assess the behavioural options provided by different social situations. As the work generated by situated identity theory has demonstrated, individuals do, indeed, have a clear-cut and consensually shared knowledge of the normative structures of different situations. This knowledge allows them to differentiate between situations that are congruent or incongruent with their personality and goals.

If an individual's personality is seen as being reflected in his or her choice of situations, then it is reasonable to expect that people will show a clear preference for situations that are congruent with their propensities. Indeed, in their review of the empirical evidence, Snyder and Ickes (1985) find strong support for the proposition that individuals actively prefer situations that are congruent with their personal qualities. Personal qualities, in this context, are conceived of not only as enduring traits but also include the person's self-concept, social attitudes and even bodily features, such as physical attractiveness.

The kind of information provided by the situational strategy about the influence of individuals upon the situations of their lives, is illustrated in two studies reported by Snyder and Gangestad (1982). The theoretical starting point for their analysis is the concept of 'self-monitoring'. This concept suggests that individuals differ reliably in the extent to which they orientate their behaviour towards meeting the expectations of their social environment (high self-monitoring individuals) or towards expressing their personal characteristics, attitudes, and values (low self-monitoring individuals). Snyder and Gangestad argue that this difference in orientation towards the self versus the social environment should find its reflection in individuals' choices of situations as well as attempts to change them. More specifically, they predict that high self-monitoring individuals should show a clear preference for situations which contain unambiguous behavioural specifications as opposed to situations which are ambiguous as to the exact nature of the behaviours considered to be appropriate in them. Low self-monitoring individuals, in contrast, should be less responsive to the clarity of behavioural specifications but should, instead, prefer to enter situations that are congruent with their personalities.

Both hypotheses were supported in a study in which introverted and extroverted subjects scoring either high or low on self-monitoring were offered a choice to enter or not to enter a situation requiring the display of sociable behaviours, whereby the nature of these behaviours was defined in either highly precise or very vague terms. As predicted, high self-monitoring individuals were much more willing to enter the clearly defined than the vaguely described situation irrespective of their level of introversion/extroversion. In contrast, the choices made by the low self-monitoring individuals were congruent with their introverted versus extroverted dispositions. In this group, readiness to join a situation requiring the expression of sociable behaviours was much higher for extroverts than for introverts, irrespective of the clarity with which behavioural requirements were described.

As far as traditional trait measures are concerned, there is further evidence to support the idea that people seek out situations that are most likely to meet their personal inclinations. For example, it has been demonstrated that extroverts prefer and feel more at ease in situations which provide opportunities for extroverted behaviour (Diener et al., 1984; Furnham, 1981), that a person's generalized locus of control determines his or her preference for situations where their outcomes are determined by their own skills as opposed to chance (Feather and Volkmer, 1988; Kahle, 1980), and that sensation seekers are particularly attracted by sensation-providing leisure activities (Mehrabian, 1978; Zuckerman, 1974). Studying the interaction between biological sex and sex-role orientation, Kenrick and Stringfield (1980) report that highly sex-typed, that is, 'masculine', men seek out sexually stimulating situations, while highly sex-typed, that is, 'feminine', women actively try to avoid those situations (see also Reis et al., 1980). Looking at specific classes of situations, Emmons et al. (1985) found further support for the situation choice model in the domains of recreation and work. One of their findings, for instance, was that extroverts showed a significantly stronger preference for studying in the library than for studying at home, suggesting that situational preferences as a function of personal dispositions manifest themselves even at a fine-grained level of analysis. On the other hand, the same principles seem to apply to highly complex and far-reaching types of situational choice like the selection of mates. Buss (1987) reports evidence that individuals show a clear preference for mates who are similar to themselves on certain central personality dimensions (see also Caspi and Bem's (1990) concept of 'proactive interaction'). Cantor et al. (1983–84) found that when individuals are given the chance to choose between different, though equally likeable, partners for different activities, they show a clear preference for partners perceived as particularly well-suited for the activity in question.

Similarly, it has been argued that people tend to seek situations that are likely to confirm their central attitudes. Furthermore, they readily seize the opportunity to influence the situation in such a way that their respective attitudes are made salient, for instance, by suggesting them as topics for discussion (Snyder, 1981). In a study by Snyder and Kendzierski (1982), individuals who were either in favour of or against affirmative action were invited to participate in a small group discussion on the benefits of affirmative action programmes for women and minorities. Within the two groups holding relatively favourable versus unfavourable attitudes on the issue, participants were further divided into high versus low self-monitoring individuals. Acceptance or rejection of the invitation to participate constituted the dependent variable of situational choice. On this basis, the following hypotheses were tested.

First, for low self-monitoring individuals, that is, those who feel that their behaviour should be a reflection of their personal attitudes, the decision to join a discussion group on affirmative action should be a function of the extent to which they endorse a favourable attitude on the subject. That is, the more favourable the attitude, the greater the likelihood that the low self-monitoring individual agrees to join the group. Secondly, for high self-monitoring individuals, that is, those who aim to bring their behaviour in line with socially accepted standards of behavioural appropriateness in a given situation, attitude towards affirmative action should be unrelated to their readiness to join the discussion. Instead, role considerations should be more salient for this group, resulting in a greater likelihood for women than for men to participate in the discussion.

Both hypotheses were clearly supported by the data, suggesting a reciprocal relationship between situational affordances and requirements on the one hand and individual predispositions on the other. As Snyder and Kendzierski argue, high self-monitoring individuals readily seize the opportunity to behave in a way that conforms to the expectations of their social environments. To the extent that affirmative action is seen as a topic particularly relevant to members of underprivileged groups, there is a normative expectation for members of these groups – women, in this case – to be actively involved in promoting the issue. In contrast, low self-monitors may be characterized by a distinct preference for attitude-congruent situations which provide them with opportunities not only to express their attitudes in behaviour (for example, presenting their case in a group discussion) but also to confirm their self-concepts as individuals who highly value the congruence between their private views and overt actions.

The functional significance of situational choice for confirming and verifying a person's self-conceptions is also stressed by Swann and Reid (1981). In a series of experiments, they examined the proposition that a central motive underlying individuals' social interactions is to confirm and stabilize their self-conceptions through social feedback. In the first experiment, subjects were shown to devote significantly more attention to social feedback that was in accordance with their self-conceptions than to feedback reflecting disagreement of the partner's evaluations with the subject's self-concept. In the second study, it was demonstrated that individuals were able deliberately to elicit responses from their interaction partners that confirmed their self-conception. Those subjects who thought of themselves as 'likeable' persons managed to elicit significantly more favourable evaluations from their partners following a 'getting-acquainted' conversation than subjects who had a self-conception of being 'dislikeable'. A closer inspection of the strategies used to elicit such confirmatory feedback revealed that the former group gave significantly more praise and compliments to their partners than members of the latter group. Similar processes of 'behavioural confirmation', that is, the elicitation of particular behaviours from a partner on the basis of prior expectations, are reported by Snyder et al. (1977). In their final experiment, Swann and Reid (1981) showed that the proposed self-verifying function of social interaction even extends beyond the boundaries of the actual encounter. Subjects were found to have significantly better recall for social feedback that confirmed their self-conceptions than for disconfirming feedback, suggesting that the motive to create a relatively stable and predictable social world runs as a pervasive thread through the different stages of an interaction from anticipation to recall.

Thus, there is considerable evidence to suggest a correspondence between personal dispositions and preference for situations providing congruent affordances. Examining this correspondence in terms of a causal chain, it becomes evident that the situational strategy is concerned with precisely the type of reciprocal interaction stressed by the dynamic version of modern interactionism (see Chapter 4). An individual's personal dispositions induce him or her actively to prefer congruent situational settings that would facilitate the behavioural expression of those dispositions. This situational choice, in turn, is likely to lead to a perpetuation of the respective dispositions, as it reinforces congruent behavioural orientations and does not provide incentives or challenges for change (Snyder, 1983). The fact that self-conceptions are highly resistant to change when studied in natural settings is explained in a similar way by Swann and Reid (1981).

However, as much as individuals are shown to be motivated to seek out situations that are congruent with their personalities, Snyder and Ickes (1985) point out that they may sometimes be equally attracted to incongruent situations. In particular, the search for and decision to enter incongruent settings provides two essential opportunities. First, entering situations which are incongruent with the person's existing self-concept enables him or her to use the shaping potential of those situations in the attempt to acquire and practise new skills and behavioural patterns conducive to change towards how the person would like to be. An example would be the shy person who persuades himself or herself to go out to discos to become more skilful in socializing with members of the opposite sex. In this case, while being incongruent with the person's real self, the chosen situation is congruent with the person's ideal self (see Cantor, 1990: 740). A second concern which may motivate individuals to enter situations incongruent with their personalities refers to attempts at changing an existing unsatisfactory situation into a more desirable one from the point of view of the actor. Thus, a liberal pro-abortion campaigner may deliberately choose the (incongruent) company of strict anti-abortionists in order to change their views on the issue. In this case, the emphasis is on changing the 'real' situation, including the attitudes and behaviours of its participants, into an 'ideal' situation, that is, one that is congruent with the individual's attitudes and values.

Even these last examples, however, are illustrative of the general claim that people, through their personalities and behaviours, exert a powerful influence on their social worlds rather than being merely influenced by them. At any point in time, their traits, attitudes, and self-conceptions affect the way in which they approach the situations of their lives, interact with different partners and cope with the constraints imposed on them by the demands of a 'strong' situation. Compared with the analysis of how individuals are influenced by situations, the complementary perspective of how situations are influenced by individuals has clearly received less attention. However, as the work reviewed in the present section has shown, the potential contribution of this perspective to our understanding of the dynamic interaction of the person and the situation is, at last, becoming recognized.

Summary

The present chapter examined the role of the situation as an emerging key concept in the study of personality. Starting from a brief review of different units of situational analysis and their implications for empirical research, the first part of the chapter was devoted to the analysis of situations in objective or quasi-objective (consensual) terms. The central concern of researchers in this area was shown to be the development of descriptive taxonomies of situations and their main defining features. It became clear that different sources of information (natural language, diary records, experimental manipulations, etc.) can be used as starting points for developing comprehensive lists of situations subsequently to be reduced into a limited set of distinct situational categories. At the same time, thinking about the usefulness of such taxonomies it became clear that they can only provide a first step towards approaching the psychologically more relevant question of the meaning of situations for individuals.

Consequently, the second section offered a review of the work designed to explore the 'psychological situation', that is, the subjective meaning assigned as part of an interpretative process to the objective, physical properties of a given situation. From this perspective, the search for a taxonomic description of situations is replaced by the search for central perceptual dimensions along which the interpretation of situations is cognitively organized. At the same time, recent models in cognitive social psychology have offered an answer to the question of how situational knowledge is stored and accessed in the course of a person's everyday experience. One respect in which a better understanding of the principles of situation cognition is essential for personality psychologists refers to the relationship between perceived situational meaning and subsequent behaviour. Therefore, a series of studies was presented examining the correspondence between perceived situational similarity and behavioural similarity across situations, as postulated in the interactionist concept of 'coherence'. Here, it became obvious that high levels of coherence can be shown if the situations involved are representative samples from an individual's personal experience. This research underlines once more the case for a greater idiographic orientation in personality psychology made in Chapter 7.

Most of the research devoted to the analysis of situations from the perspective of personality psychology has treated the situation as the 'independent' variable affecting the person's cognitive, affective, and behavioural responses. In the final section, this perspective was reversed, acknowledging people's active role in the selection and modification of situations. The distinctive ways in which individuals handle situational choices and challenges are at least as informative about their personalities as their characteristic ways of responding to given situational circumstances. At the cognitive level, they were shown to construct and anticipate 'situated identities' resulting from their choice of particular behavioural actions and then to implement the option conveying the most favourable identity. At the behavioural level, individuals actively seek out situations that are congruent with their personal dispositions while generally trying to avoid incongruent situations. Evidence was reviewed showing that specific dispositional constructs furnish accurate predictions of an individual's situational choices. This research stressing the active involvement of people in the creation and shaping of their social environment is an important complement to the more traditional perspective adopted in the first two sections which focused on the effects of situations on the individual. Altogether, the present chapter illustrated a broad spectrum of possibilities for advancing the study of personality through the systematic study of situations, giving rise to the optimistic belief that the conflict between situationist and dispositional explanations of behaviour will be finally laid to rest.

Note

1   Alexander and Rudd point out a difficulty involved in applying situated identity theory to this task: 'A potential difficulty arises when the orientations that define the important situated identities in a field are idiosyncratic. We will be in nomothetic trouble if persons attend to the orientational perspectives of uniquely imagined or implied others who are only privately present. To obviate this possibility we limit the scope of situated identity hypotheses to situations where actions are consensually defined – that is where actors of similar sociocultural backgrounds agree in their selections of situated identity dimensions and also concur in ratings along those dimensions (1981: 85–86).

9

Personality Psychology in the Nineties: An Outlook

The preceding chapters have covered a broad range of themes, theories, and methods that make up the current picture of personality psychology. In so doing, the discussion has progressed from issues that have traditionally been regarded as core ingredients of the discipline to research developments originally located at the fringes or even outside the field. There is no doubt that the notion of consistency, which provided the point of departure for the present analysis, has always been crucial to the self-definition of personality psychology in relation to other psychological domains. This is reflected not least in the force of the situationist attack on the consistency concept and the ensuing controversy that has preoccupied personality psychologists for decades. A closer inspection of the different meanings attached to the concept of consistency and the positions advanced in the controversy showed that little has been gained for the progress of personality psychology from the juxtaposition of dispositions on the one hand and situations on the other.

In contrast, several lines of development have emerged in the last decade which go beyond the search for empirical evidence of consistency and elaborate the theoretical foundations of the trait concept. As part of these efforts, the search for a taxonomy of basic trait categories acknowledges the close link between trait attributes and the everyday language of personality and has yielded a limited set of trait dimensions which incorporate a wide range of dispositional constructs. At the same time, researchers have pursued the idea that individual differences, as captured by different trait patterns, have a genetic basis. By showing that a number of traits are passed on from one generation to the next in a way that cannot be explained conclusively by learning and socialization effects, they have underlined the significance of traits as substantive constructs in personality research. A third facet of traits, which refers to their importance in communicating impressions of personality, has been explored as part of the social constructionist approach. Here, the focus is on the knowledge of trait meanings shared by members of a cultural community to explain how personal characteristics displayed by an individual are perceived and interpreted by an observer.

While the efforts of trait researchers have been directed at defending the study of personality in terms of dispositional constructs, the modern interactionist movement has been guided by the aim of reconciling dispositions and situations within one common frame of analysis. Behaviour is seen as the joint product of individual characteristics and the distinctive features of the situation which mutually influence one another in determining the person's actions. The inspection of three domains of personality analysis – anxiety, emotions, and prosocial behaviour – provided compelling evidence that the simultaneous consideration of personal and situational aspects leads to substantially improved predictions of behaviour. A number of recent contributions were reviewed showing how the development of personality can be approached from an interactionist perspective. Here, the continuous interplay of individual characteristics and environmental challenges is seen as holding the key to the understanding of personality development over the life course. What also became apparent, though, was that the sophisticated theorizing of the modern interactionist approach is not matched by equally sophisticated methods capable of capturing the proposed dynamic flow of person–situation interactions.

As far as methodological progress is concerned, a division of the field was identified which, in a way, parallels the dispute between advocates of the trait approach and their situationist challengers. This division refers to the appropriateness of a nomothetic versus idiographic level of analysis in personality. By exploiting the traditional range of methodological principles, such as aggregation of observations and use of multiple raters, researchers in the nomothetic mainstream have advanced strategies for enhancing the reliability and validity of personality measurement. At the same time, the development of measures directed at the individual person has made significant progress, reviving Allport's (1937) plea for a greater concern with the idiographic analysis of personality. Growing numbers of personality psychologists are now recognizing the need for a more complex analysis of persons' unique ways of handling their lives at different levels, from short-term responses and emotions to long-term life plans.

If the search for idiographic measures of personality is one example of a minority view gaining increasing acceptance in the field, then the call for incorporating situations into the study of personality is a second one. Situations affect behaviour in multiple ways, through their objective properties in time and space, through their psychological significance for the person and as behavioural platforms chosen and shaped by the individual according to his or her personal characteristics. The last two aspects in particular are of genuine concern to the personality psychologist. In the course of the consistency controversy, the situationist argument with its emphasis on objective (experimental) situations affecting all participants in more or less the same way prevented the subjective meaning of situations from being recognized and explored as a major force of individual behaviour. It also prevented personality psychologists from embarking on a more thorough analysis of the defining features of situations from which relevant situation taxonomies could be derived. This state of affairs has slowly begun to change over the last ten years or so, and the work reviewed in Chapter 8 bears witness to the growing prominence of the situation as a construct of personality psychology. In the search for coherence in individual behaviour across situations, the subjective perception of situational meaning has been demonstrated to be systematically related to behavioural regularities. Awareness has also been growing that individuals are not passively exposed to situational influences. They are constructively engaged in a continuous process of selecting those settings that are best suited for the expression and satisfaction of their personal dispositions and motives. Thus, personality psychology is no longer only about what people are per se but about what they are *in relation to* the particular settings and situations in which they find themselves or which they choose for themselves.

Judging from the breadth and diversity of research developments directed, in one way or another, at improving psychologists' knowledge of individual characteristics and behaviour, the field of personality psychology seems to be alive and well as it enters the 1990s. Introducing their volume on *Personality Psychology: Recent Trends and Emerging Directions*, Buss and Cantor (1989: 11) envisage 'an exciting future for the field of personality', a prospect expressed in almost the same words by other recent reviewers of the field (Angleitner, 1991; Magnusson, 1990b; Pervin, 1990c). Summarizing the contributions to his *Handbook of Personality*, Pervin (1990c: 723) stresses two major impressions that furnish his optimistic appraisal. The first is a shared emphasis on the complexity of personality. It is reflected in the view of behaviour as determined by multiple factors, including variables not traditionally assigned to the realm of personality psychology, such as physiological processes and environmental influences. The second characteristic of the current picture of personality research is closely linked to the first one and refers to a growing conceptual and methodological pluralism. If it is generally accepted that explanation and prediction of an indivi-

dual's characteristic way of behaving involves multiple determinants, then it is clear that no single methodology or central construct
will be successful in achieving this goal. Instead, the limits of
traditional personality psychology need to be, and indeed have
been, expanded to include a broader range of concepts and
methods, an endeavour clearly reflected in the readiness to forge
closer links with other fields. This development has had the
beneficial effect of lifting handed-down restrictions as to what
constitutes the germane subject matter of personality psychology:
'At least for the present [. . .] (and, we may hope, for the future),
the time of dismissal of some phenomena as not legitimate for
investigation and of hegemony of some research methods over
others have passed' (Pervin, 1990c: 725).

Overall, it appears fair to say that over the last fifteen years, the
field of personality has been successful in overcoming the state of
crisis triggered, in large part, by the fundamental critique of the trait
concept in the course of the consistency debate. There has been a
steady increase in publications in virtually every area of personality
psychology (see Angleitner, 1991: 186), with research on the trait
concept, psychoanalytic work and biologically oriented contributions showing particularly impressive growth rates. As far as the
trait concept is concerned, it was seen in Chapter 3 that traits are
now firmly re-established as *the* core constructs of personality
analysis. While their utility as basic units for conceptualizing
personality structure is corroborated by the converging evidence on
the 'Big Five' factor structure, their explanatory power in accounting for individual differences in behaviour is backed by an impressive body of research pinpointing the genetic origins of those
differences.

At the same time, however, dispositional concepts from related
fields have been gaining prominence. The recent emphasis on goals
as *motivational* categories (Pervin, 1989b) and on *sociocognitive*
variables (Higgins, 1990; Mischel, 1990) is indicative of the trend to
supplement trait-based analyses of personality by distinctly dynamic
and process-oriented conceptualizations of personality dispositions.

The growing pluralism of methods and perspectives identified by
many recent reviewers of the field has become most evident in the
last two chapters of this volume. These chapters focused on
idiographic research strategies, long considered inferior and in-
appropriate by many personality psychologists, and on the analysis
of situational influences and their cognitive representations that had
been regarded as alien territory to the field of personality through
much of the consistency debate.

Emphasizing the need to incorporate the study of situational variables into the research agenda of personality psychologists was one of the major achievements of the modern interactionist movement. It is interesting, in this context, to examine the fate of this approach in the period covered by the present volume. Advocates of an interactionist understanding of personality in terms of the joint effect of intrapersonal and situational influences were the first to come up with an answer to the serious challenges levelled at the field in the situationist argument. They brought together evidence from a variety of sources and personality domains to support their claim that behaviour can be explained more accurately by the interactive influence of person and situation variables than by either type of variable alone. For quite a while, the apparent unanimity with which personality researchers committed themselves to the interactionist ticket concealed their failure to tackle convincingly a number of fundamental tasks. Among these, the development of methods for studying the proposed reciprocal interaction of personality variables and situations and the conceptual refinement of the subjective interpretation of situational meaning have posed the greatest difficulties. At the moment, one gets the impression that enthusiam for modern interactionism as an overarching paradigm for the study of personality is fading in view of the scale of the problems yet unanswered. As far as the analysis of the 'psychological situation' is concerned, it appears that the task has been taken over by social psychologists. From a social–cognitive point of view, they have explored the relationship between the individual and the situation as a bidirectional process: persons' subjective interpretation of the situations which they encounter in the course of their everyday lives *and* their active role in choosing and shaping situations according to their personal goals and preferences. Thus, the issue of person–situation interaction remains a central one, but it has gradually moved from the centre of personality psychology to another branch of research, namely social cognition (see the discussion of the social constructionist view in Chapter 3 as a parallel development with respect to the trait concept). The one area where the interactionist perspective does seem to be flourishing and accumulating a coherent body of knowledge is the study of personality development across the life-span. Whether or not both the methods and the findings from this line of research will eventually be channelled back into the cross-sectional analysis of person–situation interactions is likely to be crucial in deciding the future role of the modern interactionist approach.

At the level of personality measurement, the work reviewed in this volume gives rise to an optimistic outlook into the future. Despite notable progress in the development of more appropriate strategies for detecting behavioural consistency within a nomothetic framework, the limitations of such normative methodologies in understanding the personalities of individuals are felt more and more acutely. There can be no doubt that measurement error is reduced by aggregating behavioural information across multiple-act criteria or multiple raters, and that validity is enhanced by basing the search for behavioural regularities on a sample of acts whose representativeness for the trait in questions has been established empirically. At the same time, such variable-centred approaches (Mischel, 1983) inevitably and deliberately dismiss any variance due to the peculiar characteristics of the individual members of the sample as psychologically uninformative. In contrast, recent years have witnessed a steady growth in the number of investigators who regard the understanding of individual personalities as a central aspect of personality psychology. This shift in emphasis from a variable-centred to a person-centred perspective referring to systematic relationships of psychological constructs *within* the individual requires a fundamentally different methodological approach. The challenge is to devise a new range of research methods which treat the individual person as the primary unit of analysis without sacrificing accepted criteria of methodological rigour and the accumulation of more general knowledge about the principles of personality functioning.

Of the many implications entailed by the growing concern with individual persons and their characteristic ways of feeling, thinking and acting, one aspect stands out as particularly important. This aspect refers to the relationship between the investigator and his or her subjects in the process of psychological inquiry. Traditionally, there has been a clear-cut division of roles in the process of empirical research. The investigator formulates hypotheses, translates them into operational definitions, and selects appropriate instruments representing the operational definitions. The subject's role is to deliver valid data by dutifully completing the instrument(s). Interaction between the two parties is typically limited to two forms – instructions and debriefings.

From an idiographic point of view, this role division appears neither appropriate nor fruitful because it makes little use of the competence of the individual as expert on his or her personality. Some researchers have made explicit calls for assigning a more active and cooperative role to the subject in the process of personality research (Hermans, 1991; Hermans and Bonarius, 1991; Krahé, 1990; Mischel, 1984b; Zevon and Tellegen, 1982). However, the growing reliance on strategies asking subjects to generate samples of their own experiences – for example, in the form of personal projects, life tasks or life narratives – can be interpreted as indirect reflections of researchers' acknowledgement of subjects' intimate knowledge of their own personalities as an invaluable source of information. Looking at the issue from the social constructionist perspective described in Chapter 3, one could say that treating the individual as a 'co-investigator in personality psychology' (Hermans and Bonarius, 1991) institutionalizes the social construction of personality as a communicative process between the psychologist and the subject.

Thus, the traditional range of methodologies for studying personality has been enriched substantially by the growing acceptance of idiographic research methods. Rather than replacing nomothetic strategies of personality measurement, the development of methods in which the unique responses of the individual are retained in the subsequent analyses of the data represents significant progress towards methodological multiplicity in personality psychology.

As noted above, pluralism in both theoretical and methodological developments is a key feature of the current state of personality research. However, having a range of diverse constructs and methods is not, in itself, a guarantee for progress. For such diversity to be a genuine asset it is essential that the different aspects are integrated into a coherent framework so as to complement each other, rather than compete or just co-exist, in their contributions to understanding personality (Magnusson, 1990b: 3). As one critic points out with respect to the level of theoretical explanation,

> the field of personality psychology often appears to consist of several subdisciplines lacking a common vision or goal, rather than as a unified scientific discipline. . . . Thus, the ideological tensions between the different approaches represent a failure by the field to achieve a metalevel understanding of the mutual dependence of the approaches in the overall personological enterprise. (Wakefield, 1989: 333–334)

Wakefield (1989) identifies three levels of explanation whose integration into a comprehensive model of personality he sees as imperative for the progress of the discipline. The first is a motivational perspective on the analysis of *intentional* behaviour (that is, action) which is considered as the ultimate object of personological explanation. At the second level of analysis, the trait concept is invoked to explain why certain individuals consistently and recurrently *form* certain intentions. From this point of view, traits are understood as constructs referring to an individual's enduring disposition to generate particular intentions. Thus, the link between traits and behaviour is mediated by the concept of intentions: 'Traits explain actions, but they do so indirectly, by explaining the reasons that motivated the actions' (Wakefield, 1989: 338). However, in order to understand why individuals develop characteristic and relatively stable patterns of intentions guiding their behavioural performance, we need a third level of analysis that offers a *functional* explanation of observed trait–intention–behaviour sequences.

Evolutionary psychology represents an increasingly prominent functional account of personality and social behaviour seeking to provide *ultimate* explanations of genetic differences as well as differences in behaviour (for example, Buss, 1991; Gangestad, 1989; Hettema and Kenrick, 1989). According to this approach one key process, *natural selection*, explains the emergence of personality characteristics in the evolutionary history of the human species. In line with the Darwinian principle of natural selection, the survival of personality characteristics, such as dominance or extroversion, is explained as a function of their adaptive value, that is, their instrumentality for the survival of the individual or the reproduction of the species. The adaptive value of a behaviour for individual survival is high if it enables the person to cope successfully with the demands and challenges of his or her environment. Prime criteria for successful coping are the acquisition of power and status as well as reproductive success, that is, the ability of the organism to pass his or her genetic make-up on to the next generation. Thus, the guiding question for understanding the ultimate causes of individual differences is directed at the specific adaptive problems confronting an organism in a particular domain and the analysis of tactics and strategies used to address these problems. For example, the fact that the formation of social hierarchies is a pervasive feature of human societies poses the adaptive problem of devising mechanisms that control and regulate positions and transitions within the hierarchy. For the individual members of the society, this should result in the natural selection of those attributes that are most likely to provide access to the higher levels of the hierarchy. By referring to the principle of natural selection as the basic mechanism underlying the phylogenetic emergence of personality attributes, evolutionary psychology is proffered by its advocates as a powerful metatheory which 'provides for personality psychology the grand framework it seeks, and which has been missing almost entirely from its core formulations' (Buss, 1991: 486). As this quotation illustrates, if there is a zeitgeist in personality psychology today, it undoubtedly lies in the rapidly growing acceptance of biologically based models of personality functioning.

As the field presents itself in the variety of research developments reviewed in the preceding chapters, it is evident that personality psychology is currently experiencing a time of new departures.

These departures, however, do not involve a radical break with the past. On the contrary, locating the roots of one's work in the seminal contributions of leading figures of some fifty years ago, such as Allport, Murray, or Lewin, has become almost commonplace and is implied to add extra significance to the authors' own approach. In between the distant past and the last decade, however, personality psychology went through a period of 'dark years', less readily acknowledged, which was marked by controversies both within the field itself and with other theoretical perspectives. In dealing with this chequered history, a new generation of 'spirited young' personality psychologists appears to be rising that 'is not mired in the problems of the past, but rather extracts the best from the past while pushing optimistically towards the future' (Buss and Cantor, 1989: 11). It is hoped that the present volume provides some help in making informed guesses on the themes, concepts and methods most likely to shape the appearance of personality psychology in the year 2000.

References

Abelson, R.P. (1981) The psychological status of the script concept. *American Psychologist*, 36: 715–729.

Abramson, P.R. (1980) *Personality*. New York: Holt, Rinehart & Winston.

Ackerman, C.A. and Endler, N.S. (1985) The interaction model of anxiety and dental treatment. *Journal of Research in Personality*, 19: 78–88.

Acock, A.C. and Scott, W.J. (1980) A model for predicting behavior: The effect of attitude and social class on high and low visibility political participation. *Social Psychology Quarterly*, 43: 59–72.

Ajzen, I. (1987) Attitudes, traits, and actions: Dispositional prediction of behavior in personality and social psychology. In L. Berkowitz (ed.), *Advances in Experimental Social Psychology*, vol. 20, pp. 1–63. San Diego, CA: Academic Press.

Ajzen, I. (1988) *Attitudes, Personality, and Behavior*. Milton Keynes: Open University Press.

Alexander, C.N. and Beggs, J.J. (1986) Disguising personal inventories: A situated identity strategy. *Social Psychology Quarterly*, 49: 192–200.

Alexander, C.N. and Lauderdale, P. (1977) Situated identities and social influence. *Sociometry*, 40: 225–233.

Alexander, C.N. and Rudd, J. (1981) Situated identities and response variables. In J.T. Tedeschi (ed.), *Impression Management Theory and Social Psychological Research*, pp. 83–103. New York: Academic Press.

Alexander, C.N. and Rudd, J. (1984) Predicting behaviors from situated identities. *Social Psychology Quarterly*, 47: 172–177.

Alexander, C.N. and Scriven, G.D. (1977) Role playing: An essential component of experimentation. *Personality and Social Psychology Bulletin*, 3: 455–466.

Alexander, C.N. and Wiley, M.G. (1981) Situated activity and identity formation. In M. Rosenberg and R.H. Turner (eds), *Social Psychology: A Sociological Perspective*, pp. 269–289. New York: Basic Books.

Allen, B.P. and Potkay, C.R. (1981) On the arbitrary distinction between states and traits. *Journal of Personality and Social Psychology*, 41: 916–928.

Allen, B.P. and Potkay, C.R. (1983) Just as arbitrary as ever: Comments on Zuckerman's rejoinder. *Journal of Personality and Social Psychology*, 44: 1087–1098.

Allport, G.W. (1937) *Personality: A Psychological Interpretation*. New York: Holt.

Allport, G.W. (1961) *Pattern and Growth in Personality*. New York: Holt, Rinehart & Winston.

Allport, G.W. (1966) Traits revisited. *American Psychologist*, 21: 1–10.

Allport, G.W. and Odbert, H.S. (1936) Trait names: A psycho-lexical study. *Psychological Monographs*, 47: No. 1.

Alston, W.P. (1975) Traits, consistency and conceptual alternatives for personality theory. *Journal for the Theory of Social Behaviour*, 5: 17–48.

Amato, P.R. and Pearce, P. (1983) A cognitively-based taxonomy of helping. In

M. Smithson, P.R. Amato and P. Pearce, *Dimensions of Helping Behaviour*, pp. 22–36. Oxford: Pergamon.

Amato, P.R. and Saunders, J. (1985) The perceived dimensions of help-seeking episodes. *Social Psychology Quarterly*, 48: 130–138.

Amelang, M. and Borkenau, P. (1984) Constructing cross-situational consistencies in behavior: Some tests on Bem's thoughts on social desirability as a moderator variable. In H. Bonarius, G. van Heck and N. Smid (eds), *Personality Psychology in Europe*, pp. 101–110. Lisse: Swets & Zeitlinger.

Andrews, K.H. and Kandel, D.B. (1979) Attitude and behavior: A specification of the contingent consistency hypothesis. *American Sociological Review*, 44: 298–310.

Angleitner, A. (1991) Personality psychology: Trends and developments. *European Journal of Personality*, 5: 185–197.

Angleitner, A. and Demtröder, A.I. (1988) Acts and dispositions: A reconsideration of the act frequency approach. *European Journal of Personality*, 2: 121–141.

Angleitner, A., Buss, D.M. and Demtröder, A.I. (1990) A cross-cultural comparison using the act frequency approach (AFA) in West Germany and the United States. *European Journal of Personality*, 4: 187–207.

Angleitner, A., Ostendorf, F. and John, O.P. (1990) Towards a taxonomy of personality descriptors in German: A psycho-lexical study. *European Journal of Personality*, 4: 89–118.

Argyle, M. (1977) Predictive and generative rule models of person × situation interaction. In D. Magnusson and N.S. Endler (eds), *Personality at the Crossroads*, pp. 353–370. Hillsdale, NJ: L. Erlbaum.

Argyle, M. and Little, B.R. (1972) Do personality traits apply to social behaviour? *Journal for the Theory of Social Behaviour*, 2: 1–35.

Argyle, M., Furnham, A. and Graham, J.A. (1981) *Social Situations*. Cambridge: Cambridge University Press.

Argyle, M., Graham, J.A., Campbell, A. and White, P. (1979) The rules of different situations. *New Zealand Psychology*, 8: 13–22.

Aronoff, J. and Wilson, J.P. (1985) *Personality and the Social Process*. Hillsdale, NJ: L. Erlbaum.

Asendorpf, J.B. (1988) Individual response profiles in the behavioural assessment of personality. *European Journal of Personality*, 2: 155–167.

Athay, M. and Darley, J.M. (1981) Toward an interaction-centered theory of personality. In N. Cantor and J.F. Kihlstrom (eds), *Personality, Cognition, and Social Interaction*, pp. 281–303. Hillsdale, NJ: L. Erlbaum.

Ball, D.W. (1972) 'The definition of situation': Some theoretical and methodological consequences of taking W.I. Thomas seriously. *Journal for the Theory of Social Behaviour*, 2: 61–82.

Baltes, P.B., Reese, H.W. and Lipsitt, L.P. (1980) Life-span developmental psychology. *Annual Review of Psychology*, 31: 65–110.

Bandura, A. (1969) *Principles of Behavior Modification*. New York: Holt, Rinehart & Winston.

Bandura, A. (1977) *Social Learning Theory*. Englewood Cliffs, NJ: Prentice Hall.

Bandura, A. (1986) *Social Foundations of Thought and Action*. Englewood Cliffs, NJ: Prentice Hall.

Bandura, A., Ross, D. and Ross, S.A. (1963) Imitation of film-mediated aggressive models. *Journal of Abnormal and Social Psychology*, 66: 3–11.

Baron, R.M. and Boudreau, L.A. (1987) An ecological perspective on integrating personality and social psychology. *Journal of Personality and Social Psychology*, 53: 1222–1228.

Baron, R.M. and Kenny, D.A. (1986) The moderator–mediator variable distinction in social psychological research: Conceptual, strategic, and statistical considerations. *Journal of Personality and Social Psychology*, 51: 1173–1182.

Batson, C.D. and Coke, J.S. (1981) Empathy: A source of altruistic emotion for helping? In J.P. Rushton and R.M. Sorrentino (eds), *Altruism and Helping Behavior: Social, Personality, and Developmental Perspectives*, pp. 167–198. Hillsdale, NJ: L. Erlbaum.

Batson, C.D., Batson, J.G., Griffit, C.A., Barrientos, S., Brandt, J.R., Sprengelmeyer, P. and Bayly, M. (1989) Negative state relief and the empathy altruism hypothesis. *Journal of Personality and Social Psychology*, 56: 922–933.

Batson, C.D., Bolen, M., Cross, J.A. and Neuringer-Benefiel, H.E. (1986) Where is the altruism in the altruistic personality? *Journal of Personality and Social Psychology*, 50: 212–220.

Batson, D.J., Duncan, B.D., Ackerman, P., Buckely, T. and Birch, K. (1981) Is empathetic emotion a source of altruistic motivation? *Journal of Personality and Social Psychology*, 40: 290–302.

Battistich, V.A. and Thompson, E.G. (1980) Students' perceptions of the college milieu: A multidimensional scaling analysis. *Personality and Social Psychology Bulletin*, 6: 74–82.

Baumeister, R.F. (1982) A self-presentation view of social phenomena. *Psychological Bulletin*, 91: 3–26.

Baumeister, R.F. and Tice, D.M. (1985) Toward a theory of situational structure. *Environment and Behavior*, 17: 147–192.

Baumeister, R.F. and Tice, D.M. (1988) Metatraits. *Journal of Personality*, 56: 571–598.

Beck, S.J. (1953) The science of personality: Nomothetic or idiographic? *Psychological Review*, 60: 353–359.

Bem, D.J. (1983a) Toward a response style theory of persons in situations. In M.M. Page (ed.), *Personality – Current Theory and Research*, pp. 201–231. 1982 Nebraska Symposium on Motivation. Lincoln, NB: University of Nebraska Press.

Bem, D.J. (1983b) Further déjà vu in the search for cross-situational consistency: A response to Mischel and Peake. *Psychological Review*, 90: 390–393.

Bem, D.J. (1983c) Constructing a theory of the triple typology: Some (second) thoughts on nomothetic and idiographic approaches to personality. *Journal of Personality*, 51: 566–577.

Bem, D.J. and Allen, A. (1974) On predicting some of the people some of the time: The search for cross-situational consistencies in behavior. *Psychological Review*, 81: 506–520.

Bem, D.J. and Funder, D.C. (1978) Predicting more of the people more of the time: Assessing the personality of situations. *Psychological Review*, 85: 485–502.

Bem, D.J. and Lord, C.G. (1979) Template matching: A proposal for probing the ecological validity of experimental settings in social psychology. *Journal of Personality and Social Psychology*, 37: 833–846.

Berger, P. and Luckmann, T. (1966) *The Social Construction of Reality*. Garden City, NY: Doubleday.

Berkowitz, L. and LePage, A. (1967) Weapons as aggression eliciting stimuli. *Journal of Personality and Social Psychology*, 7: 202–207.

Bishop, D.W. and Witt, P.A. (1970) Sources of behavioral variance during leisure time. *Journal of Personality and Social Psychology*, 16: 352–360.

Blass, T. (1984) Social psychology and personality: Towards a convergence. *Journal of Personality and Social Psychology*, 47: 1013–1027.

Block, J. (1961) *The Q-Sort Method in Personality Assessment and Psychiatric Research*. Springfield, IL: Thomas.

Block, J. (1968) Some reasons for the apparent inconsistency of personality. *Psychological Bulletin*, 70: 210–212.

Block, J. (1977) Advancing the psychology of personality: Paradigmatic shift or improvement of the quality of research. In D. Magnusson and N.S. Endler (eds), *Personality at the Crossroads*, pp. 37–63. Hillsdale, NJ: L. Erlbaum.

Block, J. (1982) Assimilation, accommodation, and the dynamics of personality development. *Child Development*, 53: 281–295.

Block, J. (1989) Critique of the act frequency approach to personality. *Journal of Personality and Social Psychology*, 56: 234–245.

Block, J. and Block, J.H. (1981) Studying situational dimensions: A grand perspective and some limited empiricism. In D. Magnusson (ed.), *Toward a Psychology of Situations*, pp. 85–102. Hillsdale, NJ: L. Erlbaum.

Block, J., Buss, D.H., Block, J.H. and Gjerde, P.F. (1981) The cognitive style of breadth of categorization: Longitudinal consistency of personality correlates. *Journal of Personality and Social Psychology*, 40: 770–779.

Borgatta, E.F. (1964) The structure of personality characteristics. *Behavioral Science*, 12: 8–17.

Borkenau, P. (1985) Vergleich einiger Verfahren zum Nachweis von Moderatoreffekten. *Zeitschrift für Differentielle und Diagnostische Psychologie*, 6: 79–87.

Borkenau, P. (1986) Towards an understanding of trait interrelations. Acts as instances of several traits. *Journal of Personality and Social Psychology*, 51: 371–381.

Borkenau, P. (1988) The multiple classification of acts and the big five factors of personality. *Journal of Research in Personality*, 22: 337–352.

Borkenau, P. (in press, a) Implicit personality theory and the five-factor model. *Journal of Personality*.

Borkenau, P. (in press, b) To predict some of the people more of the time: Individual traits and the prediction of behavior. In K.H. Craik, R. Hogan and R. Wolfe (eds), *50 Years of Personality Psychology. A Festschrift in Honour of Gordon Allport*. New York: Plenum.

Borkenau, P. and Liebler, A. (in press) Trait inferences: Sources of validity at zero acquaintance. *Journal of Personality and Social Psychology*.

Borkenau, P. and Ostendorf, F. (1990) Comparing exploratory and confirmatory factor analysis: A study on the five-factor model of personality. *Personality and Individual Differences*, 11: 515–524.

Botwin, M.D. and Buss, D.M. (1989) Structure of act report data: Is the five-factor model of personality recaptured? *Journal of Personality and Social Psychology*, 56: 988–1001.

Bouchard, T.J. and McGue, M. (1990) Genetic and rearing environmental influences on adult personality: An analysis of adopted twins reared apart. *Journal of Personality*, 58: 263–292.

Bower, G., Black, J. and Turner, T. (1979) Scripts in text comprehension and memory. *Cognitive Psychology*, 11: 307–336.

Bowers, K.S. (1973) Situationism in psychology: An analysis and critique. *Psychological Review*, 80: 307–336.

Brewer, M.B., Dull, V. and Lui, L. (1981) Perceptions of the elderly: Stereotypes as prototypes. *Journal of Personality and Social Psychology*, 41: 656–670.

Briggs, S.R. (1989) The optimal level of measurement for personality constructs. In D.M. Buss and N. Cantor (eds), *Personality Psychology: Recent Trends and Emerging Directions*, pp. 246–260. New York: Springer.

Briggs, S.R. and Cheek, J.M. (1986) The role of factor analysis in the development and evaluation of personality scales. *Journal of Personality*, 54: 106–148.

Bringle, R.G., Renner, P., Terry, R.L. and Davis, S. (1983) An analysis of situation and person components of jealousy. *Journal of Research in Personality*, 17: 354–368.

Brody, N. (1988) *Personality: In Search of Individuality*. San Diego, CA: Academic Press.

Broughton, R. (1984) A prototype strategy for construction of personality scales. *Journal of Personality and Social Psychology*, 47: 1334–1346.

Burke, P.A., Kraut, R.E. and Dworkin, R.H. (1984) Traits, consistency, and self-schemata. *Journal of Personality and Social Psychology*, 47: 568–579.

Burns, M.O. and Seligman, M.E.P. (1989) Explanatory style across the life-span: Evidence for stability over 52 years. *Journal of Personality and Social Psychology*, 56: 471–477.

Burton, R.V. (1963) The generality of dishonesty reconsidered. *Psychological Bulletin*, 70: 481–499.

Buss, A.H. (1989) Personality as traits. *American Psychologist*, 44: 1378–1388.

Buss, A.H. and Finn, S.E. (1987) Classification of personality traits. *Journal of Personality and Social Psychology*, 52: 432–444.

Buss, A.H. and Plomin, R. (1984) *A Temperament Theory of Personality Development* (rev. edn). New York: Wiley.

Buss, A.R. (1977) The trait–situation controversy and the concept of interaction. *Personality and Social Psychology Bulletin*, 3: 196–201.

Buss, D.M. (1984) Toward a psychology of person–environment (PE) correlation: The role of spouse selection. *Journal of Personality and Social Psychology*, 47: 361–377.

Buss, D.M. (1985) The act frequency approach to the interpersonal environment. In R. Hogan and W.H. Jones (eds), *Perspectives in Personality*, vol. 1, pp. 173–200. Greenwich, CT: JAI Press.

Buss, D.M. (1987) Selection, evocation, and manipulation. *Journal of Personality and Social Psychology*, 53: 1214–1221.

Buss, D.M. (ed.) (1990) *Biological Foundations of Personality: Evolution, Behavioral Genetics, and Psychophysiology*. Special Issue. *Journal of Personality*, 58.

Buss, D.M. (1991) Evolutionary personality psychology. *Annual Review of Psychology*, 42: 459–491.

Buss, D.M. and Cantor, N. (1989) Introduction. In D.M. Buss and N. Cantor (eds), *Personality Psychology: Recent Trends and Emerging Directions*, pp. 1–12. New York: Springer.

Buss, D.M. and Craik, K.H. (1980) The frequency concept of disposition: Dominance and prototypically dominant acts. *Journal of Personality*, 48: 380–392.

Buss, D.M. and Craik, K.H. (1983a) The act frequency approach to personality. *Psychological Review*, 90: 105–126.

Buss, D.M. and Craik, K.H. (1983b) Act prediction and the conceptual analysis of personality scales: Indices of act density, bipolarity, and extensity. *Journal of Personality and Social Psychology*, 45: 1081–1095.

Buss, D.M. and Craik, K.H. (1983c) The dispositional analysis of everyday conduct. *Journal of Personality*, 51: 393–412.

Buss, D.M. and Craik, K.H. (1984) Acts, dispositions, and personality. In B.A. Maher and W.B. Maher (eds), *Progress in Experimental Personality Research*, vol. 13, pp. 241–301. New York: Academic Press.

Buss, D.M. and Craik, K.H. (1986) The act frequency approach and the construction of personality. In A. Angleitner, A. Furnham and G. van Heck (eds), *Personality Psychology in Europe*, vol. 2, pp. 141–156. Lisse: Swets & Zeitlinger.

Buss, D.M. and Craik, K.H. (1989) On the cross-cultural examination of acts and dispositions. *European Journal of Personality*, 3: 19–30.

Butler, J.M. and Haigh, G.V. (1954) Changes in the relation between self-concepts and ideal concepts. In C.R. Rogers and R.F. Dymond (eds), *Psychotherapy and Personality Change*, pp. 55–75. Chicago: University of Chicago Press.

Campbell, A., Muncer, S. and Bibel, D. (1987) For disaggregation: A reply to Rushton and Erdle. *British Journal of Social Psychology*, 26: 90–92.

Campus, N. (1974) Transsituational consistency as a dimension of personality. *Journal of Personality and Social Psychology*, 29: 593–600.

Cantor, N. (1981) Perceptions of situations: Situation prototypes and person–situation prototypes. In D. Magnusson (ed.), *Toward a Psychology of Situations*, pp. 229–244. Hillsdale, NJ: L. Erlbaum.

Cantor, N. (1990) From thought to behavior: 'Having' and 'doing' in the study of personality and cognition. *American Psychologist*, 45: 735–750.

Cantor, N. and Kihlstrom, J.F. (1987) *Personality and Social Intelligence*. Englewood Cliffs, NJ: Prentice Hall.

Cantor, N. and Langston, C.A. (1989) Ups and downs of life tasks in a life transition. In L.A. Pervin (ed.), *Goal Concepts in Personality and Social Psychology*, pp. 127–167. Hillsdale, NJ: L. Erlbaum.

Cantor, N. and Mischel, W. (1979a) Prototypes in person perception. In L. Berkowitz (ed.), *Advances in Experimental Social Psychology*, vol. 12, pp. 4–52. New York: Academic Press.

Cantor, N. and Mischel, W. (1979b) Prototypicality and personality: Effects on free recall and personality impression. *Journal of Research in Personality*, 13: 187–205.

Cantor, N. and Zirkel, S. (1990) Personality, cognition, and purposive behavior. In L.A. Pervin (ed.), *Handbook of Personality: Theory and Research*, pp. 135–164. New York: Guilford Press.

Cantor, N., Mackie, D. and Lord, C.G. (1983–84) Choosing partners and activities: The social perceiver decides to mix it up. *Social Cognition*, 2: 256–272.

Cantor, N., Mischel, W. and Schwartz, J. (1982) A prototype analysis of psychological situations. *Cognitive Psychology*, 14: 45–77.

Cantor, N., Norem, J.K., Niedenthal, P.M., Langston, C.A. and Brower, A.M. (1987) Life tasks, self-concept ideals, and cognitive strategies in a life transition. *Journal of Personality and Social Psychology*, 53: 1178–1191.

Caprara, G.V. (1987) The disposition–situation debate and research on aggression. *European Journal of Personality*, 1: 1–16.

Carlson, M. and Miller, M. (1987) Explanation of the relation between negative mood and helping. *Psychological Bulletin*, 102: 91–108.

Carlson, M., Charlin, V. and Miller, N. (1988) Positive mood and helping behavior: A test of six hypotheses. *Journal of Personality and Social Psychology*, 55: 211–229.

Carlson, R. (1971) Where is the person in personality research? *Psychological Bulletin*, 75: 203–219.

Carlson, R. (1975) Personality. *Annual Review of Psychology*, 26: 393–414.

Carlson, R. (1984) What's social about social psychology? Where's the person in personality research? *Journal of Personality and Social Psychology*, 47: 1304–1309.

Carson, R.C. (1989) Personality. *Annual Review of Psychology*, 40: 227–248.

Cartwright, D.S. (1979) *Theories and Models of Personality*. Dubuque, IA: Brown.

Caspi, A. (1987) Personality in the life course. *Journal of Personality and Social Psychology*, 53: 1203–1213.

Caspi, A. (1989) On the continuities and consequences of personality: A life-course perspective. In D.M. Buss and N. Cantor (eds), *Personality Psychology: Recent Trends and Emerging Directions*, pp. 85–98. New York: Springer.

Caspi, A. and Bem, D.J. (1990) Personality continuity and change across the life course. In L.A. Pervin (ed.), *Handbook of Personality: Theory and Research*, pp. 549–575. New York: Guilford Press.

Caspi, A. and Moffitt, T.E. (1991) Individual differences are accentuated during periods of social change: The sample case of girls at puberty. *Journal of Personality and Social Psychology*, 61: 157–168.

Caspi, A., Bem, D.J. and Elder, G.H. (1989) Continuities and consequences of interactional style across the life course. *Journal of Personality*, 57: 375–406.

Caspi, A., Elder, G.H. and Bem, D.J. (1988) Moving away from the world: Life-course patterns of shy children. *Developmental Psychology*, 24: 824–831.

Casselden, P.A. and Hampson, S.E. (in press) Forming impressions from incongruent traits. *Journal of Personality and Social Psychology*.

Cattell, R.B. (1943) The description of personality: Basic traits resolved into clusters. *Journal of Abnormal and Social Psychology*, 38: 476–506.

Cattell, R.B. (1944) Psychological measurement: Normative, ipsative, interactive. *Psychological Review*, 51: 292–303.

Cattell, R.B. (1950) *Personality*. New York: McGraw-Hill.

Cattell, R.B. (1957) *Personality and Motivation Structure and Measurement*. Yonkers-on-Hudson, NY: World Book Company.

Champagne, B.M. and Pervin, L.A. (1987) The relationship of perceived situation similarity to perceived behavior similarity: Implications for social learning theory. *European Journal of Personality Psychology*, 1: 79–91.

Chaplin, W.F. (1991) The next generation of moderator research in personality psychology. *Journal of Personality*, 59: 143–178.

Chaplin, W.F. and Buckner, K.E. (1988) Self-ratings of personality: A naturalistic comparison of normative, ipsative, and idiothetic standards. *Journal of Personality*, 56: 509–530.

Chaplin, W.F. and Goldberg, L.R. (1985) A failure to replicate the Bem and Allen study of individual differences in cross-situational consistency. *Journal of Personallity and Social Psychology*, 47: 1074–1090.

Chatman, J. (1989) Improving interactional organizational research: A model of person–organization fit. *Academy of Management Review*, 14: 333–349.

Cheek, J.M. (1982) Aggregation, moderator variables, and the validity of personality tests: A peer-rating study. *Journal of Personality and Social Psychology*, 43: 1254–1269.

Chesterfield, P.D.S., Earl of (n.d.) *Letters to His Son*, ed. by O.H. Leigh, vol. 2, pp. 82–85. New York: Tudor.

Church, T.A. and Katigbak, M.S. (1989) Internal, external, and self-report structure of personality in a Non-Western culture: An investigation of cross-language and cross-cultural generalizability. *Journal of Personality and Social Psychology*, 57: 857–872.

Cialdini, R.B., Kenrick, D.T. and Baumann, D.J. (1982) Effect of mood on prosocial behavior in children and adults. In N. Eisenberg (ed.), *The Development of Prosocial Behavior*, pp. 339–359. New York: Academic Press.

Cohen, C.E. (1983) Inferring characteristics of other people: Categories and attribute accessibility. *Journal of Personality and Social Psychology*, 44: 34–44.

Colvin, C.R. and Funder, D.C. (1991) Predicting personality and behavior: A boundary on the acquaintanceship effect. *Journal of Personality and Social Psychology*, 60: 884–894.

Conley, J.J. (1984a) The hierarchy of consistency: A review and model of longitudinal findings on adult individual differences in intelligence, personality, and self-opinion. *Personality and Individual Differences*, 5: 11–26.

Conley, J.J. (1984b) Relation of temporal stability and cross-situational consistency in personality: Comment on the Mischel–Epstein debate. *Psychological Review*, 91: 491–496.

Conger, A.J. (1983) Toward a further understanding of the intuitive personologists: Some critical evidence on the diabolical quality of subjective psychometrics. *Journal of Personality*, 51: 248–258.

Corsini, R.J. (ed.) (1977) *Current Personality Theories*. Itasca, IL: F.E. Peacock.

Costa, P.T. and McCrae, R.R. (1985) *The NEO Personality Inventory*. Odessa, FL: Psychological Assessment Resources.

Costa, P.T. and McCrae, R.R. (1988a) Personality in adulthood: A six-year longitudinal study of self-reports and spouse ratings on the NEO personality inventory. *Journal of Personality and Social Psychology*, 54: 853–863.

Costa, P.T. and McCrae, R.R. (1988b) From catalog to classification: Murray's needs and the five-factor model. *Journal of Personality and Social Psychology*, 55: 258–265.

Costa, P.T., McCrae, R.R. and Arenberg, D. (1980) Enduring dispositions in adult males. *Journal of Personality and Social Psychology*, 38: 793–800.

Craik, K. H. (1986) Personality research methods: An historical perspective. *Journal of Personality*, 54: 18–51.

Crowne, D.P. and Marlowe, D. (1964) *The Approval Motive: Studies in Evaluative Dependence*. New York: Wiley.

D'Andrade, R.G. (1965) Trait psychology and componential analysis. *American Anthropologist*, 67: 149–170.

Davis, M.H. (1983) The effects of dispositional empathy on emotional reactions and helping. *Journal of Personality*, 51: 167–184.

Deaux, K. and Major, B. (1977) Sex-related patterns in the unit of perception. *Personality and Social Psychology Bulletin*, 3: 297–300.

Deluty, R.H. (1985) Consistency of assertive, aggressive, and submissive behavior for children. *Journal of Personality and Social Psychology*, 49: 1054–1065.

De Raad, B. and Hoskins, M. (1990) Personality-descriptive nouns. *European Journal of Personality*, 4: 131–146.

Diener, E. and Larsen, R. (1984) Temporal stability and cross-situational consistency of affective, behavioral, and cognitive responses. *Journal of Personality and Social Psychology*, 47: 871–883.

Diener, E., Larsen, R.J. and Emmons, R.A. (1984) Person × situation interactions: Choice of situations and congruence response models. *Journal of Personality and Social Psychology*, 47: 580–592.

Digman, J.M. (1988) Classical theories of trait organization and the Big Five Factors of personality. Paper presented at the Annual Meeting of the APA, Atlanta.

Digman, J.M. (1989) Five robust trait dimensions: Development, stability, and utility. *Journal of Personality*, 57: 195–214.

Digman, J.M. (1990) Personality structure: Emergence of the five-factor model. *Annual Review of Psychology*, 41: 417–440.

Digman, J.M. and Inouye, J. (1986) Further specification of the five robust factors of personality. *Journal of Personality and Social Psychology*, 50: 116–123.

Digman, J.M. and Takemoto-Chock, N.K. (1981) Factors in the natural language of personality: Re-analysis, comparison, and interpretation of six major studies. *Multivariate Behavioral Research*, 16: 149–170.

Dobson, K.S. (1983) A regression analysis of the interactional approach to anxiety. *Canadian Journal of Behavioral Science*, 15: 163–173.

Dolan, C.A. and White, J.W. (1988) Issues of consistency and effectiveness in coping with daily stressors. *Journal of Research in Personality*, 22: 395–407.

Donat, D.C. (1983) Predicting state-anxiety: A comparison of multidimensional and unidimensional trait approaches. *Journal of Research in Personality*, 17: 256–262.

Dweck, C.S. and Legett, E.L. (1988) A social-cognitive approach to motivation and personality. *Psychological Review*, 95: 256–273.

Dworkin, R.H. and Goldfinger, S.H. (1985) Processing bias: Individual differences in the cognition of situations. *Journal of Personality*, 53: 480–501.

Dworkin, R.H. and Kihlstrom, J.F. (1978) An S–R inventory of dominance for research on the nature of person–situation interactions. *Journal of Personality*, 46: 43–56.

Eckes, T. (1986) Eine Prototypenstudie zur natürlichen Kategorisierung sozialer Situationen. *Zeitschrift für Differentielle und Diagnostische Psychologie*, 7: 145–161.

Edwards, J.M. (1984) Situational determinants of behavior. In N.S. Endler and J. McV. Hunt (eds), *Personality and the Behavioral Disorders*, vol. 1, pp. 147–182. New York: Wiley.

Edwards, J.M. and Endler, N.S. (1983) Personality research. In M. Hersen, A.E. Kazdin and A.S. Bellack (eds), *The Clinical Psychology Handbook*, pp. 223–238. New York: Pergamon.

Edwards, J.M. and Endler, N.S. (1989) Appraisal of stressful situations. *Personality and Individual Differences*, 10: 7–10.

Edwards, L.A. and Klockars, A.J. (1981) Significant others and self-evaluation: Relationships between perceived and actual observations. *Personality and Social Psychology Bulletin*, 7: 244–251.

Ekehammar, B. (1974) Interactionism in psychology from a historical perspective. *Psychological Bulletin*, 81: 1026–1048.

Ekehammar, B., Schalling, D. and Magnusson, D. (1975) Dimensions of stressful situations: A comparison between a response analytical and stimulus analytical approach. *Multivariate Behavioral Research*, 10: 155–164.

Elder, G.H. and Caspi, A. (1988) Human development and social change: An emerging perspective on the life course. In N. Bolger, A. Caspi, G. Downey and M. Moorehouse (eds), *Persons in Context*, pp. 77–113. Cambridge: Cambridge University Press.

Elms. A.C. (1975) The crisis of confidence in social psychology. *American Psychologist*, 30: 967–976.

Emmons, R.A. (1986) Personal strivings: An approach to personality and subjective well-being. *Journal of Personality and Social Psychology*, 51: 1058–1068.

Emmons, R.A. (1989a) Exploring the relation between motives and traits: The case of narcissism. In D.M. Buss and N. Cantor (eds), *Personality Psychology: Recent Trends and Emerging Directions*, pp. 32–44. New York: Springer.

Emmons, R.A. (1989b) The personal strivings approach to personality. In L.A. Pervin (ed.), *Goal Concepts in Personality and Social Psychology*, pp. 87–126. Hillsdale, NJ: L. Erlbaum.

Emmons, R.A. (1991) Personal strivings, daily life events, and psychological and physical well-being. *Journal of Personality*, 59: 453–472.

Emmons, R.A. and Diener, E. (1986a) An interactional approach to the study of personality and emotion. *Journal of Personality*, 54: 371–384.

Emmons, R.A. and Diener, E. (1986b) Situation selection as a moderator of response consistency and stability. *Journal of Personality and Social Psychology*, 51: 1013–1019.

Emmons, R.A. and King, L.A. (1989) Personal strivings and affective reactivity. *Journal of Personality and Social Psychology*, 56: 478–484.

Emmons, R.A., Diener, E. and Larsen, R.J. (1985) Choice of situations and congruence models of interactionism. *Personality and Individual Differences*, 6: 693–702.

Emmons, R.A., Diener, E. and Larsen, R.J. (1986) Choice and avoidance of everyday situations and affect congruence: Two models of reciprocal interactionism. *Journal of Personality and Social Psychology*, 51: 815–826.

Endler, N.S. (1973) The person versus the situation – A pseudo-issue? A response to Alker. *Journal of Personality*, 41: 287–303.

Endler, N.S. (1975) A person–situation interaction model of anxiety. In C.D. Spielberger and I.G. Sarason (eds.), *Stress and Anxiety*, vol. 1, pp. 145–164. Washington, DC: Hemisphere.

Endler, N.S. (1980) Person–situation interaction and anxiety. In I.L. Kutash and L.B. Schlesinger (eds), *Handbook of Stress and Anxiety*, pp. 249–266. San Francisco: Jossey-Bass.

Endler, N.S. (1982) Interactionism comes of age. In M.P. Zanna, E.T. Higgins and C.P. Herman (eds), *Consistency in Social Behavior: The Ontario Symposium*, vol. 2, pp. 209–249. Hillsdale, NJ: L. Erlbaum.

Endler, N.S. (1983) Interactionism: A personality model, but not yet a theory. In M.M. Page (ed.), *Personality: Current Theory and Research*, pp. 155–200. 1982 Nebraska Symposium on Motivation. Lincoln, NB: University of Nebraska Press.

Endler, N.S. and Hunt, J.McV. (1968) S–R-inventories of hostility and comparisons of the proportions of variance from persons, responses, and situations for hostility and anxiousness. *Journal of Personality and Social Psychology*, 9: 309–315.

Endler, N.S. and Magnusson, D. (eds) (1976a) *Interactional Psychology and Personality*. New York: Hemisphere.

Endler, N.S. and Magnusson, D. (1976b) Toward an interactional psychology of personality. *Psychological Bulletin*, 83: 956–974.

Endler, N.S. and Okada, M. (1975) A multidimensional measure of trait-anxiety:

The S–R inventory of general trait anxiousness. *Journal of Consulting and Clinical Psychology*, 43: 319–329.

Endler, N.S., Hunt, J.McV. and Rosenstein, A.J. (1962) An S–R-Inventory of anxiousness. *Psychological Monographs*, 76: whole No. 536.

Endler, N.S., King, P.R., Edwards, J.M., Kuczynski, M. and Diveky, S. (1983) Generality of the interaction model of anxiety with respect to two social evaluation field studies. *Canadian Journal of Behavioral Science*, 15: 60–69.

Endler, N.S., Magnusson, D., Ekehammar, B. and Okada, M. (1976) The multidimensionality of state and trait anxiety. *Scandinavian Journal of Psychology*, 17: 81–96.

Endler, N.S., Parker, J.D., Bagby, R.M. and Cox, B.J. (1991) Multidimensionality of state and trait anxiety: Factor structure of the Endler Multidimensional Anxiety Scales. *Journal of Personality and Social Psychology*, 60: 919–926.

Epstein, S. (1979) The stability of behavior: I. On predicting most of the people much of the time. *Journal of Personality and Social Psychology*, 37: 1097–1126.

Epstein, S. (1980) The stability of behavior: II. Implications for psychological research. *American Psychologist*, 35: 790–806.

Epstein, S. (1983a) The stability of confusion. A reply to Mischel and Peake. *Psychological Review*, 90: 179–184.

Epstein, S. (1983b) Aggregation and beyond: Some basic issues on the prediction of behavior. *Journal of Personality*, 51: 360–392.

Epstein, S. (1983c) A research paradigm for the study of personality and emotions. In M.M. Page (ed.), *Personality: Current Theory and Research*, pp. 91–154. 1982 Nebraska Symposium on Motivation. Lincoln, NB: University of Nebraska Press.

Epstein, S. (1984) The stability of behavior across time and situations. In R.A. Zucker, J. Aronoff and A.I. Rabin (eds), *Personality and the Prediction of Behavior*, pp. 209–268. New York: Academic Press.

Epstein, S. and O'Brien, E. J. (1985) The person–situation debate in historical and current perspective. *Psychological Bulletin*, 98: 513–537.

Erikson, E.H. (1963) *Childhood and Society*, 2nd edn. New York: Norton.

Erkut, S., Jaquette, D.S. and Staub, E. (1981) Moral judgment–situation interaction as a basis for predicting prosocial behavior. *Journal of Personality*, 49: 1–14.

Eysenck, H.J. (1952) *The Scientific Study of Personality*. London: Routledge & Kegan Paul.

Eysenck, H.J. (1954) The science of personality: Nomothetic! *Psychological Review*, 61: 339–342.

Eysenck, H.J. (1970) *The Structure of Human Personality*, 3rd edn. London: Methuen.

Eysenck, H. (1990) Genetic and environmental contributions to individual differences: The three major dimensions of personality. *Journal of Personality*, 58: 245–261.

Falk, J.L. (1956) Issues distinguishing idiographic from nomothetic approaches to personality. *Psychological Review*, 63: 53–62.

Feather, N.T. and Volkmer, R.E. (1988) Preference for situations involving effort, time pressure, and feedback in relation to type A behavior, locus of control, and test anxiety. *Journal of Personality and Social Psychology*, 55: 266–271.

Fenigstein, A., Scheier, M. and Buss, A. (1975) Public and private self-consciousness: Assessment and theory. *Journal of Consulting and Clinical Psychology*, 43: 522–527.

Feshbach, S. (1984) The 'personality' of personality theory and research. *Personality and Social Psychology Bulletin*, 10: 446–456.

Fiedler, F.E. (1977) What triggers the person–situation interaction in leadership? In D. Magnusson and N.S. Endler (eds), *Personality at the Crossroads*, pp. 151–263. Hillsdale, NJ: L. Erlbaum.

Fiedler, F.E., Chemers, M.M. and Mahar, L. (1976) *Improving Leadership Effectiveness: The Leader Match Concept*. New York: Wiley.

Finn, S.E. (1986) Stability of personality self-ratings over 30 years: Evidence for an age/cohort interaction. *Journal of Personality and Social Psychology*, 50: 813–818.

Fiske, D.W. (1949) Consistency of the factorial structure of trait ratings from different sources. *Journal of Abnormal and Social Psychology*, 44: 329–344.

Fiske, D.W. (1978a) *Strategies for Personality Research*. San Francisco: Jossey-Bass.

Fiske, D.W. (1978b) Cosmopolitan constructs and provincial observations: Some prescriptions for a chronically ill specialty. In H. London (ed.), *Personality – A New Look at Metatheories*, pp. 21–43. Washington, DC: Hemisphere.

Fiske, S.T. and Taylor, S.E. (1984) *Social Cognition*. Reading, MA: Addison-Wesley.

Flavell, J.H. (1963) *The Developmental Psychology of Jean Piaget*. Princeton, NJ: D. van Nostrand.

Flood, M. and Endler, N.S. (1980) The interaction model of anxiety: An empirical test in an athletic competition situation. *Journal of Research in Personality*, 14: 329–339.

Forgas, J.P. (1976) The perception of social episodes: Categorical and dimensional representations of two different social milieus. *Journal of Personality and Social Psychology*, 34: 199–209.

Forgas, J.P. (1978) Social episodes and social structure in an academic setting: The social environment of an intact group. *Journal of Experimental Social Psychology*, 14: 434–448.

Forgas, J.P. (1979a) *Social Episodes: The Study of Interaction Routines*. London: Academic Press.

Forgas, J.P. (1979b) Multidimensional scaling: A discovery method in social psychology. In G.P. Ginsburg (ed.), *Emerging Strategies in Social Psychological Research*, pp. 254–288. New York: Academic Press.

Forgas, J.P. (1982) Episode cognition: Internal representations of interaction routines. In L. Berkowitz (ed.), *Advances in Experimental Social Psychology*, vol. 15, pp. 59–101. New York: Academic Press.

Forgas, J.P. (1983a) Episode cognition and personality: A multidimensional analysis. *Journal of Personality*, 51: 34–48.

Forgas, J.P. (1983b) Social skills and the perception of social episodes. *British Journal of Clinical Psychology*, 22: 195–207.

Forgas, J.P., Brown, L.B. and Menyhart, J. (1980) Dimensions of aggression: The perception of aggressive episodes. *British Journal of Social and Clinical Psychology*, 19: 215–227.

Frederiksen, N. (1972) Toward a taxonomy of situations. *American Psychologist*, 27: 114–123.

Funder, D.C. (1980) On seeing ourselves as others see us: Self–other agreement and discrepancy in personality ratings. *Journal of Personality*, 48: 473–493.

Funder, D.C. (1982) On assessing social psychological theories through the study of individual differences: template matching and forced compliance. *Journal of Personality and Social Psychology*, 43: 100–110.

Funder, D.C. (1983a) The 'consistency' controversy and the accuracy of personality judgments. *Journal of Personality*, 51: 346–359.

Funder, D.C. (1983b) Three issues in predicting more of the people: A reply to Mischel and Peake. *Psychological Review*, 90: 283–289.

Funder, D.C. (1989) Accuracy in personality judgment and the dancing bear. In D.M. Buss and N. Cantor (eds), *Personality Psychology: Recent Trends and Emerging Directions*, pp. 210–223. New York: Springer.

Funder, D.C. and Colvin, C.R. (1988) Friends and strangers: Acquaintanceship, agreement, and the accuracy of personality judgment. *Journal of Personality and Social Psychology*, 55: 149–158.

Funder, D.C. and Colvin, C.R. (1991) Explorations in behavioral consistency: Properties of persons, situations, and behavior. *Journal of Personality and Social Psychology*, 60: 773–794.

Funder, D.C. and Ozer, D.J. (1983) Behavior as a function of the situation. *Journal of Personality and Social Psychology*, 44: 107–112.

Furnham, A. (1981) Personality and activity preference. *British Journal of Social Psychology*, 20: 57–68.

Furnham, A. and Argyle, M. (eds) (1981) *The Psychology of Social Situations*. Oxford: Pergamon.

Furnham, A. and Jaspers, J. (1983) The evidence for interactionism in psychology: A critical analysis of the situation–response inventories. *Personality and Individual Differences*, 6: 627–644.

Furth, H. (1981) *Piaget and Knowledge*, 2nd edn. Chicago: Chicago University Press.

Gadlin, H. and Rubin, S.H. (1979) Interactionism: A nonresolution of the person–situation controversy. In A. R. Buss (ed.), *Psychology in Social Context*, pp. 213–238. New York: Irvington.

Gangestad, S.W. (1989) The evolutionary history of genetic variation: An emerging issue in the behavioral genetic study of personality. In D.M. Buss and N. Cantor (eds), *Personality Psychology: Recent Trends and Emerging Directions*, pp. 320–332. New York: Springer.

Geis, F.L. (1978) The psychological situation and personality traits in behavior. In H. London (ed.), *Personality – A New Look at Metatheories*, pp. 123–152. Washington, DC: Hemisphere.

Gergen, K.J. (1985) The social constructionist movement in modern personality. *American Psychologist*, 40: 266–275.

Gergen, K.J. and Davis, K.E. (eds) (1985) *The Social Construction of the Person*. New York: Springer.

Gibbons, F.X. and Wicklund, R.A. (1982) Self-focused attention and helping behaviour. *Journal of Personality and Social Psychology*, 43: 462–477.

Gibson, E.J. (1979) *The Ecological Approach to Visual Perception*. Boston, MA: Houghton Mifflin.

Gifford, R. (1982) Affiliativeness: A trait measure in relation to single-act and multiple-act behavioral criteria. *Journal of Research in Personality*, 16: 128–134.

Goffman, E. (1959) *The presentation of self in everyday life*. New York: Doubleday.

Goldberg, L. (1981) Language and individual differences: The search for universals in personality lexicons. In L. Wheeler (ed.), *Review of Personality and Social Psychology*, vol. 1, pp. 141–165. Beverly Hills, CA: Sage.

Goldberg, L. (1990) An alternative 'description of personality': The Big-Five factor structure. *Journal of Personality and Social Psychology*, 59: 1216–1229.

Golding, S.L. (1975) Flies in the ointment: Methodological problems in the analysis of the percentage of variance due to persons and situations. *Psychological Bulletin*, 82: 278–288.

Golding, S.L. (1977) The problem of construal styles in the analysis of person–situation interactions. In D. Magnusson and N.S. Endler (eds), *Personality at the Crossroads*, pp. 401–407. Hillsdale, NJ: L. Erlbaum.

Gormly, J. (1983) Predicting behavior from personality trait scores. *Personality and Social Psychology Bulletin*, 9: 267–270.

Gormly, J. (1984) Correspondence between personality traits ratings and behavioural events. *Journal of Personality*, 52: 220–232.

Gough, H.G. (1957) *Manual for the California Psychological Inventory*. Palo Alto, CA: Consulting Psychologists Press.

Gough, H.G. and Heilbrun, A.B. (1980) *The Adjective Check List Manual*, rev. edn. Palo Alto, CA: Consulting Psychologists Press.

Graesser, A.C., Wolls, S.B., Kowalski, D.J. and Smith D.A. (1980) Memory for typical and atypical actions in scripted activities. *Journal of Experimental Psychology: Human Learning and Memory*, 6: 503–513.

Greaner, J.L. and Penner, L.A. (1982) The reliability and validity of Bem and Allen's measure of cross-situational consistency. *Social Behavior and Personality*, 10: 241–244.

Guilford, J.P. (1959) *Personality*. New York: McGraw-Hill.

Guilford, J.P. (1975) Factors and factors of personality. *Psychological Bulletin*, 82: 802–814.

Hampson, S.E. (1988) *The Construction of Personality*, 2nd edn. London: Routledge & Kegan Paul.

Hampson, S.E. (1989) Using traits to construct personality. In D.M. Buss and N. Cantor (eds), *Personality Psychology: Recent Trends and Emerging Directions*, pp. 286–293. New York: Springer.

Hampson, S.E. (1990) Reconciling inconsistent information: Impressions of personality from combinations of traits. *European Journal of Personality*, 4: 157–172.

Hampson, S.E., Goldberg, L.R. and John, O.P. (1987) Category-breadth and social desirability values for 573 personality terms. *European Journal of Personality*, 1: 241–258.

Hampson, S.E., John, O.P. and Goldberg, L.R. (1986) Category breadth and hierarchical structure in personality: Studies of asymmetries in judgments of trait implications. *Journal of Personality and Social Psychology*, 51: 37–54.

Harris, J.G. jr. (1980) Nomovalidation and idiovalidation: A quest for the true personality profile. *American Psychologist*, 35: 729–744.

Harris, J.G. jr. (1984) Congruence and stability of multimethod profiles: A new pair of personality variables. *Journal of Personality*, 53: 586–602.

Hartshorne, H. and May, M.A. (1928) *Studies in the Nature of Character (Vol. 1): Studies in Deceit*. New York: Macmillan.

Heck, G.L. van (1989) Situation concepts. Definitions and classification. In P.J. Hettema (ed.), *Personality and Environment*, pp. 53–69. Chichester: Wiley.

Heilizer, F. (1980) Psychodigms of theory in personality and social psychology. *Psychological Reports*, 46: 63–85.

Hermans, H.J.M. (1988) On the integration of nomothetic and idiographic research methods in the study of personal meaning. *Journal of Personality*, 56: 785–812.

Hermans, H.J.M. (1991) The person as co-investigator in self-research: Valuation theory. *European Journal of Personality*, 5: 217–233.

Hermans, H.J.M. and Bonarius, H. (1991) The person as co-investigator in personality research. *European Journal of Personality*, 5: 199–216.

Hettema, J. and Kenrick, D.T. (1989) Biosocial interaction and individual adaptation. In P.J. Hettema (ed.), *Personality and Environment*, pp. 3–29. Chichester: Wiley.

Hettema, J., Heck, G.L. van, and Brandt, C. (1989) The representation of situations through films. In P.J. Hettema (ed.), *Personality and Environment*, pp. 113–127. Chichester: Wiley.

Higgins, E.T. (1990) Personality, social psychology, and person–situation relations: Standards and knowledge activation as a common language. In L.A. Pervin (ed.), *Handbook of Personality: Theory and Research*, pp. 302–338. New York: Guilford Press.

Hirschberg, N. (1978) A correct treatment of traits. In H. London (ed.), *Personality – A New Look at Metatheories*, pp. 48–68. Washington, DC: Hemisphere.

Hoffmann, M.L. (1981) Is altruism part of human nature? *Journal of Personality and Social Psychology*, 40: 121–137.

Hofstee, W.K.B. (1990) The use of everyday personality language for scientific purposes. *European Journal of Personality*, 4: 77–88.

Hogan, R. (1986) *Hogan Personality Inventory*. Minneapolis, MN: National Computer Systems.

Hogan, R.T. and Emler, N.P. (1978) The biases in contemporary social psychology. *Social Research*, 45: 478–534.

Hogan, R., Hogan, J., Briggs, S. and Jones, W. (1983) Sense, nonsense, and the use of personality measures. *Journal of Research in Personality*, 17: 451–456.

Holt, R.R. (1962) Individuality and generalization in the psychology of personality. *Journal of Personality*, 30: 377–404.

Houts, A.C., Cook, T.D. and Shaddish, W.R. (1986) The person–situation debate: A critical multiplist perspective. *Journal of Personality*, 54: 52–105.

Howard, J.A. (1979) Person–situation interaction models. *Personality and Social Psychology Bulletin*, 5: 191–195.

Howe, M.J.A. (1982) Biographical evidence and the development of outstanding individuals. *American Psychologist*, 37: 1071–1081.

Hoy, E. and Endler, N.S. (1969) Types of stressful situations and their relation to trait anxiety and sex. *Canadian Journal of Behavioural Science*, 1: 207–214.

Huesman, L.R. and Eron, L.D. (1989) Individual differences and the trait of aggression. *European Journal of Personality*, 3: 95–106.

Huesman, L.R., Eron, L.D., Lefkowitz, M.M. and Walder, L.O. (1984) The stability of aggression over time and generations. *Developmental Psychology*, 20: 1120–1134.

Hyland, M.E. (1984) Interactionism and the person × situation debate. In J.R. Royce and L.P. Mos (eds), *Annals of Theoretical Psychology*, vol. 2, pp. 303–328. New York: Plenum Press.

Hyland, M.E. (1985) Traits, processes, and the purpose of templates. *Journal of Research in Personality*, 19: 72–77.

Jaccard, J. (1979) Personality and behavioral prediction: An analysis of behavioral criterion measures. In L.R. Kahle (ed.), *Methods for Studying Person–Situation Interactions*, pp. 73–91. New Directions for Methodology of Behavioral Science, 2. San Francisco: Jossey-Bass.

Jaccard, J. and Dittus, P. (1990) Idiographic and nomothetic perspectives on research methods and data analysis. In C. Hendrick and M. S. Clark (eds),

Research Methods in Personality and Social Psychology, pp. 312–351. Newbury Park, CA: Sage.

Jaccard, J. and Wood, G. (1986) An idiothetic approach to behavioral decision making. In D. Brinberg and R. Lutz (eds), *Perspectives on Methodology in Consumer Behavior*, pp. 67–106. New York: Springer.

Jaccard, J., Wan, C.K. and Wood, G. (1988) Idiothetic methods for the analysis of behavioral decision making. In J.C. Mancuso and M.L. Shaw (eds), *Cognition and Personal Structures*, pp. 137–167. New York: Praeger.

Jackson, D.N. (1967) *Personality Research Form Manual*. Goshen, NY: Research Psychologists Press.

Jackson, D.N. (1984) *Personality Research Form Manual*, 3rd edn. Port Huron, MI: Research Psychologists Press.

Jackson, D.N. and Paunonen, S.V. (1985) Construct validity and the predictability of behavior. *Journal of Personality and Social Psychology*, 49: 554–570.

Jaspers, J.M. (1985) The future of social psychology: Taking the past to heart. In A. Furnham (ed.), *Social Behavior in Context*, pp. 273–310. Boston: Allyn and Bacon.

Jessor, R. (1981) The perceived environment in psychological theory and research. In D. Magnusson (ed.), *Toward a Psychology of Situations*, pp. 297–317. Hillsdale, NJ: L. Erlbaum.

John, O.P. (1990) The 'big five' factor taxonomy: Dimensions of personality in the natural language and in questionnaires. In L.A. Pervin (ed.), *Handbook of Personality: Theory and Research*, pp. 66–100. New York: Guilford Press.

John, O.P., Angleitner, A. and Ostendorf, F. (1988) The lexical approach to personality: A historical review of trait taxonomic research. *European Journal of Personality*, 2: 171–205.

John, O.P., Hampson, S.E. and Goldberg, L.R. (1991) The basic level in personality-trait hierarchies: Studies of trait use and accessibility in different contexts. *Journal of Personality and Social Psychology*, 60: 348–361.

Jung, C.G. (1923) *Psychological Types*. London: Routledge & Kegan Paul.

Kagan, J. (1988) The meaning of personality predicates. *American Psychologist*, 43: 614–620.

Kahle, L.R. (ed.) (1979) *Methods for Studying Person–Situation Interactions*. New Directions for Methodology of Behavioral Science, vol. 2. San Francisco: Jossey-Bass.

Kahle, L.R. (1980) Stimulus condition self-selection by males in the interaction of locus of control and skill-chance situations. *Journal of Personality and Social Psychology*, 38: 50–56.

Kahle, L.R. (1984) *Attitudes and Social Adaptation. A Person–Situation Interaction Approach*. Oxford: Pergamon Press.

Kantor, J.R. (1924) *Principles of Psychology*, vol. 1. Bloomington: Principia Press.

Kantor, J.R. (1926) *Principles of Psychology*, vol. 2. Bloomington: Principia Press.

Kaplan, H.B. (1986) *Social Psychology of Self-Referent Behavior*. New York: Plenum Press.

Kelly, G.A. (1955) *The Psychology of Personal Constructs*, vol. 1. New York: Norton.

Kendall, P.C. (1978) Anxiety: States, traits – situations? *Journal of Consulting and Clinical Psychology*, 46: 280–287.

Kenrick, D.T. (1986) How strong is the case against contemporary social and personality psychology? A response to Carlson. *Journal of Personality and Social Psychology*, 50: 839–844.

Kenrick, D.T. (1989) A biosocial perspective on mates and traits: Reuniting personality and social psychology. In D.M. Buss and N. Cantor (eds), *Personality Psychology: Recent Trends and Emerging Directions*, pp. 308–319. New York: Springer.

Kenrick, D.T. and Braver, S.L. (1982) Personality: Idiographic and nomothetic! A rejoinder. *Psychological Review*, 89: 182–186.

Kenrick, D.T. and Dantchik, A. (1983) Interactionism, idiographics, and the social psychological invasion of personality. *Journal of Personality*, 51: 286–307.

Kenrick, D.T. and Funder, D.C. (1988) Profiting from controversy: Lessons from the person–situation debate. *American Psychologist*, 43: 23–34.

Kenrick, D.T. and Stringfield, D.O. (1980) Personality traits and the eye of the beholder: Crossing some traditional philosophical boundaries in the search for consistency in all of the people. *Psychological Review*, 87: 88–104.

Kenrick, D.T., McCreath, H.E., Govern, J., King, R. and Bordin, J. (1990) Person–environment intersections: Everyday settings and common trait dimensions. *Journal of Personality and Social Psychology*, 58: 685–698.

Kenrick, D.T., Montello, D.R. and MacFarlane, S. (1985) Personality: Social learning, social cognition, or social biology? In R. Hogan and W.J. Jones (eds), *Perspectives in Personality*, vol. 1, pp. 201–243. Greenwich, CT: JAI Press.

Kihlstrom, J.F. (1987) Introduction to the special issue: Integrating personality and social psychology. *Journal of Personality and Social Psychology*, 53: 989–992.

King, G.A. and Sorrentino, R.M. (1983) Psychological dimensions of goal-oriented interpersonal situations. *Journal of Personality and Social Psychology*, 44: 140–162.

King, P.R. and Endler, N.S. (1982) Medical intervention and the interaction model of anxiety. *Canadian Journal of Behavioral Science*, 14: 82–91.

King, P.R. and Endler, N.S. (1989) Improving the assessment of situation perception with respect to anxiety. *Personality and Individual Differences*, 10: 1063–1069.

Klinger, E. (1977) *Meaning and Void: Inner Experience and the Incentives in People's Lives*. Minneapolis, MN: University of Minnesota Press.

Klirs, E.G. and Revelle, W. (1986) Predicting variability from perceived situational similarity. *Journal of Research in Personality*, 20: 34–50.

Knapp, J.R. and Sebes, J.M. (1982) Self-reported variability and enhancement of prediction. *Psychological Reports*, 51: 735–741.

Koestner, R., Bernieri, F. and Zuckerman, M. (1989) Trait-specific versus person-specific moderators of cross-situational consistency. *Journal of Personality*, 57: 1–16.

Koffka, K. (1935) *Principles of Gestalt Psychology*. New York: Harcourt, Brace.

Kohlberg, L. (1981) *The Philosophy of Moral Development: Moral stages and the Idea of Justice*. San Francisco: Harper and Row.

Koretzky, M.B., Kohn, M. and Jeger, A.M. (1978) Cross-situational consistency among problem adolescents: An application of the two-factor model. *Journal of Personality and Social Psychology*, 36: 1054–1059.

Krahé, B. (1986) Similar perceptions, similar reactions: An idiographic approach to cross-situational coherence. *Journal of Research in Personality*, 20: 349–361.

Krahé, B. (1990) *Situation Cognition and Coherence in Personality: An Individual-Centred Approach*. Cambridge: Cambridge University Press.

Krauskopf, C. (1978) Comment on Endler and Magnusson's attempt to redefine personality. *Psychological Bulletin*, 85: 280–283.

Kreitler, S. and Kreitler, H. (1990) *The Cognitive Foundations of Personality Traits*. New York: Plenum Press.

Kulka, R.A. (1979) Interaction as person–environment fit. In L.R. Kahle (ed.), *Methods for Studying Person–Situation Interactions*, pp. 55–71. New Directions for Methodology of Behavioral Science, vol. 2. San Francisco: Jossey-Bass.

Lamiell, J.T. (1981) Toward an idiothetic psychology of personality. *American Psychologist*, 36: 276–289.

Lamiell, J.T. (1982) The case for an idiothetic psychology of personality: A conceptual and empirical foundation. In B.A. Maher and W.B. Maher (eds), *Progress in Experimental Personality Research*, vol. 11, pp. 1–64. New York: Academic Press.

Lamiell, J.T. (1986) Epistemological tenets of an idiothetic psychology of personality. In A. Angleitner, A. Furnham and G. van Heck (eds), *Personality Psychology in Europe*, vol. 2, pp. 3–22. Lisse: Swets & Zeitlinger.

Lamiell, J.T. (1987) *The Psychology of Personality: An Epistemological Inquiry*. New York: Columbia University Press.

Lamiell, J.T. and Trierweiler, S.J. (1986) Interactive measurement, idiographic inquiry, and the challenge to conventional 'nomothetism'. *Journal of Personality*, 54: 460–469.

Lamiell, J.T., Foss, M.A., Larsen, R.J. and Hempel, A.M. (1983) Studies in intuitive personology from an idiographic point of view: Implications for personality theory. *Journal of Personality*, 51: 438–467.

Lamiell, J.T., Foss, M.A., Trierweiler, S.J. and Leffel, G.M. (1983) Toward a further understanding of the intuitive personologist: Some preliminary evidence for the dialectical quality of subjective personality impressions. *Journal of Personality*, 51: 214–235.

Lamiell, J.T., Trierweiler, S.J. and Foss, M.A. (1983) Detecting inconsistencies in personality: Reconciling intuitions and empirical evidence. *Journal of Personality Assessment*, 47: 380–389.

Lantermann, E.D. (1980) *Interaktionen – Person, Situation und Handlung*. München: Urban & Schwarzenberg.

Larsen, R.J. (1987) The stability of mood variability: A spectral analytical approach to daily mood assessments. *Journal of Personality and Social Psychology*, 52: 1195–1204.

Larsen, R.J. (1989) A process approach to personality psychology: Utilizing time as a facet of data. In D.M. Buss and N. Cantor (eds), *Personality Psychology: Recent Trends and Emerging Directions*, pp. 177–193. New York: Springer.

Latham, G.P. and Saari, L.M. (1984) Do people do what they say? Further studies on the situational interview. *Journal of Applied Psychology*, 69: 569–573.

Laux, L. and Weber, H. (1987) Person-centred coping research. *European Journal of Personality*, 1: 193–214.

Lazarus, R.S. and Launier, R. (1978) Stress-related transactions between person and environment. In L.A. Pervin, and M. Lewis (eds), *Perspectives in Interactional Psychology*, pp. 287–327. New York: Plenum Press.

Lerner, J.V. (1983) The role of temperament in psychosocial adaptation in early adolescents: A test of a 'goodness of fit' model. *Journal of Genetic Psychology*, 143: 149–157.

Lerner, R.M. (1983) A 'goodness of fit' model of person–context interaction. In

D. Magnusson and V.L. Allen (eds), *Human Development: An Interactional Perspective*, pp. 279–294. New York: Academic Press.

Lerner, R.M. (1987) A life-span perspective for early adolescence. In R.M. Lerner and T.T. Foch (eds), *Biological-Psychological Interactions in Early Adolescence*, pp. 9–34. Hillsdale, NJ: L. Erlbaum.

Lerner, R.M. and Busch-Rossnagel, N.A. (1981) *Individuals as Producers of Their Development*. New York: Academic Press.

Lerner, R.M. and Lerner, J.V. (1987) Children in their contexts: A goodness of fit model. In J.B. Lancaster, J. Altmann, A.S. Ross and L.R. Sherrod (eds), *Parenting across the Lifespan: Biosocial Perspectives*, pp. 377–404. New York: Aldine de Gruyter.

Lerner, R.M. and Tubman, J.G. (1989) Conceptual issues in studying continuity and discontinuity in personality development across life. *Journal of Personality*, 52: 343–373.

Levy, L.H. (1983) Trait approaches. In M. Hersen, A.E. Kazdin and A.S. Bellack (eds), *The Clinical Psychology Handbook*, pp. 123–142. New York: Pergamon.

Lewin, K. (1936) *Principles of Topological Psychology*. New York: McGraw-Hill.

Lippa, R. and Donaldson, S.I. (1990) Self-monitoring and idiographic measures of behavioral variability across interpersonal relationships. *Journal of Personality*, 58: 467–479.

Little, B.R. (1983) Personal projects: A rationale and method for investigation. *Environment and Behavior*, 15: 273–309.

Little, B.R. (1987) Personality and the environment. In D. Stokols and I. Altman (eds), *Handbook of Environmental Psychology*, vol. 1, pp. 205–244. New York: Wiley.

Little, B.R. (1989) Personal project analysis: Trivial pursuits, magnificent obsessions, and the search for coherence. In D.M. Buss and N. Cantor (eds), *Personality Psychology: Recent Trends and Emerging Directions*, pp. 15–31. New York: Springer.

Livneh, H. and Livneh, C. (1989) The five-factor model of personality: Is evidence for its cross-measure validity premature? *Personality and Individual Differences*, 10: 75–80.

Loehlin, J.C. (1989) Partitioning environmental and genetic contributions to behavioral development. *American Psychologist*, 44: 1285–1292.

Loehlin, J.C. and Nichols, R.C. (1976) *Heredity, Environment and Personality*. Austin: University of Texas Press.

Loehlin, J.C., Horn, J.M and Willerman, L. (1990) Heredity, environment and personality: Evidence from the Texas adoption project. *Journal of Personality*, 58: 221–243.

Loehlin, J.C., Willerman, L. and Horn, J.M. (1988) Human behavior genetics. *Annual Review of Psychology*, 39: 101–133.

Loevinger, J. and Knoll, E. (1983), Personality: Stages, traits and the self. *Annual Review of Psychology*, 34: 195–222.

Lord, C.G. (1982) Predicting behavioral consistency from an individual's perception of situational similarities. *Journal of Personality and Social Psychology*, 42: 1076–1088.

Lorr, M. (1986) *Interpersonal Style Inventory: Manual*. Los Angeles: Western Psychological Services.

Magnusson, D. (1971) An analysis of situational dimensions. *Perceptual and Motor Skills*, 32: 851–867.

Magnusson, D. (1974) The individual in the situation: Some studies on individuals' perception of situations. *Studia Psychologica*, 16: 124–136.

Magnusson, D. (1976) The person and the situation in an interactional model of behaviour. *Scandinavian Journal of Psychology*, 17: 253–271.

Magnusson, D. (1978) *On the Psychological Situation*. Reports from the Department of Psychology, University of Stockholm, No. 544.

Magnusson, D. (1980) Personality in an interactional paradigm of research. *Zeitschrift für Differentielle und Diagnostische Psychologie*, 1: 17–34.

Magnusson, D. (ed.) (1981a) *Toward a Psychology of Situations*. Hillsdale, NJ: L. Erlbaum.

Magnusson, D. (1981b) Wanted: A psychology of situations. In D. Magnusson (ed.), *Toward a Psychology of Situations*, pp. 115–137. Hillsdale, NJ: L. Erlbaum.

Magnusson, D. (1988) *Individual Development from an Interactional Perspective: A Longitudinal Study*. Hillsdale, NJ: L. Erlbaum.

Magnusson, D. (1990a) Personality development from an interactional perspective. In L.A. Pervin (ed.), *Handbook of Personality: Theory and Research*, pp. 193–222. New York: Guilford Press.

Magnusson, D. (1990b) Personality research – challenges for the future. *European Journal of Personality*, 4: 1–17.

Magnusson, D. and Allen, V.L. (eds) (1983a) *Human Development: An Interactional Perspective*. New York: Academic Press.

Magnusson, D. and Allen, V.L. (1983b) An interactional perspective for human development. In D. Magnusson and V.L. Allen (eds), *Human Development: An Interactional Perspective*, pp. 3–31. New York: Academic Press.

Magnusson, D. and Ekehammar, B. (1975) Perceptions of and reactions to stressful situations. *Journal of Personality and Social Psychology*, 31: 1147–1154.

Magnusson, D. and Ekehammar, B. (1978) Similar situations – similar behaviors? *Journal of Research in Personality*, 12: 41–48.

Magnusson, D. and Endler, N.S. (eds) (1977a) *Personality at the Crossroads*. Hillsdale, NJ: L. Erlbaum.

Magnusson, D. and Endler, N.S. (1977b) Interactional psychology: Present status and future prospects. In D. Magnusson and N.S. Endler (eds), *Personality at the Crossroads*, pp. 3–35. Hillsdale, NJ: L. Erlbaum.

Magnusson, D. and Stattin, H. (1982) Methods for studying stressful situations. In H.W. Krohne and L. Laux (eds), *Achievement, Stress, and Anxiety*, pp. 317–331. Washington, DC: Hemisphere.

Maller, J.B. (1934) General and specific factors in character. *Journal of Social Psychology*, 5: 97–102.

Malloy, T.E. and Kenny, D.A. (1986) The social relations model: An integrative method for personality research. *Journal of Personality*, 54: 199–225.

Manucia, G.K., Baumann, D.J. and Cialdini, R.B. (1984) Mood influences on helping: Direct effects or side effects? *Journal of Personality and Social Psychology*, 46: 357–364.

Marceil, J.C. (1977) Implicit dimensions of idiography and nomothesis: A reformulation. *American Psychologist*, 32: 1046–1055.

Marcus, R.F. (1986) Naturalistic observation of cooperation, helping, and sharing and their associations with empathy and affect. In C. Zahn-Wexler, M.E. Cummings and R. Iannotti (eds), *Altruism and Aggression: Biological and Social Origins*, pp. 256–279. Cambridge: Cambridge University Press.

McAdams, D.P. (1988) *Power, Intimacy, and the Life Story*. New York: Guilford Press.

McAdams, D.P. (1989) The development of a narrative identity. In D.M. Buss and N. Cantor (eds), *Personality Psychology: Recent Trends and Emerging Directions*, pp. 160–174. New York: Springer.

McAdams, D.P., Ruetzel, K. and Foley, J.M. (1986) Complexity and generativity at mid-life: Relations among social motives, ego development, and adults' plans for the future. *Journal of Personality and Social Psychology*, 50: 800–807.

McClelland, D.C. (1981) Is personality consistent? In A.I. Rabin, A.M. Barclay and R.A. Zucker (eds), *Further Explorations in Personality*, pp. 87–113. New York: Wiley.

McClelland, D. C. (1985) *Human Motivation*. Glenview, IL: Scott, Foresman & Co.

McCrae, R.R. (1982) Consensual validation of personality traits: Evidence from self-reports and ratings. *Journal of Personality and Social Psychology*, 43: 293–303.

McCrae, R.R. (1990) Traits and trait names: How well is openness represented in natural language? *European Journal of Personality*, 4: 119–129.

McCrae, R.R. and Costa, P.T. (1982) Self-concept and the stability of personality: Cross-sectional comparisons of self-reports and ratings. *Journal of Personality and Social Psychology*, 43: 1282–1292.

McCrae, R.R. and Costa, P.T. (1985) Updating Norman's 'adequate taxonomy': Intelligence and personality dimensions in natural language and questionnaires. *Journal of Personality and Social Psychology*, 49: 710–721.

McCrae, R.R. and Costa, P.T. (1987) Validation of the five–factor model of personality across instruments and observers. *Journal of Personality and Social Psychology*, 52: 81–90.

McCrae, R.R. and Costa, P.T. (1989) The structure of interpersonal traits: Wiggins' circumplex and the five-factor model. *Journal of Personality and Social Psychology*, 56: 586–595.

McCrae, R.R. and Costa, P.T. (1991) Adding *Liebe und Arbeit*: The full five-factor model and well-being. *Personality and Social Psychology Bulletin*, 17: 227–232.

Meehl, P.E. (1986) Trait language and behaviorese. In T. Thompson and M.D. Zeiler (eds), *Analysis and Integration of Behavioral Units*, pp. 315–334. Hillsdale, NJ: L. Erlbaum.

Mehrabian, A. (1978) Characteristic individual reactions to preferred and unpreferred environments. *Journal of Personality*, 46: 717–731.

Mervielde, I. and Pot, E. (1989) Perceiver and target effects in personality ratings. *European Journal of Personality*, 3: 1–13.

Mervis, C.B. and Rosch, E. (1981) Categorization of natural objects. *Annual Review of Psychology*, 32: 89–115.

Miller, L.C., Berg, J.M. and Archer, R.L. (1983) Openers: Individuals who elicit intimate self-disclosure. *Journal of Personality and Social Psychology*, 44: 1234–1244.

Mischel, W. (1968) *Personality and Assessment*. New York: Wiley.

Mischel, W. (1973) Toward a cognitive social learning reconceptualization of personality. *Psychological Review*, 81: 252–283.

Mischel, W. (1977) On the future of personality measurement. *American Psychologist*, 32: 246–254.

Mischel, W. (1979) On the interface of cognition and personality. *American Psychologist*, 34: 740–754.

Mischel, W. (1983) Alternatives in the pursuit of the predictability and consistency of persons: Stable data that yield unstable interpretations. *Journal of Personality*, 51: 578–604.

Mischel, W. (1984a) Convergences and challenges in the search for consistency. *American Psychologist*, 39: 351–364.

Mischel, W. (1984b) On the predictability of behavior and the structure of personality. In R.A. Zucker, J. Aronoff and A.I. Rabin (eds), *Personality and the Prediction of Behavior*, pp. 269–305. New York: Academic Press.

Mischel, W. (1986) *Introduction to Personality*, 4th edn. New York: CBS.

Mischel, W. (1990) Personality dispositions revisited and revised: A view after three decades. In L.A. Pervin (ed.), *Handbook of Personality: Theory and Research*, pp. 111–134. New York: Guilford Press.

Mischel, W. and Peake, P.K. (1982a) Beyond déjà vu in the search for cross-situational consistency. *Psychological Review*, 89: 730–755.

Mischel, W. and Peake, P.K. (1982b) The search for consistency: Measure for measure. In M.P. Zanna, E.T. Higgins and C.P. Herman (eds), *Consistency in Social Behavior: The Ontario Symposium*, vol. 2, pp. 187–207. Hillsdale, NJ: L. Erlbaum.

Mischel, W. and Peake, P.E. (1983a) Analyzing the construction of consistency in personality. In M.M. Page (ed.), *Personality – Current Theory and Research*, pp. 233–262. The 1982 Nebraska Symposium on Motivation. Lincoln, NB: University of Nebraska Press.

Mischel, W. and Peake, P.E. (1983b) Some facets of consistency: Replies to Epstein, Funder, and Bem. *Psychological Review*, 90: 394–402.

Monson, T.C., Hesley, J.W. and Chernick, L. (1982) Specifying when traits can and cannot predict behavior: An alternative to abandoning the attempt to predict single acts. *Journal of Personality and Social Psychology*, 43: 385–399.

Moser, K. (1989) The act-frequency approach: A conceptual critique. *Personality and Social Psychology Bulletin*, 15: 73–83.

Moskowitz, D.S. (1982) Coherence and cross-situational generality in personality: A new analysis of old problems. *Journal of Personality and Social Psychology*, 43: 754–768.

Moskowitz, D.S. (1986) Comparison of self-reports, reports by knowledgeable informants, and behavioral observation data. *Journal of Personality*, 54: 294–317.

Moskowitz, D.S. (1988) Cross-situational generality in the laboratory: Dominance and friendliness. *Journal of Personality and Social Psychology*, 54: 829–839.

Moskowitz, D.S. (1990) Convergence of self-reports and independent observers: Dominance and friendliness. *Journal of Personality and Social Psychology*, 58: 1096–1106.

Moskowitz, D.S. and Schwartz, J.C. (1982) Validity comparisons of behavior counts and ratings by knowledgeable informants. *Journal of Personality and Social Psychology*, 42: 518–528.

Mothersill, K.J., Dobson, K.S. and Neufeld, R.W. (1986) The interactional model of anxiety: An evaluation of the differential hypothesis. *Journal of Personality and Social Psychology*, 51: 640–648.

Mumford, M.D., Stokes, G.S. and Owens, W.A. (1990) *Patterns of Life Adaptation: The Ecology of Human Individuality*. Hillsdale, NJ: L. Erlbaum.

Murray, H.A. (1938) *Explorations in Personality*. New York: Oxford University Press.

Newtson, D. (1973) Attribution and the unit of perception of ongoing behavior. *Journal of Personality and Social Psychology*, 28: 28–38.

Newtson, D. and Engquist, G. (1976) The perceptual organization of ongoing behavior. *Journal of Experimental Social Psychology*, 12: 436–450.

Newtson, D., Hairfield, J., Bloomingdale, J. and Cutino, S. (1987) The structure of action and interaction. *Social Cognition*, 5: 191–237.

Nicholls, J.G., Licht, B.G. and Pearl, R.A. (1982) Some dangers of using personality questionnaires to study personality. *Psychological Bulletin*, 92: 572–580.

Niedenthal, P.M., Cantor, N. and Kihlstrom, J.F. (1985) Prototype-matching: A strategy for social decision making. *Journal of Personality and Social Psychology*, 48: 575–584.

Nisbett, R.E. (1980) The trait construct in lay and professional psychology. In L. Festinger (ed.), *Retrospections on Social Psychology*, pp. 109–130. New York: Oxford University Press.

Noller, P., Law, H. and Comrey, A.L. (1987) Cattell, Comrey and Eysenck personality factors compared: More evidence for five robust factors? *Journal of Personality and Social Psychology*, 53: 775–782.

Norem, J.K. (1989) Cognitive strategies as personality: Effectiveness, specificity, flexibility, and change. In D.M. Buss and N. Cantor (eds), *Personality Psychology: Recent Trends and Emerging Directions*, pp. 45–60. New York: Springer.

Norman, W.T. (1963) Toward an adequate taxonomy of personality attributes: Replicated factor structure in peer nomination personality ratings. *Journal of Abnormal and Social Psychology*, 66: 574–583.

Olweus, D. (1977) A critical analysis of the 'modern' interactionist position. In D. Magnusson and N.S. Endler (eds), *Personality at the Crossroads*, pp. 221–233. Hillsdale, NJ: L. Erlbaum.

Olweus, D. (1979) The stability of aggressive reaction patterns in human males: A review. *Psychological Bulletin*, 86: 852–875.

Olweus, D. (1980) The consistency issue in personality psychology revisited – with special reference to aggression. *British Journal of Social and Clinical Psychology*, 19: 377–390.

Ozer, D.J. (1986) *Consistency in Personality: A Methodological Framework*. New York: Springer.

Ozer, D.J. and Gjerde, P.F. (1989) Patterns of personality consistency and change from childhood to adolescence. *Journal of Personality*, 57: 483–507.

Passini, F.T. and Norman, W.T. (1966) A universal conception of personality structure? *Journal of Personality and Social Psychology*, 4: 44–49.

Paunonen, S.V. (1984) Optimizing the validity of personality assessments: The importance of aggregation and item content. *Journal of Research in Personality*, 18: 411–431.

Paunonen, S.V. (1988) Trait relevance and the differential predictability of behavior. *Journal of Personality*, 56: 599–619.

Paunonen, S.V. (1989) Consensus in personality judgments: Moderating effects of target–rater acquaintanceship and behavior observability. *Journal of Personality and Social Psychology*, 56: 823–833.

Paunonen, S.V. (1991) On the accuracy of ratings of personality by strangers. *Journal of Personality and Social Psychology*, 61: 471–477.

Paunonen, S.V. and Jackson, D.N. (1985) Idiographic measurement strategies for personality and prediction: Some unredeemed promissary notes. *Psychological Review*, 92: 486–511.

Paunonen, S.V. and Jackson, D.N. (1986a) Nomothetic and idiographic measurement in personality. *Journal of Personality*, 54: 447–459.

Paunonen, S.V. and Jackson, D.N. (1986b) Idiothetic inquiry and the toil of Sisyphus. *Journal of Personality*, 54: 470–477.

Peabody, D. (1987) Selecting representative trait adjectives. *Journal of Personality and Social Psychology*, 52: 59–71.

Peabody, D. and Goldberg, L. (1989) Some determinants of factor representations of trait adjectives. *Journal of Personality and Social Psychology*, 57: 552–567.

Peake, P.K. (1984) Theoretical divergences in the person–situation debate. In J.R. Royce and L.P. Mos (eds), *Annals of Theoretical Psychology*, vol. 2, pp. 329–338. New York: Plenum Press.

Peake, P.K. and Mischel, W. (1984) Getting lost in the search for large coefficients. Reply to Conley. *Psychological Review*, 91: 497–501.

Pedersen, N.L., Plomin, R., McClearn, G.E. and Friberg, L. (1988) Neuroticism, extroversion, and related traits in adult twins reared apart and reared together. *Journal of Personality and Social Psychology*, 55: 950–957.

Pervin, L.A. (1968) Performance and satisfaction as a function of individual–environment fit. *Psychological Bulletin*, 69: 56–68.

Pervin, L.A. (1976) A free-response description approach to the analysis of person–situation interaction. *Journal of Personality and Social Psychology*, 34: 465–474.

Pervin, L.A. (1978) Definitions, measurements, and classifications of stimuli, situations, and environments. *Human Ecology*, 6: 71–105.

Pervin, L.A. (1980) *Personality: Theory, Assessment, and Research*, 3rd edn. New York: Wiley.

Pervin, L.A. (1981) The relation of situations to behavior. In D. Magnusson (ed.), *Toward a Psychology of Situations*, pp. 343–360. Hillsdale, NJ: L. Erlbaum.

Pervin, L. A. (1984a) Idiographic approaches to personality. In N. Endler and J.M. Hunt (eds), *Personality and the Behavioral Disorders*, pp. 261–282. New York: Wiley.

Pervin. L. A. (1984b) Persons, situations, interactions, and the future of personality. In J.R. Royce and L.P. Mos (eds), *Annals of Theoretical Psychology*, vol. 2, pp. 339–344. New York: Plenum Press.

Pervin, L.A. (1984c) *Current Controversies and Issues in Personality*, 2nd edn. New York: Wiley.

Pervin, L.A. (1985) Personality: Current controversies, issues, and directions. *Annual Review of Psychology*, 36: 83–114.

Pervin, L.A. (1989a) Persons, situations, interactions: The history of a controversy and a discussion of theoretical models. *Academy of Management Review*, 14: 350–360.

Pervin, L.A. (ed.) (1989b) *Goal Concepts in Personality and Social Psychology*. Hillsdale, NJ: L. Erlbaum.

Pervin, L.A. (ed.) (1990a) *Handbook of Personality: Theory and Research*. New York: Guilford Press.

Pervin, L.A. (1990b) A brief history of modern personality theory. In L.A. Pervin (ed.), *Handbook of Personality: Theory and Research*, pp. 3–18. New York: Guilford Press.

Pervin, L.A. (1990c) Personality theory and research: Prospects for the future. In L.A. Pervin (ed.), *Handbook of Personality: Theory and Research*, pp. 723–727. New York: Guilford Press.

Pervin, L.A. and Lewis, M. (eds) (1978) *Perspectives in Interactional Psychology*. New York: Plenum Press.

Peterson, C. (1988) *Personality*. San Diego: Harcourt, Brace, Jovanovich.

Peterson, D.R. (1979) Assessing interpersonal relationships in natural settings. In L.R. Kahle (ed.), *Methods for Studying Person–Situation Interactions*, pp. 33–54. New Directions for Methodology of Behavioral Science, vol. 2. San Francisco: Jossey-Bass.

Phares, E.J. and Lamiell, J.T. (1977) Personality. *Annual Review of Psychology*, 28: 113–140.

Phillips, B.J. and Endler, N.S. (1982) Academic examinations and anxiety: The interaction model empirically tested. *Journal of Research in Personality*, 16: 303–318.

Piaget, J. (1952) *The Origins of Intelligence in Children*. New York: International University Press.

Piccione, C., Hilgard, E.R. and Zimbardo, P.G. (1989) On the degree of stability of measured hypnotizability over a 25-year period. *Journal of Personality and Social Psychology*, 56: 289–295.

Piedmont, R.L., McCrae, R.R. and Costa, P.T. (1991) Adjective check list scales and the five-factor model. *Journal of Personality and Social Psychology*, 60: 630–637.

Plomin, R. (1986) Behavioral genetic methods. *Journal of Personality*, 54: 226–261.

Plomin, R. and Nesselroade, J.R. (1990) Behavioral genetics and personality change. *Journal of Personality*, 58: 191–220.

Plomin, R. and Rende, R. (1991) Human behavioral genetics. *Annual Review of Psychology*, 42: 161–190.

Plomin, R., Chipuer, H.M. and Loehlin, J.C. (1990) Behavioral genetics and personality. In L.A. Pervin (ed.), *Handbook of Personality: Theory and Research*, pp. 225–243. New York: Guilford Press.

Plutchik, R. (1980) *Emotion: A Psychoevolutionary Synthesis*. New York: Harper & Row.

Price, R.H. (1974) The taxonomic classification of behaviors and situations and the problem of behavior–environment congruence. *Human Relations*, 27: 567–585.

Price, R.H. (1981) Risky situations. In D. Magnusson (ed.), *Toward a Psychology of Situations*, pp. 103–112. Hillsdale, NJ: L. Erlbaum.

Price, R.H. and Bouffard, D.L. (1974) Behavioral appropriateness and situational constraints as dimensions of social behavior. *Journal of Personality and Social Psychology*, 30: 579–586.

Pryor, J.B. (1980) Self-reports and behavior. In D.M. Wegner and R.R. Vallacher (eds), *The Self in Social Psychology*, pp. 206–228. Oxford: Oxford University Press.

Rabin, A.I., Zucker, R.A., Emmons, R.A. and Frank, S. (eds) (1990) *Studying Persons and Lives*. New York: Springer.

Read, S.J., Jones, D.K. and Miller, J.C. (1990) Traits as goal-based categories: The importance of goals in the coherence of dispositional categories. *Journal of Personality and Social Psychology*, 58: 1048–1061.

Reis, H.T., Nezlek, J. and Wheeler, L. (1980) Physical attractiveness in social interaction. *Journal of Personality and Social Psychology*, 38: 604–617.

Rogers, J.H. and Widiger, T.A. (1989) Comparing idiothetic, ipsative, and normative indices of consistency. *Journal of Personality*, 57: 847–869.

Romer, D., Gruder, C.L. and Lizzadro, T. (1986) A person–situation approach to altruistic behavior. *Journal of Personality and Social Psychology*, 51: 1001–1012.

Rorer, L.G. (1990) Personality assessment: A conceptual survey. In L.A. Pervin (ed.), *Handbook of Personality: Theory and Research*, pp. 693–720. New York: Guilford Press.

Rorer, L.G. and Widiger, T.A. (1983) Personality structure and assessment. *Annual Review of Psychology*, 34: 431–463.

Rosch, E. (1975) Cognitive representation of semantic categories. *Journal of Experimental Psychology: General*, 104: 192–233.

Rosenberg, S. and Gara, M.A. (1983) Contemporary perspectives and future directions of personality and social psychology. *Journal of Personality and Social Psychology*, 45: 57–73.

Rosenzweig, S. (1986) Idiodynamics vis-a-vis psychology. *American Psychologist*, 41: 241–245.

Ross, A.O. (1987) *Personality. The Scientific Study of Complex Human Behavior.* New York: Holt, Rinehart & Winston.

Rothbart, M. and Park, B. (1986) On the confirmability and disconfirmability of trait concepts. *Journal of Personality and Social Psychology*, 50: 131–142.

Rotter, J.B. (1954) *Social Learning and Clinical Psychology*. Englewood Cliffs, NJ: Prentice Hall.

Rotter, J.B. (1981) The psychological situation in social-learning theory. In D. Magnusson (ed.), *Toward a Psychology of Situations*, pp. 169–179. Hillsdale, NJ: L. Erlbaum.

Rowe, D.C. (1987) Resolving the person–situation debate. *American Psychologist*, 42: 218–227.

Rowe, D.C. (1989) Personality theory and behavioral genetics: Contributions and issues. In D.M. Buss and N. Cantor (eds), *Personality Psychology: Recent Trends and Emerging Directions*, pp. 294–307. New York: Springer.

Royce, J.R. (1983) Personality integration: A synthesis of the parts and wholes of individuality theory. *Journal of Personality*, 51: 683–706.

Runyan, W.M. (1982) *Life Histories and Psychobiography*. New York: Oxford University Press.

Runyan, W.M. (1983) Idiographic goals and methods in the study of lives. *Journal of Personality*, 51: 414–437.

Runyan, W.M. (1990) Individual lives and the structure of personality. In A.I. Rabin, R.A. Zucker, R.A. Emmons and S. Frank (eds), *Studying Persons and Lives*, pp. 10–40. New York: Springer.

Rushton, J.P. (1981) The altruistic personality. In J.P. Rushton and R.M. Sorrentino (eds), *Altruism and Helping Behavior: Social, Personality, and Developmental Perspectives*, pp. 251–266. Hillsdale, NJ: L. Erlbaum.

Rushton, J.P. (1984) The altruistic personality: Evidence from laboratory, naturalistic, and self-report perspectives. In E. Staub, D. Bar-Tal, J. Karylowski, and J. Reykowski (eds), *Development and Maintenance of Prosocial Behavior*, pp. 271–290. New York: Plenum Press.

Rushton, J.P. (1990) Sir Francis Galton, epigenetic models, genetic similarity models, and human life-history. *Journal of Personality*, 58: 117–140.

Rushton, J.P. and Erdle, S. (1987) Evidence for an aggressive (and delinquent) personality. *British Journal of Social Psychology*, 26: 87–89.

Rushton, J.P., Brainerd, C.J. and Pressley, M. (1983) Behavioral development and construct validity: The principle of aggregation. *Psychological Bulletin*, 94: 18–38.

Rushton, J.P., Jackson, D.N. and Paunonen, S.V. (1981) Personality: Nomothetic or idiographic? A response to Kenrick & Stringfield. *Psychological Review*, 88: 582–589.

Russell, J.A. and Pratt, G. (1980) The description of the affective quality attributed to environments. *Journal of Personality and Social Psychology*, 38: 311–322.

Salovey, P., Mayer, J.D. and Rosenhan, D.L. (1991) Mood and helping: Mood as a motivator of helping and helping as a regulator of mood. In M.S. Clark (ed.), *Prosocial Behavior*, pp. 215–237. Newbury Park, CA: Sage.

Sarason, I.G. and Sarason, B.R. (1983) Person–situation interactions in human development: Cognitive factors and coping strategies. In D. Magnusson and V.L. Allen (eds), *Human Development: An Interactional Perspective*, pp. 187–198. New York: Academic Press.

Schaller, M. and Cialdini, R.B. (1988) The economics of helping: Support for a mood management motive. *Journal of Experimental Social Psychology*, 24: 163–181.

Schank, R. and Abelson, R. (1977) *Script, Plans, Goals, and Understanding: An Inquiry into Human Knowledge Structures*. Hillsdale, NJ: L. Erlbaum.

Scheier, M.F. (1980) Effects of public and private self-consciousness on the public expression of personal beliefs. *Journal of Personality and Social Psychology*, 39: 514–521.

Scheier, M.F., Buss, A.H. and Buss, D.M. (1978) Self-consciousness, self-report of aggressiveness, and aggression. *Journal of Research in Personality*, 12: 133–140.

Schneider, D.J., Hastorf, A.H. and Ellsworth, P.C. (1979) *Person Perception*, 2nd edn. Reading, MA: Addison-Wesley.

Schulenberg, J.E., Vondracek, F.W. and Nesselroade, J.R. (1988) Patterns of short-term changes in individual's work values: P-technique factor analyses of intra-individual variability. *Multivariate Behavioral Research*, 23: 377–395.

Schutte, N., Kenrick, D.T. and Sadalla, E.K. (1985) The search for predictable settings: Situational prototypes, constraint, and behavioral variation. *Journal of Personality and Social Psychology*, 49: 121–128.

Sechrest, L. (1976) Personality. *Annual Review of Psychology*, 27: 1–28.

Semin, G.R. and Fiedler, K. (1988) The cognitive functions of linguistic categories in describing persons: Social cognition and language. *Journal of Personality and Social Psychology*, 54: 558–568.

Semin, G.R. and Fiedler, K. (1991) The linguistic category model, its bases, applications and range. In W. Stroebe and M. Hewstone (eds), *European Review of Social Psychology*, vol. 2, pp. 1–30. Chichester: Wiley.

Semin, G.R. and Greenslade, L. (1985) Differential contributions of linguistic factors to memory-based ratings: Systematizing the systematic distortion hypothesis. *Journal of Personality and Social Psychology*, 49: 1713–1723.

Shaver, P., Schwartz, J., Kirson, D. and O'Connor, C. (1987) Emotion knowledge: Further exploration of a prototype approach. *Journal of Personality and Social Psychology*, 52: 1061–1086.

Shaw, M.E. (1976) *Group Dynamics*, 2nd edn. New York: McGraw-Hill.

Sherman, S.J. and Fazio, R.H. (1983) Parallels between attitudes and traits as predictors of behavior. *Journal of Personality*, 51: 308–345

Shoda, Y., Mischel, W. and Wright, J.C. (1989) Intuitive interactionism in person perception: Effects of situation–behavior relations on dispositional judgments. *Journal of Personality and Social Psychology*, 56: 41–53.

Showers, C. and Cantor, N. (1985) Social cognition: A look at motivated strategies. *Annual Review of Psychology*, 36: 275–305.

Shrauger, J.S. and Schoeneman, T.J. (1979) Symbolic interactionist view of the self-concept: Through the looking glass darkly. *Psychological Bulletin*, 86: 549–573.

Shweder, R.A. (1975) How relevant is the individual difference theory of personality? *Journal of Personality*, 43: 455–484.

Shweder, R.A. (1982) Fact and artifact in trait perception: The systematic distortion hypothesis. In B.A. Maher and W.B. Maher (eds), *Progress in Experimental Personality Research*, vol. 11, pp. 65–101. New York: Academic Press.

Shweder, R.A. and Bourne, E.J. (1984) Does the concept of the person vary cross-culturally? In R.A. Shweder and R.A. Levine (eds), *Culture Theory: Essays on Mind, Self, and Emotion*, pp. 158–199. Cambridge: Cambridge University Press.

Shweder, R.A. and Miller, J.G. (1985) The social construction of the person: How is it possible? In K.J. Gergen and K.E. Davis (eds), *The Social Construction of the Person*, pp. 41–69. New York: Springer.

Silverstein, A. (1988) An Aristotelian resolution of the idiographic versus nomothetic tension. *American Psychologist*, 43: 425–430.

Singer, J.L. and Kolligian, J. (1987) Personality: Developments in the study of private experience. *Annual Review of Psychology*, 38: 533–574.

Skinner, B.F. (1963) Behaviorism at fifty. *Science*, 140: 951–958.

Small, S.A., Zeldin, R.S. and Savin-Williams, R.C. (1983) In search of personality traits: A multimethod analysis of naturally occurring prosocial and dominance behavior. *Journal of Personality*, 51: 1–15.

Snyder, M. (1974) Self-monitoring of expressive behavior. *Journal of Personality and Social Psychology*, 30: 526–537.

Snyder, M. (1979) Self-monitoring processes. In L. Berkowitz (ed.), *Advances in Experimental Social Psychology*, vol. 12, pp. 86–131. New York: Academic Press.

Snyder, M. (1981) On the influence of individuals on situations. In N. Cantor and J.F. Kihlstrom (eds), *Personality, Cognition, and Social Behavior*, pp. 309–329. Hillsdale, NJ: L. Erlbaum.

Snyder, M. (1983) The influence of individuals on situations: Implications for understanding the links between personality and social behavior. *Journal of Personality*, 51: 497–516.

Snyder, M. (1987) *Public Appearances/Private Realities. The Psychology of Self-Monitoring*. New York: W.H. Freeman.

Snyder, M. and Gangestad, S. (1982) Choosing social situations: Two investigations of self-monitoring processes. *Journal of Personality and Social Psychology*, 43: 125–135.

Snyder, M. and Ickes, W. (1985) Personality and social behavior. In G. Lindzey and E. Aronson (eds), *Handbook of Social Psychology*, vol. 2, 3rd edn, pp. 883–947. New York: Random House.

Snyder, M. and Kendzierski, D. (1982) Choosing social situations: Investigating the origins of correspondence between attitudes and behavior. *Journal of Personality*, 50: 280–295.

Snyder, M., Tanke, E.D. and Berscheid, E. (1977) Social perception and interpersonal behavior: On the self-fulfilling nature of social stereotypes. *Journal of Personality and Social Psychology*, 35: 565–566.

Spielberger, C.D. (1966) The effects of anxiety on complex learning and academic achievement. In C.D. Spielberger (ed.), *Anxiety and Behavior*, pp. 361–398. New York: Academic Press.

Spielberger, C.D. (1972) Anxiety as an emotional state. In C.D. Spielberger (ed.), *Anxiety: Current Trends in Theory and Research*, vol. 1, pp. 23–49. New York: Academic Press.

Spielberger, C.D., Gorsuch, R.L. and Lushene, R.E. (1970) *Manual for the State–Trait–Anxiety Inventory*. Palo Alto, CA: Consulting Psychologists Press.

Spokane, A.R. (ed.) (1987) *Conceptual and Methodological Issues in Person–Environment Fit Research*. Special Issue, *Journal of Vocational Behavior*, 31(3).

Staats, A.W. (1980) 'Behavioural interaction' and 'interactional psychology' theories of personality: Similarities, differences, and the need for unification. *British Journal of Psychology*, 71: 205–220.

Staats, A.W. and Burns, G.L. (1982) Emotional personality repertoire as cause of behavior: Specification of personality and interaction principles. *Journal of Personality and Social Psychology*, 43: 873–881.

Staub, E. (1980) Social and prosocial behavior: Personal and situational influences and their interactions. In E. Staub (ed.), *Personality: Basic Aspects and Current Research*, pp. 237–294. Englewood Cliffs, NJ: Prentice Hall.

Staub, E. (1984) Notes on an interactionist–motivational theory of the determinants and development of (pro)social behavior. In E. Staub, D. Bar-Tal, J. Karylowski and J. Reykowski (eds), *Development and Maintenance of Prosocial Behavior*, pp. 29–49. New York: Plenum Press.

Stebbins, R.A. (1985) The definition of the situation: A review. In A. Furnham (ed.), *Social Behavior in Context*, pp. 134–154. Boston: Allyn and Bacon.

Stern, W. (1921) *Die differentielle Psychologie in ihren methodologischen Grundlagen*, 3rd edn. Leipzig: Barth.

Stewart, A.J. (1982) The course of individual adaptation to life changes. *Journal of Personality and Social Psychology*, 42: 1100–1113.

Stokes, G.S., Mumford, M.D. and Owens, W.A. (1989) Life history prototypes in the study of human individuality. *Journal of Personality*, 57: 509–545.

Swann, W.B. and Reed, S.J. (1981) Self-verification processes: How we sustain our self-conceptions. *Journal of Experimental Social Psychology*, 17: 351–372.

Taylor, R.B. (1981) Perception of density: Individual differences. *Environment and Behavior*, 13: 3–21.

Taylor, S.E. and Crocker, J. (1981) Schematic bases of social information processing. In E.T. Higgins, C.P. Herman and M.P. Zanna (eds), *Social Cognition – The Ontario Symposium*, vol. 1, pp. 89–134. Hillsdale, NJ: L. Erlbaum.

Tellegen, A. (1985) Structures of mood and personality and their relevance to assessing anxiety with an emphasis on self-report. In A. Tuma and J. Maser (eds), *Anxiety and the Anxiety Disorders*, pp. 681–706. Hillsdale, NJ: L. Erlbaum.

Tellegen, A. (1988) The analysis of consistency in personality assessment. *Journal of Personality*, 56: 621–663.

Tellegen, A., Kamp, J. and Watson, D. (1982) Recognizing individual differences in predictive structures. *Psychological Review*, 89: 95–105.

Tellegen, A., Lykken, D.T., Bouchard, T.J., Wilcox, K.J., Segal, N.L. and Rich, S. (1988) Personality similarity in twins reared together and apart. *Journal of Personality and Social Psychology*, 54: 1031–1039.

Thomae, H. (1987) Conceptualizations of responses to stress. *European Journal of Personality*, 1: 171–192.

Thomas, W.I. (1928) *The Child in America*. New York: Knopf.

Thompson, W.C., Cowan, C.L. and Rosenhan, D.L. (1980) Focus of attention mediates the impact of negative affect on altruism. *Journal of Personality and Social Psychology*, 38: 291–300.

Thorndike, E.L. (1920) A constant error in psychological ratings. *Journal of Applied Psychology*, 4: 25–29.

Thorngate, W. (1986) The production, detection, and explanation of behavioral patterns. In J. Valsiner (ed.), *The Individual Subject and Scientific Psychology*, pp. 71–93. New York: Plenum.

Tomkins, S.S. (1981) The rise, fall, and resurrection of the study of personality. *The Journal of Mind and Behavior*, 2: 443–452.

Toi, M. and Batson, C.D. (1982) More evidence that empathy is a source of altruistic motivation. *Journal of Personality and Social Psychology*, 43: 281–292.

Tooby, J. and Cosmides, L. (1990) On the universality of human nature and the uniqueness of the individual: The role of genetics and adaptation. *Journal of Personality*, 58: 17–67.

Trapnell, P.D. and Wiggins, J.S. (1990) Extension of the interpersonal adjective scales to include the big five dimensions of personality. *Journal of Personality and Social Psychology*, 59: 781–790.

Triandis, H. et al. (1984) Individual models of social behavior. *Journal of Personality and Social Psychology*, 46: 1389–1404.

Tupes, E.C. and Christal, R.E. (1961) Recurrent personality factors based on trait ratings. *USAF ASD Technical Report*, 61–97.

Turner, R. G. (1978) Consistency, self-consciousness, and the predictive utility of typical and maximal personality measures. *Journal of Research in Personality*, 12: 117–132.

Turner, R.G. and Gilliam, B.J. (1979) Identifying the situationally variable subject: Correspondence among different self-report formats. *Applied Psychological Measurement*, 3: 361–369.

Turner, R.H. (1988) Personality in society: Social psychology's contribution to sociology. *Social Psychology Quarterly*, 51: 1–10.

Underwood, B. and Moore, B.S. (1981) Sources of behavioral consistency. *Journal of Personality and Social Psychology*, 40: 780–785.

Valsiner, J. (ed.) (1986a) *The Individual Subject and Scientific Psychology*. New York: Plenum.

Valsiner, J. (1986b) Between groups and individuals: Psychologists' and laypersons' interpretation of correlational findings. In J. Valsiner (ed.), *The Individual Subject and Scientific Psychology*, pp. 113–151. New York: Plenum.

Vestewig, R. (1978) Cross-response mode consistency in risk taking as a function of self-reported strategy and self-perceived consistency. *Journal of Research in Personality*, 12: 152–163.

Vleeming, R. (1981) Some sources of behavioral variance as measured by an S–R inventory of machiavellianism. *Psychological Reports*, 48: 359–368.

Wakefield, J.C. (1989) Levels of explanation in personality theory. In D.M. Buss and N. Cantor (eds), *Personality Psychology: Recent Trends and Emerging Directions*, pp. 333–346. New York: Springer.

Wallach, M.A. and Legett, M.I. (1972) Testing the hypothesis that a person will be consistent: Stylistic consistency versus situational specificity in size of children's drawings. *Journal of Personality*, 40: 309–330.

Waller, N.G. and Ben-Porath, Y. (1987) Is it time for clinical psychology to embrace the five-factor model of personality? *American Psychologist*, 42: 887–889.

Walschburger, P. (1986) Psychophysiological activation research: An approach to assess individual stress reactions? In J. Valsiner (ed.), *The Individual Subject and Scientific Psychology*, pp. 311–345. New York: Plenum.

Watson, D. (1982) The actor and the observer: How are their perceptions of causality divergent? *Psychological Bulletin*, 92: 682–700.

Watson, D. (1988) Intraindividual and interindividual analyses of positive and negative affect: The relation to health complaints, perceived stress, and daily activities. *Journal of Personality and Social Psychology*, 54: 1020–1030.

Watson, D. (1989) Strangers' ratings of the five robust personality factors: Evidence of a surprising convergence with self-reports. *Journal of Personality and Social Psychology*, 57: 120–128.

Watson, D. and Clark, L.A. (1991) Self- versus peer ratings of specific emotional traits: Evidence of convergent and discriminant validity. *Journal of Personality and Social Psychology*, 60: 927–940.

Werner, P.D. and Pervin, L.A. (1986) The content of personality inventory items. *Journal of Personality and Social Psychology*, 51: 622–628.

West, S. (1983) Personality and prediction: An introduction. *Journal of Personality*, 51: 276–285.

West, S.G. (ed.) (1986a) *Methodological Developments in Personality Research*. Special Issue, *Journal of Personality*, 54.

West, S.G. (1986b) Introduction. In S.G. West (ed.), *Methodological Developments in Personality Research*. Special Issue, *Journal of Personality*, 54: 1–17.

West, S.G. and Graziano, W.G. (eds) (1989a) *Long-Term Stability and Change in Personality*. Special Issue, *Journal of Personality*, 57.

West, S.G. and Graziano, W.G. (1989b) Long-term stability and change in personality: An introduction. *Journal of Personality*, 57: 175–193.

Wicker, A.W. (1969) Attitudes versus actions: The relationship of verbal and overt behavioral responses to attitude objects. *Journal of Social Issues*, 4: 41–78.

Wiggins, J.S. (1979) A psychological taxonomy of trait-descriptive terms: The interpersonal domain. *Journal of Personality and Social Psychology*, 37: 395–412.

Windelband, W. (1894) *Geschichte und Naturwissenschaft*. Strassburg: Heitz.

Wish, M., Deutsch, M. and Kaplan, S.J. (1976) Perceived dimensions of interpersonal relations. *Journal of Personality and Social Psychology*, 33: 409–420.

Wohlwill, J.W. (1983) Physical and social environment as factors in development. In D. Magnusson and V.L. Allen (eds), *Human Development: An Interactional Perspective*, pp. 111–129. New York: Academic Press.

Woodruffe, C. (1984) The consistency of presented personality: Additional evidence from aggregation. *Journal of Personality*, 52: 307–317.

Woodruffe, C. (1985) Consensual validation of personality traits: Additional evidence and individual differences. *Journal of Personality and Social Psychology*, 48: 1240–1252.

Woody, E.Z. (1983) The intuitive personologist revisited: A critique of dialectical person perception. *Journal of Personality*, 51: 236–247.

Wright, J.C. and Mischel, W. (1987) A conditional approach to dispositional constructs: The local predictability of behavior. *Journal of Personality and Social Psychology*, 53: 1159–1177.

Wright, J.C. and Mischel, W. (1988) Conditional hedges and the intuitive psychology of traits. *Journal of Personality and Social Psychology*, 55: 454–469.

Wymer, W.E. and Penner, L.A. (1985) Moderator variables and different types of predictability: Do you have a match? *Journal of Personality and Social Psychology*, 49: 1002–1015.

Zavalloni, M. and Louis-Guerin, C. (1979) Social psychology at the crossroads: Its encounter with cognitive and ecological psychology and the interactive perspective. *European Journal of Social Psychology*, 9: 307–321.

Zevon, M.A. and Tellegen, A. (1982) The structure of mood change: An idiographic/nomothetic analysis. *Journal of Personality and Social Psychology*, 43: 111–122.

Zuckerman, M. (1974) The sensation seeking motive. In B. Maher (ed.), *Progress in Experimental Personality Research*, vol. 7, pp. 80–148. New York: Academic Press.

Zuckerman, M., Biernieri, F., Koestner, R. and Rosenthal, R. (1989) To predict some of the people some of the time: In search of moderators. *Journal of Personality and Social Psychology*, 57: 279–293.

Zuckerman, M., Koestner, R., DeBoy, T., Garcia, T., Maresca, B.C. and Sartoris, J.M. (1988) To predict some people some of the time: A reexamination of the moderator variable approach in personality theory. *Journal of Personality and Social Psychology*, 54: 1006–1019.

Zuroff, D.C. (1982) Person, situation, and person-by-situation interaction components in person perception. *Journal of Personality*, 50: 1–14.

Zuroff, D.C. (1986) Was Gordon Allport a trait theorist? *Journal of Personality and Social Psychology*, 51: 993–1000.

Index